MW00526749

India's Founding Moment

India's Founding Moment

The Constitution of a Most Surprising Democracy

MADHAV KHOSLA

Harvard University Press

Cambridge, Massachusetts
London, England
2020

Publication of this book has been supported through the generous provisions
of the Maurice and Lula Bradley Smith Memorial Fund.

First printing

Cataloging-in-Publication Data available from the Library of Congress

ISBN: 978-0-674-98087-7

An Indian Parliament or collection of Indian parliaments would produce undisguised, unqualified anarchy.

—JAMES FITZJAMES STEPHEN, *Foundations of the Government of India*, 1883

The end of our Indian Empire is perhaps almost as much beyond calculation as the beginning of it. There is no analogy in history either for one or the other.

—JOHN ROBERT SEELEY, *The Expansion of England*, 1883

Our major difficulties in India are due to the fact that we consider our problems—economic, social, industrial, agricultural, communal, Indian states—within the framework of existing conditions. Within that framework, and retaining the privileges and special status that are part of it, they become impossible of solution.

—JAWAHARLAL NEHRU, *The Discovery of India*, 1946

Constitutional morality is not a natural sentiment. It has to be cultivated. We must realize that our people have yet to learn it. Democracy in India is only a top-dressing on an Indian soil which is essentially undemocratic.

—B. R. AMBEDKAR, *Constituent Assembly Debates*, 1948

For Amita and Rajiv Khosla

CONTENTS

Introduction

The Indian Problem

1

India's Founding Moment

Introduction

The Indian Problem

As the year 1946 came to an end, Jawaharlal Nehru introduced the Aims and Objects Resolution in the Constituent Assembly of India. It was an act of great moment, a formal declaration of the terms under which Indians would perform the rituals of self-rule. Yet Nehru, who had been a leading participant in the anticolonial struggle and was soon to be independent India's first prime minister, spoke with a hint of regret. "One of the unfortunate legacies of the past," he observed, "has been that there has been no imagination in the understanding of the Indian problem."[1] Nehru sensed that Indians were yet to grasp the import of their revolution. For him, the Indian revolution matched the American, French, and Russian in historical meaning. Much like these defining flashes in modern constitutionalism, the event was exceptional for the problem it had to solve. This study of India's constitutional founding is an effort to take seriously Nehru's suggestion.

To appreciate why the making of modern India marked such a remarkable moment in the history of modern constitutionalism—to uncover its singularity—is to consider how ideas about democracy took shape in an age of empire. When Alexis de Tocqueville and John Stuart Mill proposed that democracy was unsuited to certain societies, that it mandated the presence of background conditions to enable its existence, they communicated in a language that was familiar to the nineteenth century.[2] Constitutional theorists like Walter Bagehot and A. V. Dicey spoke in similar terms. They found it natural that the nature of government rested on its surrounding environment.[3] In a way, such scholars committed the sin of

1

essentialism. They followed in the rich tradition of James Mill, whose *History of British India* had made it known that Indians simply were a certain kind of people.[4] Mill's *History of British India* had revealed the innate nature of Indians with astonishing detail: untold aspects of Indian social and cultural life were dissected, each attribute taken to be a mark of deviation from the Western world. In performing this task, such works had suggested that human behavior was not the consequence of politics but instead its cause. The distinction between pre-political and political passions had been turned on its head, a scenario that Thomas Hobbes would have regarded as placing the cart before the horse.

But there was more than essentialism to the nineteenth century's turn from the radical institutional imagination of the previous century. Anxieties about the spread of democracy arose in the face of two changes. The first was the discovery of society—the encounters with modes of interaction and solidarity beyond the alienating confines of political life.[5] The second was the emergence of the economy—the rise of commercial enclaves that were lively and self-assured, and promised a distinct form of collaboration.[6] The arrival of society and the economy complicated the account of sovereignty that someone like Hobbes had been able to neatly offer. At the heart of the Hobbesian project was the independence of politics. The objective was to portray a certain kind of freedom that the political sphere promised. For the nineteenth century, however, the task at hand had acquired greater complexity. To fully understand the existence of society and the economy meant interpreting the effects that these spaces had on political life. Did politics produce these spaces of energy, these fresh ways of thinking about freedom, or was politics contingent on them?

Arenas governed by social bonds or commercial exchange were not free in a technical sense. But even though the sovereign power of the state could invariably reach them, they did exert a kind of autonomous force. Their self-sufficiency called for a new conception of power. In the case of Hobbes, for example, the relationship between power and sovereignty had been relatively easy to frame. The primary threat to the domain of politics, at least in *Leviathan,* was the church and, to some extent, noble lords.[7] By the nineteenth century, however, power had become a more dynamic force. The sparkling changes in human activity released by the domains of the social and the economic could not be ignored. They forced attention on the implications that earlier conceptions of power might hold for conceptualizing sovereignty. In an array of historical contexts, attempts were made to work out the dynamic between power and sovereignty. The

2

Abbé Sieyès tried to grasp this relation in the context of representation.[8] The *Federalist Papers* tried to come to terms with it within the framework of institutions.[9] In today's world, democratic theory has taken yet another turn, with political scientists and legal scholars urging us to reconsider how power might corrode popular representation.[10]

The changing character of power in the modern world—puzzles about the relationship between the political and the social and economic spheres of life—contributed to the nineteenth-century concern with universalizing self-government. This concern is a familiar topic in our intellectual life. It has been captured by a recent outpouring of scholarship on the political theory of empire.[11] This work has engaged with a number of important ideas: the centrality of imperial ideology to wider questions in the nineteenth century; the connection between liberalism and empire; the relationship between Western categories of understanding and non-Western forms of experience; the contrast between the nineteenth century and prior centuries; the nature and meaning of universalism; and the assortment of reasons and justifications given for European expansion. This diverse set of scholarly interventions has sharpened our appreciation of major Western thinkers, given us a genealogy of imperial ways of seeing, and demystified the conceptual relationship between the imperial ideology and the idea of freedom.

There is more, however, that remains to be learned. This body of work has been striking for its historical and philosophical contributions, but it has offered us only one side of the story. We now have an appreciation of the ideological apparatus on which empires were built. But we have less sense of how those who were colonized responded to this ideology.[12] In the Indian context the search for self-government developed gradually, but from at least 1929 onward—when the leading force behind this search, the Indian National Congress, issued a call for *purna swaraj* (complete independence)—freedom from foreign rule absorbed the nationalist agenda. India's political response to colonialism has, of course, been covered in compelling ways, but the intellectual answer has been far less explored. We know less than we might expect about how Indians met the problem of self-government.

This book addresses India's founders' responses to the problem of democracy and its preconditions. How did they approach the missing foundations on which self-government was widely thought to be predicated? India's founders, I shall suggest, met the imperial argument on direct terms. They believed in the possibility of creating democratic citizens through democratic politics. A study of the constitutional vision brings to light the political apparatus that could effectuate this transition and respond to the challenge of democratization. The apparatus had three key elements: the explication of rules through codification; the existence of an overarching state; and representation centered on individuals. In each case there was an attempt to free Indians from prevailing types of knowledge and understanding, to place them in a realm of agency and deliberation that was appropriate to self-rule, and to alter the relationship that they shared with one another. In studying this schema, it is crucial to keep in mind the notion of the constitutive. Democracy was interpreted not as a sum of performances, but as a form of government where behavior had common meaning. The rules and structures and institutions were efforts not only to shape action but, more fundamentally, to provide meaning to practices that could be shared. Each feature of the framework served distinct and complementary roles in realizing this—in converting Indians from subjects into citizens.

The Turn to Democracy

The act of being governed by another involved acute psychological burdens, both for the ruler and the ruled.[13] This burden meant that responses to colonialism were inevitably varied in both form and authenticity. A noticeable feature in anticolonial thought was the turn to history.[14] Western eyes had seen India as a land of ceaseless conflict and, in some accounts, as a land without a history. In G. W. F. Hegel's lectures on the philosophy of history, to use a well-known example, one saw the ease with which India could be kept out of global transitions. For Hegel, India was a land that had "remained stationary and fixed."[15] Despotism, even in nations where it held sway, was taken to be an unnatural form of order. But in India, Hegel contended, it was a natural state of being. The distinctions imposed by caste had "condemn[ed] the Indian people to the most degrading spiritual serfdom."[16] As a result, the Indian people had no understanding of their independent existence. This meant that the land was a place without the exercise of conscious choices—it was a land without the possibility of politics. The Indian mind was littered with "confused dreams," and the ingredients of historical reasoning—an "intelligent, thoughtful comprehension of events, and fidelity in representing them"—were nowhere to be found.[17] There was, quite simply,

4

no meaning that one could attach to the phases across which the Indian civilization had voyaged.

It was precisely this permanence—the sin of essentialism—that Indians hoped to counter. History could be deployed to puncture the alleged association between Western societies and democratic ways of being.[18] To recover a new past was to anticipate a new future. Among alternative renderings of India's past, it is hard to locate a text of greater ambition than Jawaharlal Nehru's *The Discovery of India.*[19] Nehru had long acknowledged that the greatest "of all the injuries done by England to India" was the creation of "the slave mentality"—the infliction of a burden that had psychologically incapacitated Indians from asserting themselves.[20] *The Discovery of India,* a text written largely in jail—where Nehru spent nearly a decade of his life during colonial rule—and published only a few years before Indian independence, took matters further. It presented a grand image of India's past, one rich in complexity and variety. For Nehru, India had passed through centuries of change and housed countless modes of living, while nonetheless retaining "a spirit that [was] peculiar to it and that [was] impressed on all its children, however much they may differ among themselves."[21]

Colonial histories, by contrast, had imagined India's past as empty and uncivil. In their understanding, only an external authority could impose some logic on epochs of futility and madness. In locating a shared Indian experience—in capturing India's resilience in the face of changing fortunes and its accommodative potential in the face of diversity—*The Discovery of India* was a show of extraordinary intellectual imagination. The text had, to be sure, distinct limitations. Nehru barely gestured at controversies and made little of real tensions. As a work of history, the book would have been a spectacular failure. But that was never its aim. It was instead an act of nation-building with a clear message: India's varied past demonstrated the sheer contingency of its current enslavement. Across centuries, India had shown itself to be capable of change—capable of finding new ways to survive and thrive—and it could find such ways again. The study that began from ancient India was used to make a decidedly modern point: that India could be constituted and reconstituted.

The task of constituting India fell on the founders of India's Constitution. They faced a peculiar challenge. The history of modern constitutionalism is typically portrayed as consisting of specific moments, with each moment immortalizing a distinct set of fears and achievements. In the case of the American founding, for example, matters of inquiry usually include the question of large versus small republics; the possibility of constraining power through institutions; and the prospect of republicanism without monarchy.[22] The Indian founding similarly brought into focus a unique set of issues. These issues defined and exemplified the postcolonial constitutional moment. At the heart of this moment—in which constitution-making and democratization occurred simultaneously—lay the question of democracy in an environment unqualified for its existence. Democracy was being instituted in a difficult setting: poor and illiterate; divided by caste, religion, and language; and burdened by centuries of tradition. These factors placed the decolonization constitution-making process in noticeable contrast to the development of Western nation-states. In the West, the historical path of countries saw improvements in prosperity, stronger administration systems, and the subsequent extension of franchise. Universal suffrage came after a reasonable average level of income had been secured and state administrative systems were relatively well established. The historical conditions of India's creation should encourage us to see it as the paradigmatic democratic experience of the twentieth century, in much the same way that Tocqueville had seen the United States as the model nineteenth-century democracy.

The immediate coming of universal suffrage in India's settings is even more arresting, given democracy's troubled history in the decades preceding the end of British rule. The First World War had brushed aside the major continental empires only to create democratic states that readily collapsed in the 1920s and 1930s. Even where self-rule existed, its outcomes invited apprehension. "Popular government," the prominent British scholar and politician James Bryce wrote in 1921, "has not yet been proved to guarantee, always and everywhere, good government."[23] The crisis of democracy during the interwar years exposed the fragility of democracy's foundations. As one scholar recently observed while taking stock of democracy's withdrawal in the early 1930s, "Of the seventeen new democracies that had been set up in the hopeful aftermath of the First World War, only a few were left. Italy, Portugal, Poland, Brazil, Argentina, Uruguay, Japan, and Germany had all reverted to forms of authoritarianism."[24]

The uncertainty about democracy as a workable form of political organization during these years was not lost on India's leaders. They wondered what their future might look like in such a rapidly changing world.[25] Where democratic life survived—most notably during America's New

Deal—its survival was often doubted, and its victory was hardly straight-forward.[26] Similarly, when democracy did return after 1945, its arrival was anything but a foregone conclusion. Its victory over fascism in Europe was contingent, and it spoke to neither the certainty nor the stability of the democratic form.[27] The West, at this time, did not hesitate to inform Indians that democracy was an alien ideal. When the British prime minister Clement Attlee wrote to Nehru to stress the Commonwealth's worth in 1949, he advised him that monarchical arrangements best suited the Asian people: "I should have said that the general tradition in Asia is in favor of monarchy. I think this is true of India historically . . . Republicanism is an alien importation from Europe derived from nineteenth-century liberalism and appreciated and understood by a comparatively small intelligentsia. The Asiatic republics are few and of recent establishment. Their record is not very encouraging. They tend to degenerate into dictatorships or oligarchies. They offer a prize for the ambitious authoritarian individual."[28]

Others would make similar observations, at times expressing dismay at the constitutional text that was taking shape in India. Philip Spratt, a British thinker and political activist based in India since the mid-1920s, was only one among many commentators to make brave predictions. The Indian Constitution, he declared, "is in its main outlines a liberal constitution, to be imposed upon a society which is not a liberal society, and cannot be expected to make such a constitution work."[29] The brutal economic and social reality of India, one might note, made visible the contrast between the wave of decolonization in Asia and Africa in the 1950s and 1960s, and the experience in the white colonies. As M. C. Setalvad, India's first attorney general, emphasized in his Hamlyn Lectures in London a few years after the end of colonial rule: "At the advent of freedom, the position of India was in no sense comparable to that in the Dominions of Canada and Australia."[30] The contrast with other constitution-making efforts at the time was equally observable, whether one considers the factors that shaped Japan's 1947 Constitution (the *Nihonkoku Kenpō*) or West Germany's 1949 Basic Law (the *Grundgesetz*), or indeed the 1950 decision by Israel's Constituent Assembly (the first *Knesset*) to create a constitution in parts.[31]

The special nature of the Indian founding may come as a surprise to contemporary scholars of global constitutionalism. The current spate of scholarship on comparative constitution-making has sought to understand moments of creation in terms of patterns and trends, often by taking note of the incentives and interests of the various actors involved. One frequent topic of study, for example, has been the processes of constitution-making: the relationship between methods and results.[32] Various themes have been subject to interrogation, from the nature of participants included in drafting exercises to the role of knowledge and expertise to the pressures that constitution-makers face. Even though the scholarship has at times turned to particular founding episodes, little interest has been expressed in the distinct ideological significance of the postcolonial constitutional moment and the dramatic remaking of Asia and Africa in the 1950s and 1960s.[33]

This was not always the case. The specificity of India's founding was, for instance, widely noticed by constitutional thinkers at the time. The Cambridge lawyer Ivor Jennings was among the most celebrated of such figures.[34] As someone who participated in the constitution-drafting efforts in Ceylon and Pakistan and lectured on the new Indian Constitution, Jennings studied how nations liberated from colonial rule could embrace self-government. He made the case that constitutions must be written by keeping local contexts in mind. His attack was on Jeremy Bentham, "who had sat in Westminster working out constitutional principles for countries almost as far apart as China and Peru," and Jean-Jacques Rousseau, who "sitting in Geneva . . . had drafted a constitution for Poland, a country which he never visited."[35]

Jennings cautioned against indifference to regional realities when it came to writing constitutions for the decolonized world. A place like India was, after all, lacking in many of Britain's renowned features: a basic standard of education and literacy; and broad homogeneity in class, language, and religion.[36] Jennings toyed with a variety of constitutional design techniques that might facilitate self-government, highlighting the indispensable role of factors like political leadership. But it is striking that he felt—even in 1956—that the question of suffrage should remain open. When a country came to decide on suffrage, it would do well to remember that "it may be possible to minimize the risks by creating a limited franchise or by balancing representation."[37] The problems of the postcolonial world had never occurred in Britain "because the franchise was extended gradually."[38] A "narrow franchise, indirect elections, tribal representation may all be quite sensible in colonial conditions," and it would be an error to condemn them "merely because they are regarded as primitive in the Conservative Party Headquarters or Transport House."[39] Implicit in Jennings's advice was the idea that national sovereignty could be severed from the question of suffrage. A country could be free even if all its citizens did not have the right to vote.

This general view of India's political capacity had found expression in colonial assessments during the first half of the twentieth century. In the *Report on Indian Constitutional Reforms* of 1918, much was made of "the traditions and habits of thought of the people."[40] India's people were poor and incapable, and they belonged to a society that was without solidarity. The *Report* spoke the language of civilizational hierarchy and progress through instruction. India may well find itself ready for self-government on some future occasion, but that day had not yet arrived. A sustainable political culture, the *Report* contended, was based "not so much on statutes and written constitutions, as on the gradual building up of conventions, customs, and traditions."[41] And these latter ornaments were, of course, missing among the Indian people. In subsequent years, India's unpropitious conditions continued to trouble the imperial mind. The *Report of the Indian Statutory Commission,* submitted a little over a decade later, in 1930, recommended an extension of the vote to correspond to a growth in adult literacy. This reasoning captured the persistence of the colonial logic. In addition to the implications that illiteracy would have for the exercise of the vote, it would also result in a practical nightmare. One could only imagine the checks and preparations needed when one was "dealing with a mass of illiterate voters."[42] The *Report of the Indian Franchise Committee,* published two years later, observed that illiteracy prevented an informed outlook toward public affairs and political participation. The task of political education could be partly satisfied by political parties. But India could, alas, boast of little party organization. Conditions such as these led the Committee to reject universal suffrage and "seek a more manageable basis" for running the show.[43]

When Indians had turned to the suffrage question in the nineteenth century, their agenda had been greater involvement in the colonial administration. In the twentieth century, however, the question of suffrage occasionally faded into the background—concern over the internal distribution of power declined as national sovereignty became the goal. Yet, the matter did receive some attention, and mainstream texts of the Indian nationalist movement often spoke of a wide franchise. The Lucknow Pact of 1916, a famous agreement of sorts between the Indian National Congress and the Muslim League, stipulated elections to the provincial legislative councils "on as broad a franchise as possible."[44] The Motilal Nehru Report of 1928, a local response to imperial constitutional reform, committed

India to universal franchise.[45] Prior attempts at restricting the right to vote had, the *Report* claimed, only harmed those who were excluded. Moreover—and this point was fundamental—the *Report* argued that the very exercise of the right to vote was a form of education.[46] When the Sapru Committee's report—an Indian attempt to propose a constitutional scheme that could accommodate different domestic political interests—was published in 1945, it too made the case for universal suffrage. In rejecting the Franchise Committee's 1932 report, the Sapru Committee claimed that even though circumstances had changed—the party structure, for example, had evolved—substantial changes in such matters could occur "only *after* full responsible government has been introduced."[47] In keeping with this rationale, it reiterated the idea that the very exercise of franchise would provide the education necessary to enable a responsible politics.[48]

The support for universal franchise could also be seen in proclamations by major political actors. Nationalist leaders viewed restrictions on the franchise as colonial attempts to curb growing disaffection.[49] Mohandas Gandhi, who returned from South Africa in 1915 and swiftly became the face of India's entire effort at emancipation, boldly declared in 1939 that he was unworried by illiteracy and "would plump for unadulterated adult franchise for both men and women."[50] The contribution of B. R. Ambedkar, who took up the cause of the lower castes during the anticolonial struggle and later occupied a critical role in the Constituent Assembly, was significant in this regard. Ironically, the specificity of Ambedkar's political agenda—his focus on the problem of caste—made him sensitive to restrictions on the right to vote. Qualifications based on education and property during colonial rule meant the *de facto* exclusion of the lower castes. As a result, the nature and meaning of the right to vote often became a focal point in Ambedkar's negotiations with the colonial government. Before the Southborough Committee on Franchise in 1919, Ambedkar made the case that suffrage could itself serve an instructive role and that participation in political life would bring about consciousness among the lower castes. Relying on the new liberalism movement in early twentieth-century Britain, which linked collective unity and individual autonomy, Ambedkar turned to L. T. Hobhouse's 1911 text *Liberalism*.[51] His specific reference suggested that "the success of democracy depends on the response of the voters to the opportunities given to them. But, conversely, the opportunities must be given in order to call forth that response. The exercise of popular government is itself an education . . . enfranchisement itself may be precisely the stimulus needed to awaken interest."[52]

A decade later Ambedkar proposed that the exercise of the franchise was not a privilege but a right. To treat it as a privilege, he argued, would mean that the "political emancipation of the un-enfranchised will be entirely at the mercy of those that are enfranchised."[53] To limit the suffrage on account of illiteracy was a kind of perversity, because literacy had first been denied to a segment of the population and now that segment was being denied suffrage because it was illiterate.[54] Moreover, such a limitation mistakenly presumed that formal literacy was equivalent to a capacity to determine one's own choices.[55] A close study of the gradual extension of the suffrage in the West, Ambedkar argued, showed that it had not been based on any philosophy. The staggered expansion of voting rights had occurred for political reasons. It took place because the ruling classes wanted to preserve their power. The stages through which transitions ensued were not driven by rationales or ideologies.[56] There was no larger lesson to be drawn from this history; there was no deeper truth that carried weight. Moreover, the apparent relationship between restrictions on the franchise and good government had little truth. All one needed to do, Ambedkar claimed at the First London Roundtable Conference in 1930, was "take the trouble of reading the life of Lord Shaftsbury, and the social and political history of England" to see that "the unreformed Parliament was not a blessing to anyone."[57]

To limit the franchise, Ambedkar believed, was to misunderstand the meaning of democracy. It was to proclaim that democracy was solely about the expression of preferences at the ballot box. Instead of falling prey to this vision, which he saw as impoverished, Ambedkar turned to John Dewey to underline the relationship between democracy and participation. Dewey had regarded a democratic society as entailing more than a specific kind of government. At a deeper level, what such a society offered was "a mode of associated living, of conjoint communicated experience."[58] A democracy involved many different avenues of shared interest among its people. This sharing meant that one always had to consider the actions of others, just as the actions of others informed how one chose to act. Such a process meant the end of isolation. One had to react to a world that possessed far greater variety—this process led to progress and released a great number of capacities that prior forms of narrow behavior had curbed.

11

It is easy to see why Ambedkar found this account compelling. It was focused, after all, on moving beyond the segregation imposed by rigid group differentiation. Drawing on Dewey, Ambedkar saw in the right to vote the power to regulate the terms on which one's life would be lived with regard to others. To have such a right was to have the opportunity to determine the conditions on which interpersonal relationships would be directed. If democracy was about shaping the associations in one's life, a limitation on suffrage would place the lower classes under the control of the powerful. It would mean that such classes would be deprived of the chance to shape interactions in their life. Rather than enabling responsible government, suffrage restrictions were therefore a form of coercion: "Just as the capitalist must have the power, if he is to have any constitution, to dictate how he shall live on terms of associated life with the labor, surely the laborer is entitled also to have the power to regulate the terms on which he shall live with his capitalist master."[59]

When British rule ended two decades later, such arguments no longer needed to be made. Universal franchise was a fait accompli for India's political elite. A century earlier, Indian political thought had been preoccupied with understanding how the nation had fallen prey to foreign hands. This nineteenth-century inquiry led to an astonishing degree of self-reflection. It produced numerous individuals who were critics of both alien rule and Indian society. The critique of the British often went alongside systematic assessments of the costs imposed by their rule. A noteworthy strain of thinking, for example, showed how British economic development was made possible by the transfer of wealth from India.[60] As the twentieth century unfolded, Indians turned their attention away from the loss of freedom to how it might be regained. The turn came alongside new forms of public engagement as well as political organization. This shift resulted in intense disagreements over political action, as seen in the divide between the moderate and extremist camps of the Indian National Congress that split the party in 1907, and in broader debates over the extent to which Indian nationalism should embrace constitutional means for revolution.

After Mohandas Gandhi's transformation of the nationalist movement from 1919 onward, the focus shifted from an increase in local participation to a thoroughgoing attack on the foundations of the colonial state. As self-rule became the objective of India's political struggle, a body that would draft a constitutional text for the new nation began to acquire a place in the nationalist imagination. It was only when "the Indian people settle their own constitution in a popularly elected constituent assembly," Jawaharlal Nehru noted in 1933, that India's various political conflicts could be resolved.[61] The call for an assembly was a call for noninterference from the British. Gandhi's draft resolution in 1940, which was approved by the Congress party's Working Committee, declared that the "people of India alone can properly shape their own constitution and determine their relations to other countries of the world, through a constituent assembly elected on the basis of adult suffrage."[62] It confirmed the faith that such an assembly might solve the problem of communal representation. This assembly would be, the Working Committee declared in May 1946, "sovereign in so far as the framing of the Constitution is concerned."[63]

A body to prepare a constitution was eventually formed as per the Cabinet Mission Plan of 1946—a proposal that kept British India undivided, grouped provinces according to their religious composition, limited the federal government's role to select national matters like foreign policy, and left unresolved crucial matters like the position of the princely states. The Muslim League boycotted the early sessions of the Constituent Assembly, demanding two assemblies that would draft texts for two separate nations. In time the Assembly acquired legal status under the Indian Independence Act of 1947, which created two separate dominions, India and Pakistan. Its deliberations lasted from December 1946 to November 1949—amid civil war, one of the largest migrations in human history, and the incorporation of nearly 600 princely states into the Indian Union.

The body was indirectly elected based on the elections to the provincial legislatures in 1945–1946. It is estimated that under these elections only around one-fourth or one-fifth of the adult population had been eligible to vote.[64] It also included nearly a hundred representatives of the princely states, chosen by way of a process of consultation. The Assembly had limited socioeconomic diversity. Moreover, the creation of Pakistan and exit of the Muslim League left the Indian National Congress with an overwhelming majority. Despite this, however, the body emerged as a remarkable forum for the articulation of intellectual disagreements and contrasting viewpoints. It consisted of nearly 400 members, and its work was conducted through various committees and subcommittees that undertook much of the real composition. When in session, the Assembly considered submissions and reports of the committees and subcommittees, and reviewed versions of draft provisions and the overall text. It finally adopted a document with 395 provisions and eight schedules. No ratification was undertaken, and the Constitution of India came into force on January 26, 1950.

Numerous individuals were vital to the constitution-making process. B. R. Ambedkar chaired the crucial drafting committee. In addition to Jawaharlal Nehru, three other senior Indian National Congress leaders— Abul Kalam Azad, Vallabhbhai Patel, and Rajendra Prasad—are also credited with having played major parts.[65] Each was influential in the anticolonial struggle and held a distinguished position in the postcolonial nation-making endeavor. Azad was a significant voice for Hindu-Muslim unity and served as India's minister of education. Patel, the nation's deputy prime minister, was central to the integration of the princely states into the Indian Union. Prasad, a teacher and lawyer, served as the president of the Constituent Assembly, and later become the president of India. Others in the Assembly also intervened in ways that often proved decisive. These included two prominent lawyers, Alladi Krishnaswami Ayyar and K. M. Munshi; the social activist and reformer Hansa Mehta, who was a notable female voice in the Assembly; and the economist K. T. Shah. An incomparable role was played by the civil servant B. N. Rau. Rau's distinguished career in the colonial civil service included both bureaucratic and judicial offices. Though not formally a member of the Assembly, he served as the Constitutional Adviser to the body. He would later be appointed as a judge of the Permanent Court of International Justice at The Hague. During the constitution-making process, Rau was responsible both for his own substantive contributions, based on serious comparative research, and for incorporating the submissions of different committees and subcommittees into a single document. Importantly, the Constituent Assembly also served as India's first provisional parliament. It performed its dual roles separately, capturing the fact that *constitution-making* was taken to be a distinct task. The body enjoyed a significant degree of political legitimacy throughout its existence. Even Gandhi, otherwise a fierce critic of Western political institutions, came around to having some faith in the body. At a time of intense conflict among communities, he hoped that it would manage the problem of representation, though he remained skeptical of whether it would affirm his vision of a decentralized India.[66]

An unrestricted suffrage may have been a fait accompli for India's founders, but its meaning could not be overlooked. As the Constituent Assembly took up the third and final reading of the draft constitutional text on November 17, 1949, the adoption of democracy gripped its imag-

14

ination. Even if one were to cast aside illiteracy and societal divisions, there was the brutal administrative matter of conducting elections for such a large electorate. Prasad, the Assembly's president, acknowledged that "the mere act of printing [the electoral roll] is such a big and tremendous job that the governments are being hard put to it, to find the presses which will undertake this big job."[67] For several members, the choice of an unrestricted franchise was an act of courage.[68] But not everyone was equally impressed. Some felt that it was simply an impractical endeavor.[69] Another described it as "a dangerous weapon" in the absence of education and patriotism.[70] One member went so far as to regard it "a monstrous experiment."[71]

Some members felt that a more sensible approach would have been to extend the franchise gradually, as had been done in Britain.[72] Inventive options, such as imposing literacy requirements on candidates seeking election, were sometimes offered as means to ensure better government.[73] But such suggestions were few and far between. The Assembly never seriously countenanced the idea of limiting suffrage. As one member put it, qualifications based on property or education were impossible in a country where few had either—the result would not be government based on consent in any sense of the term.[74] Rather than limiting suffrage, the challenge was to resolve the problems posed by universal franchise. The outstanding feature of India's constitutional founding is the seriousness with which this challenge was acknowledged.

India's Overlooked Origins

It is a matter of some surprise that India's democratic origins have been neglected within the history of political ideas. Among scholars of the period, the constitutional founding itself has provoked hardly any curiosity. Instead, much of the available energy has been expended on the partition of British India and on Indian nationalism. Though the division of territory was dramatic and the emergence of nationalist ideology outside the West was noteworthy, the constitutional moment has been snubbed for a deeper reason: It has been thought to lack any historical significance. Early reflections on the Indian Constitution presented narratives of steady progression: one British statute was followed by another, each successive law marking a shift toward greater Indian involvement, with the process culminating in self-government.[75] The development was viewed as a sign of evolution rather than repudiation. More recent studies often repeat the plot lines of these early reflections, deemphasizing historical ruptures by weaving a longer history.[76] The 1950 constitutional text borrowed several ideas from the Government of India Act of 1935. It replicated many of the Act's provisions and adopted familiar elements of the British constitutional schema. This fact has led some historians to conclude that the Constitution is a mere extension of the 1935 Act.[77]

Such a view rests on an impoverished reading of legal documents. In legal documents, all words do not have the same value—some matter more than others. Regardless of the number of words that were taken from the 1935 Act, democratization signified a major break from the past. From 1858 until 1920, when the Government of India Act of 1919 came into force, India's constitutional scheme had no form of executive responsibility to the legislature. The changes introduced by the 1919 Act were severely limited. The arrangement at the central level remained, by and large, the same. At the provincial level, a new system of dyarchy meant that ministers were only given control of select "transferred" subjects, and the governor still retained vast powers. As V. S. Srinivasa Sastri, a founding member of the moderate Indian Liberal Party, put it, the executive was "highly pampered."[78] Moreover, provincial autonomy was circumscribed by provisions that allowed the central government to supervise and veto provincial legislation.[79] Though the Government of India Act of 1935 ushered in responsible government at the provincial level, its federal scheme at the center failed to start, leaving the arrangement of power at this tier essentially unchanged. The 1935 Act introduced dyarchy at the center but, yet again, kept vital matters within executive control. Legislatures at the provincial level had greater powers than before, but the power of the governors was by no means trivial. Above all, they could dismiss a validly elected government. For all its changes, throughout its tenure British rule in India remained what James Fitzjames Stephen once described as "an absolute government, founded not on consent but on conquest"[80] and what the Earl of Minto had termed a "constitutional autocracy."[81] What bears emphasizing is that even if specific measures introduced into the colonial structure over time had enabled the government to become minimally representative, that government was in no way a responsible government.[82] Furthermore, there were no rights, and judicial review was permissible only on extremely narrow grounds.[83]

The effort to deny any ideological weight to India's origins relates, in some ways, to trends that once infected studies of Indian nationalism. Some decades ago it was suggested that modern India was born out of a series of self-interested compromises and arrangements between the Raj and locals.[84] The ills committed by this scholarship were not those committed by men like John Strachey, who had seen nationalism as an elite trick played on the masses.[85] Yet both strands were similar in one respect: they held that the Indian story had nothing to offer in the realm of ideas. The formal legal structure of the colonial state was underlined, the incentives that shaped local politics were highlighted, and Indian nationalism was denied rather than explained. Under this frame of reasoning, Indians revolted not because of any philosophical disagreement, but because of a failure to succeed under the colonial system. As per this account, Indians initially sought to work together with the Raj. In due course, tensions arose from internal local rivalry and frustrated desires led to anticolonial sentiments. The opposition that emerged resulted in some locals benefiting and others losing out. This, in turn, led to forms of agitation and to specific kinds of allowances, and the eventual outcome was the end of British rule. Such studies took Indian nationalism to be, in Tapan Raychaudhuri's vivid phrase, a kind of "animal politics."[86] In denying the role of ideas, they mistakenly assumed that historical changes were necessitated by political life, and they ignored sets of arguments on which actions rested. Though such studies have been subject to devastating responses, the general idea that they embodied—that Indian outbursts are best seen as banal self-interested schemes for power—has cast a long shadow.

On occasion India's constitutional founding has been downplayed not by privileging tactics over ideology but by claiming a different kind of historical continuity. Here the argument is not that India's postcolonial framework neatly followed the colonial model, but instead that Indian liberal ideas had a long history and pre-dated the 1950 Constitution. Such a narrative places features of India's founding within a longer historical trajectory and portrays the constitutional founding as natural and inevitable.[87] It is certainly true that the Constitution embraced several ideas associated with modern constitutional liberalism—the recognition of rights, the power of judicial review, the principle of separation of powers, and so forth. But this fact is a puzzle, not an explanation. Indeed, it is precisely the puzzle at the heart of Indian intellectual history. In the decades preceding the drafting of the constitutional text, Indian intellectual life comprised an assortment of traditions that would be hard to characterize as liberal in contemporary understandings of the term.[88] Mohandas Gandhi's anti-statist vision is the example with which we are most acquainted, but even figures like B. R. Ambedkar and Jawaharlal Nehru were hardly preoccupied with the liberal distinction between the public and the private. If scholars of the American founding could once assert that the nation's birth arose in circumstances ordained for liberalism, as Louis Hartz did, such a claim is impossible to make in the Indian case.[89] The question to be asked is why India's political elite converged on a set of liberal constitutional values without the inheritance of any major liberal tradition.[90] This is a question different from the one at the core of this book, but it is not an unrelated one. It was the problem of democratization under Indian conditions, the following chapters shall show, that offers at least part of the answer to this question. The principles of liberal constitutionalism—the centrality of the state, noncommunal political representation, and so on—were seen as responsive to the challenges posed by the burden of democracy.

Scholars of contemporary India, one should acknowledge, have been alive to its unprecedented democratic form. This theme has often been the framing device for historical studies of India's postcolonial life.[91] Similarly, political scientists have investigated the inexplicable survival of Indian democracy.[92] There have been attempts at rationalizing this survival to see how India might fit into the universal rules of politics. The question has also been posed comparatively, typically comparing the nation's fortunes with those of its neighbor Pakistan.[93] Such inquiries are part of a broader conversation. In historical and comparative studies of politics, there has long been an interest in many stages of modernization occurring at once.[94] Much effort has been made to understand why democratic transitions occur as well as why some transitions are successful, with some resulting in democracies that consolidate whereas others result in breakdowns. Which variables best explain such divergent realities? Do democratic fortunes turn on wealth and income? Are they shaped by different class interests? What role is played by countermajoritarian institutions that can protect old elites? How do political parties influence regime outcomes?[95] These are unavoidable questions—and why the sudden expansion in political participation in India's fragile climate did not go haywire is a query that is hard to ignore when one attends to the experience of so many other postcolonial experiments. A recent meditation on global democracy put the matter plainly when it recognized that India is "the most surprising democracy there has ever been: surprising in its scale, in its persistence among a huge and, for most of its existence, still exceedingly poor population, and in its tensile strength in the face of fierce centrifugal pressures and high levels of violence, corruption, and human oppression throughout most of its existence."[96] But such observations, as the tenor of this passage confirms, have been invitations to comprehend how democracy has been domesticated in a strange land. The absence of secularization, the low levels of literacy, the lack of a liberal tradition, and so forth have invited assessment of how democracy works in different settings. Such an assessment is far from irrelevant, but it is concerned with the working of Indian democracy rather than the decision to be democratic. Simply put, one cannot help but notice how little has been said about the founding approach toward democratization. The endurance of self-government in India may have encouraged much work within the disciplines of history and political science, but it has failed to inspire interest in how all of this initially came to pass.[97] There is, it would seem, an understanding that even though the founders embraced democracy with intent, the choice "was unwitting in the sense that the elite who introduced it was itself surprisingly insouciant about the potential implications of its actions."[98]

This was hardly the case. As Alladi Krishnaswami Ayyar, a frequent and crucial voice in the Assembly, put it in his final address before the body, "The principle of adult suffrage was adopted in no lighthearted mood but with the full realizations of its implications."[99] One member portrayed the risks of blind legal transplantation in vivid terms: "There is said to be a tribe of monkeys in Africa which copy faithfully the houses of men and then live on the outside of them instead of inside. The transplantation of political institutions is not free from this danger of copying the obvious and leaving out the essential."[100] In a speech in the Bombay Legislature in 1939, B. R. Ambedkar had similarly cautioned against constitutional arrangements that copied the West without sensitivity to India's conditions:

> Jeremy Bentham must be known to every lawyer, if not to the outside world. Jeremy Bentham was a great legislator; he was a man who indulged in formularies; he was a man who indulged in symmetrical classification of things; he wanted to reform the English law on the basis of pure rationalism. The South American colonies thought that a man who believed in nothing but applying reason and who believed in doing things a priori was a proper person who would be asked to frame a constitution for themselves. They sent emissaries with briefs, I believe, marked, as they usually are for counsel, to draft the constitution. There were innumerable colonies

19

in South America, all spilt out of the old Spanish empire. Jeremy Bentham jumped at the opportunity of drafting constitutions for these new countries in South America. He took great pains and framed the most elaborate documents. I see the Prime Minister laughing because he knows the facts. And, sir, they were shipped all these documents, constitutional documents framed by Jeremy Bentham, were shipped over to South America, for the protection of the life and liberty of the people and for the intonement, if I may say so, of the democratic principle. When they went there, they were tried by the South American people for a few years. And afterward every constitution that was framed by Jeremy Bentham broke to pieces, and they did not know what to do with the surplus copies that had arrived; and all the South American people decided that they should be burnt publicly.[101]

The answer to the Indian problem could not be found in thoughtless duplication. The challenge of postcolonial constitutionalism was to attend to both the meaning and the impact of Western ideas and the reality of local traditions and circumstances.[102] India's founding moment called for a schema that could meet the challenges of constituting democracy in an inhospitable environment. This book is a study of the plan that emerged. It focuses on three distinct themes—codification, centralization, and representation—that lay at the heart of the Constituent Assembly's deliberations. They capture at once the concerns that democratization cast on the political imagination at the time, and the promise that it offered for a political order on new terms.

The Architecture of Democracy

Thus far, in speaking of democracy in India, we have spoken primarily of the immediate granting of universal suffrage. This granting of suffrage was issued, though, alongside the construction of a specific institutional framework. This framework could not, of course, guarantee the success of the constitutional project—any such success must contend with external factors. But the project was crucial to shaping the political horizons of the future. The framework would channel and structure the exercise of the suffrage, and it would provide the means by which democratic politics could result in the creation of a democratic citizen. A feature of this conception was that *popular authorization*—that is, the exercise of the

20

vote—was necessary but insufficient for a political system to have *legiti-mate authority*.[103] The mechanism of free and fair elections would give individuals the agency to determine their political destiny, but more was required from the terms of the exercise of that agency. One must ask not merely what kind of postcolonial structure was conceptualized by India's founders but also how such a structure was seen as validating the use of authority and legitimizing the application of coercive power. This ques-tion matters in all constitutional democracies, but it might be a salient one for those that involve radical transformations.

Attention to how authority was legitimized allows us to make some sense of the liberal characteristics of India's founding. An idea familiar since at least Jean-Jacques Rousseau is that freedom turns not only on our consent but also on the conditions that our consent engenders.[104] It is not enough to assert that democracy has moral force because it allows for all to participate equally. More is usually required for us to accept the law's claim to authority and its exercise of coercive power. This sentiment is gestured at during instances when we ask whether a democracy is func-tioning democratically.[105] If we are to address the legitimization of au-thority beyond popular authorization, we must attend to the arrangement that India's founders put in place, and we must consider the role it played in the task of justification. As we shall see, the founding schema had fea-tures that we would associate with contemporary liberal thought: it com-mitted itself to a common language of the rule of law, executed through codification; it constructed a centralized state and rejected localism; and it instituted a model of representation whose units were individuals rather than groups. The following chapters will demonstrate how these features were seen to enable legitimization—that is, how they would allow Indians to arrive at outcomes agreeable to free and equal individuals. The archi-tecture would make possible democratization in the deeper sense of the term, for it would not only guarantee popular authorization but provide the mechanisms by which authority might be sustained.

Each aspect of the founding scheme articulated a distinct kind of moral imagination that allowed Indians to see each other differently and placed them in a new relationship with one another. Chapter 1 looks at the very act of drafting a constitutional text. The founding orientation toward written constitutionalism was aimed at more than simply guiding and in-forming political action. The impulse toward the codification of rules into a single canonical text was intended to create common meanings and explicate norms that other societies could take for granted. Codification was less a way to empower and limit specific actors and institutions, though empower and limit them it did, and more an attempt to generate an understanding of the meaning of such actors and institutions. The text was conceived not simply as a means to enable or prohibit action but as a device that could define the nature of political actions and the concepts that such actions implicated. The text would have to provide, rather than assume as established, the shared norms on which self-government was predicated. The Constitution was, in other words, conceptualized as a pedagogical tool. It would be an instrument of political education—aspiring to nothing short of building a new civic culture.

The codification of rules was one way to liberate Indians from existing forms of thought and understanding. But liberation was required from other constraints as well. One such constraint was the narrow horizons imposed by localism. Chapter 2 considers this concern and studies the choice of a strong centralized state. All constitutions limit political authority in some fashion or another. But they also, perhaps more importantly, create such authority. Such instances of creation necessarily involve judgments over what it means for a body to be a political authority, and which kinds of bodies can become such authorities. The choice of a strong centralized state was hardly a self-evident one. Indian intellectual history had a long tradition of local government thought, and several proposals for the reconstruction of India drew on this tradition. The contest over centralization, we shall find, was a contest between the state and society. Supporters of a strong centralized state did not trust that Indian society had the internal capacity for order and change. Their conception of Indian society made the centrality of the state inevitable. The founders of India's Constitution believed that a centralized state was the only mechanism that could stand above all other forces and restructure the relationship among those it governed. And only such restructuring could further a common politics devoted to social and economic transformation, because municipal structures—governmental and nongovernmental alike—were thought to be captured by rigid social and cultural bonds and prejudices.

Self-determination required Indians to be released from still further pressures. Chapter 3 examines the understanding of Indians as political agents in the context of representation. India's awesome diversity was routinely referenced as a reason for its incompatibility with self-government. In the colonial era, Indian society was taken to be held together by different groups. It was a space where one's identity was asserted through one's community, and power was shared between communities. The founding replaced this imagery of the nation by a different one. The decades preceding India's independence experienced a profound crisis over representation, one that culminated in the partition of British India. Partition marked the failure of years of negotiations performed on communal terms, and it opened the door to a conception of citizenship that was free from the power of predefined identities. The founding approach toward religion and caste—the two principal divisions—helps us see how participation was imagined in a shared political life. The new logic for political mediation involved a transition from the balancing of communities to the affirmation of the individual. This shift created a political subject whose interests and identity would be forged in the battlefield of politics.

These themes were the major fault lines in the Constituent Assembly debates. They capture the self-awareness of India's hostile environment as well as the attempt to address the dangers that this environment posed. Codification could serve an educative role in a country without established constitutional conventions; centralization could liberate a society seized by local antidemocratic sentiments; and a theory of representation unmediated by forced identities could meet the challenges of difference. Taken together, these themes highlight the internal cogency of the Indian constitutional project. The liberation from localism was, for instance, a spatial form of the representation story. Both centralization and non-communal representation were attempts to rescue individualism from other pressures. In a similar way, codification expressed a commitment to the exercise of power through forms that involved a different kind of interaction than, say, kinship relations. The breakdown of prevailing structures of power would allow for different allegiances to be brought into the service of a collective political form. And such collective agency would enable a kind of deliberation that would be suitable to democratic politics. The relationship between these themes is thrown into relief when we recall that the Muslim League leader Mohammad Ali Jinnah's concern with the particularistic use of power in an undivided India implicated both matters of territory and identity. Indeed, it was the territorializing of communal representation that would eventually redesign the topography of South Asia. Jinnah's crucial arguments are considered in the discussion of representation in Chapter 3 because their key feature was the mediation of representation through a community lens, but the historical link between representation and territory affirms the interrelation between the different elements of the Indian constitutional enterprise. In their own distinct way, the codification of norms, the existence of a centralized state, and the freedom from communal groupings would allow Indians to engage in a new form of reasoning and participation. Each was a path to the creation of a polity. Together, the different mechanisms could produce *democratic* citizens.

The birth of modern India marked the historical node at which democracy, constitutionalism, and modernity occurred simultaneously. The Indian revolution combined a set of concerns that had proceeded at separate rates in the West, and it signaled a time at which a set of processes—the introduction of popular authorization, the creation of rules constituting public authority and participation, the concentration of authority in the state, the identification of self-determination with individual freedom, the separation of the public and the private—emerged at a single moment. The moment was a historical response to both eighteenth-century failures and nineteenth-century critics of democracy. The fact that India encountered troubles that earlier moments of democratic creation were able to avoid makes it the new paradigm for what it means to create a democracy in the modern world. This is what makes the experience of Indian democracy not just the experience of one nation but the experience of *democracy itself.*

Whether the inattention to India's birth is an ideological consequence of continued Western condescension toward the universalization of self-government or a contingent fallout of the dynamics that govern the production of knowledge is neither here nor there. The point is that scholars of democracy cannot avoid a consideration of India's birth. In the few studies that exist, India's constitutional moment has been interpreted variously. Some—most notably Granville Austin in his defining history of the event, *The Indian Constitution: Cornerstone of a Nation*—see it as a vehicle for social revolution; some regard it as a monument to state power; and some, as I have noted, consider it to be a continuation of the colonial legacy.[106] Each of these studies has its finger on some aspect of the truth, and each identifies some special element that was present. But they all miss how democracy was seen as constructed through three mutually reinforcing elements: the rule of law, the modern state, and the individualization of identity.

This book is neither a work of historical reconstruction offering a sequential, causal account of actors and events, nor an exploration of power dynamics that shaped specific choices. It is instead a study of certain traditions of thought about democracy and constitutionalism at the moment of India's creation. It probes self-conscious ways of thinking about the meaning of these ideas under very unusual circumstances. There are two assumptions at work here that should be mentioned. The first assumption is quite simply that ideas matter, and that the choices underlying the birth of modern India were not forced by historical forces or strategic currents. They emerged, at least in part, from agents' theoretical understanding of the history that was unfolding. This book sheds light on some of that understanding and proceeds on the belief that the study of ideas offers one way to comprehend events in history. The second assumption is a certain account of historical change, an account that is revealed by the very subject matter of this book. One reason the Indian founding has rarely been interrogated is that it has often not been regarded as the site of revolution. The emphasis has been on social processes rather than political forms. Studies have focused on institutional continuity between the colonial and the postcolonial state, the evolution of agrarian structures, the place of the peasantry in the anticolonial struggle, and so on.[107] Though such work has made signal contributions to our understanding of the past, it has displaced the study of the political. In this book I take a different stance, and share in the self-conscious belief held by India's founders that political forms do indeed carry influence.

The three themes in this book express both the means and the end of the Indian pedagogical project. Each theme involves an aspect of the educated citizen that India's founders wanted to create. The imperial project had never been serious at the level of pedagogy. It was about the co-option of elites rather than the transformation of subjects. The Indian answer to the imperial project was a critique of the earlier language of pedagogy. The critique was driven by the fact that the British had no solution to how one overcame the problems of Indian society. The imperialist imagination, that is, had no answer to the problem of *political education*. India's founders were troubled by the circumstances of the country they were creating. Though this meant that they shared a widespread view about democracy's preconditions, it was their very attack on India's sociological reality that made them radicals.

The two animating sentiments in this book—the claim about political education and the claim about constitutional mechanisms that could make India safe for democracy—thus run together in important ways. The imperial argument against self-government had been, in the ultimate analysis, an argument about the impossibility of collective political agency under certain conditions. The suffrage question in Europe had, after all, been framed through the language of capacity.[108] The fears in the Indian case were not altogether different from those in the West: the unraveling of social harmony; the unintelligent and irresponsible exercise of the right to vote; the exploitation of power by those elected to office; the lack of enforcement of a political mandate; and above all the misuse of public power. But the Indian political project answered these fears differently. The conditions thought to infect political activity turned on how that activity had been ordered. A different ordering could make possible a different politics. The relationship between India's historical and sociological reality and its politics was a contingent one. It was a construction of the imperial ideology, and there were other possibilities of existence. The making of India's Constitution was a determined struggle to work through what an alternative arrangement might be.

The imperial state was predicated on the belief that India would have to be mediated by a superior class of peoples. As far as the imperialists were concerned, the only way to acquaint Indians with alien ideals was by subjecting them to political absolutism. But what were imagined to be immutable facts about Indian life were in fact the product of a certain kind of politics. A set of beliefs shaped and constructed by imperialism were assumed and rationalized as being universal truths. After all, the power of politics was precisely that it would find ways to create its own form of essentialism. The great imperial advocates of Britain's civilizing mission were, in one crucial respect, correct. The Indian elite shared the sense that the people had to be educated. But the British had offered the wrong remedy, for the path to education lay not in the deferment of freedom and the imposition of foreign rule. Instead, it lay in the very creation of a self-sustaining democratic politics.

1

The Grammar of Constitutionalism

Constitutions are ubiquitous but they come in many sizes. The Indian Constitution has substantial length. The original text contained 395 articles and eight appendixes. Over time, the word count has only grown, and the document is often referred to as the world's longest written constitution.[1] Though the length of India's founding text is mentioned in popular and scholarly writings, it rarely provokes any real curiosity. This was not always the case. In the late 1950s, for example, the document's word count caught the attention of the controversial critic of liberal constitutionalism Carl Schmitt when he turned to revise his 1932 work *Legality and Legitimacy*. Written just prior to the fall of the Weimar Republic, *Legality and Legitimacy* had categorized the various constitutional schemas in the modern world, contrasting legislative, jurisdictional, and governmental-administrative states. But on returning to his original study more than two decades later, Schmitt noticed that it had become dated. To remedy matters, he added an afterword that acknowledged two arresting developments in the interim period.

The first development was the emergence of the welfare state. Such a state required law by decree, thereby leaving behind the traditional separation of powers model. One could not continue to rely on a structure in which the legislature had the exclusive authority to make laws. A bureaucracy, Schmitt observed, "no longer gets by with the concept of law, which stems from the classical separation of state and society. Instead, it adapts legal concepts to the welfare state's level of development."[2] This fusion of administrative and constitutional law took place alongside a further development: a change in the character of constitutions themselves. Constitutions, Schmitt noticed, had moved beyond simply setting the basic framework for politics. Once known by their focus on procedural rules, they had started to take on a substantive character. To demonstrate this shift in identity, Schmitt turned to the newly enacted Indian Constitution:

> The father of the liberal *Rechtsstaat,* John Locke, in an oft-quoted expression directed against enabling acts and legislative delegations, pointedly remarked that the legislature is not there to make legislatures, but rather laws. Analogously, one can say that the constitution-maker and even the constitutional legislature are there to make good legislatures and legislative procedures, and not to make the laws themselves. Otherwise, it would be consistent to issue the constitution immediately as a type of Corpus Juris with a multiyear plan included as an appendix. As noted, there is certainly a tendency in this direction, and constitutions are becoming even longer. Indeed, the new Indian Constitution already has 315 articles and eight appendixes. Whoever finds that right and proper should at least know that it is no longer here a matter of the type of constitution on whose foundation past European constitutional law and its theory of the *Rechtsstaat* and of the separation of powers were formed.[3]

In these few sentences Schmitt held up for consideration an unusual feature of India's Constitution—its size. Indians had shown an interest in written constitutionalism for some years prior to the end of colonial rule. The Swaraj Bill of 1895—typically viewed as the earliest attempt at an Indian constitutional text—was drafted over five decades before the Constituent Assembly first met. Yet little in the decades prior to the formal constitution-making process suggested that codification was to become a defining feature of India's Constitution. Similarly, India's founders drew on a range of constitutional models in exercising the choices that they faced, but no model quite resembled the approach to constitution-writing that they finally took. This chapter examines the founding impulse toward codification.

The promise of codification was that it could create common meanings around democratic principles where few such meanings existed. The writing of India's founding text aimed at capturing what consensus formation would look like under ordinary conditions of democratization. It expressed the common knowledge that would obtain were this to happen.[4] I will begin with a general examination of the codification enterprise in order to set out some of the overarching motivations behind the constitution-making endeavor and to contrast that endeavor with both the writing of legal materials during the colonial era and the standard view of constitutions among contemporary scholars. I will then illustrate the *theory* of codification through a study of three specific decisions. First, the decision to recognize numerous socioeconomic rights in the constitutional text—to commit to such rights in writing—but to disallow their judicial enforcement. In other words, the realization of such rights was kept outside of the domain of courts. Second, the decision to guarantee several enforceable rights that were primarily civil-political in character, such as the right to free speech and expression. Here the puzzle was the provision of such rights alongside the textual insertion of the exceptions and limitations to which such rights would be subject. That is, the rights were recognized and limited at the same moment. Or so it seemed. Third, decisions regarding the contest between what are referred to as procedural due process and substantive due process. Under the former framework, courts would have the power to review whether an action by the state conformed to the procedure laid down by a law, but they would have no power to review the law itself. Under the latter framework, the power vested in courts was substantially enlarged. They could, under conditions of substantive due process, not only assess whether actions by the executive fell within the ambit of an enacted law, but also consider whether the law itself was valid. Here, the contest between procedural and substantive due process was played out in the context of the right to life and personal liberty.

To capture the import of codification, one must attend not only to words but more fundamentally to the idea of *shared practices*. In order to participate in common practices, one needs to be within a certain orbit of understanding. The actions that people perform within that orbit are actions in the field of certain common meanings. The creation of common meaning is the creation of a new intersubjective relationship. In a new orbit of understanding, the participants see themselves and each other differently. The codification of the constitutional text was seen as crucial to the creation of common meaning because the ambit of understanding that a people come to form shares a relationship to the language that people employ. The vocabulary that is put into use has a constitutive relationship to the social reality that comes into being.[5]

The distinct approach toward constitutional codification was motivated, above all, by the fear of uncertainty. The effort to provide the constitutional text with content was a response to the creation of a new *demos* traveling in uncharted territory. The fear extended across the board, whether one had in mind the behavior of voters, legislators, or judges. Regardless of the actor or arena that it targeted, codification sought to provide action with meaning, and to thereby guide, inform, and shape behavior under conditions of sudden empowerment. The creation of rules and their specific form would enable learning, and the shared understanding that was provided by codification made possible individual action across a host of domains. And, naturally, the writing of the constitutional text was linked to a specific conception of the state. Codification was employed to give the exercise of state power a normative direction, making it clear that certain commitments and conditions were necessary for such power to hold legitimacy.

The Impulse toward Codification

It is now commonplace to assert, thanks largely due to H. L. A. Hart, that even though societies might exist without the legal institutions that surround us, only small and relatively simple societies can operate without some basic set of rules. Such communities do establish legal relationships, such as relationships based on kinship ties. But unless they have mechanisms for the creation and identification of rules, for settling differences over the existence and meaning of rules, and for changing and developing rules, their collective life will be burdened by unclarity, stagnation, and inefficiency.[6] Modern legal systems, partly to prevent such problems, are structured around a set of general rules. Generality enables rules to have broad application and allows them to be impersonal in their operation. The reasons in favor of rules are familiar. Even though rules are necessarily overinclusive and underinclusive, and even though their application will now and again breach the background justification for the rules, they have several virtues: they enable reliance, facilitate agency, further efficiency by establishing tests for determining action, and so on.[7]

While a great deal is common about rules, the precise shape that they take can vary considerably. The detail that they embody, in both form and substance, will have major implications for the actors involved. A fear of how actors might behave—a fear based on the actors' lack of knowledge or understanding, their deep-seated prejudices and customary tendencies, and so forth—will encourage rule-makers in the direction of greater rule specification. Considerable effort may be made to lay down the conditions under which the background justification for a rule applies. Rule-makers will, in other words, acknowledge the absence of a consensus on this justification. It would seem to be the case that when rule-makers undertake such an effort, they perceive that the negative consequences of greater specification are preferable to those that would follow in the absence of the guidance that specification provides.[8] Rules, after all, require background conditions to work. For a rule to be a source of reliance, for example, both the enforcer and the addressee of the rule must possess some shared understanding.[9] Where shared understandings are not prevalent, rule-makers will have much work to do.

A striking feature of India's founding was the orientation toward constitutional rules. In general, constitutions are understood as a set of rules that relate to the system of government and are incorporated in one or a few documents.[10] More precisely, one might say that the rules included in a constitution create and regulate institutions whose powers have not been delegated to them from any other institution.[11] To the extent that their powers are delegated rather than inherent, they have, at least in modern democratic societies, been delegated from the people. This much is as true of the Indian Constitution as it is of others. But the Indian text does more than simply create institutions of inherent power. By and large, exercises of power contain some internal standard for its use, and every constitution legitimizes the exercise of power by establishing certain forms of justification. During India's constitution-making process, there was a determination to specify the internal standards that apply to different powers. The constitutional text was a means for democratic constitutionalism to set up its own test of legitimacy: codification was used to explicate what constitutionalism within a democratic society meant. In other words, the creation of rules focused on enabling actors to form an understanding of the actions that they were performing.[12]

To appreciate the constitution-making exercise at India's founding, one must contrast it with the codification efforts during colonial rule. The colonial state committed extraordinary intellectual and administrative resources to the collation and organization of legal rules.[13] Indeed, the creation of a modern legal system has been regarded as a defining feature of British rule in India.[14] Codification began with the religious laws. For eighteenth-century figures like Warren Hastings, who served as the governor of the Presidency of Fort William, and William Jones, a major scholar and judge, India was an ancient civilization with long-established practices of governance and social ordering. The methodical gathering of such practices—their classification and publication—held the promise of providing guidance to the rulers. Codification offered a way by which the colonized could be controlled. It could rescue the British from depending on natives who understood such practices and profited from their special claims to knowledge. India's rulers could be liberated from the interpretive tricks played by local legal experts, and earlier uncorrupted legal norms could be restored.[15]

The aim of the enterprise was to take a body of existing or forgotten social practices and give them concrete legal expression. Such an enterprise would enable them to survive in a new institutional environment. When Thomas Macaulay delivered his noteworthy address on British rule in India in the House of Commons in 1833, he described the sheer chaos that made codification necessary. The situation in India after the fall of the Mughal dynasty was, Macaulay claimed, akin to the state of Europe after the fall of the Roman Empire. At the end of the dynasty, India had contained other parallel and competing legal orders, as had Europe at the end of the Roman Empire. Just as Italy had to contend with the simultaneous presence of Roman law, Lombard law, Bavarian law, and so on, India had to deal with Hindu law, Islamic law, English law, and such. The result was anarchic:

> In one and the same cause the process and pleadings are in the fashion of one nation, the judgment is according to the laws of another. An issue is evolved according to the rules of Westminster, and decided according to those of Benares. The only Mohametan book in the nature of a code is the Koran; the only Hindoo book the Institutes. Everybody who knows those books, knows that they provide for a very small part of the cases which must arise in every community. All beyond them is comment and tradition. If a point of Hindoo law arises, the Judge calls on the Pundit for an option. If a point of Mohametan law arises, the Judge applies to the Cauzee. What the integrity of these functionaries is, we may learn from Sir William Jones. That eminent man declared, that he could not answer it to his conscience to decide any point of law on the faith of the Hindoo expositor . . . Sir Francis Macnaghten tells us that it is a delusion to fancy that there is any known and fixed law under which the Hindoo people live; that texts may be produced on any

side of any question ... in practice the decisions of the tribunals are altogether arbitrary. What is administered is not law, but a kind of rude and capricious equity.[16]

Macaulay became a central actor in the codification project that was introduced by the Charter Act of 1833. Macaulay and his kindred nineteenth-century reformers saw their task differently than Hastings and Jones did. These new reformers were driven by a Benthamite zeal for rationalism. Their intention was no longer to make sense of different legal orders but instead to create a code of legal rules that could structure social relations in logically intelligible ways. Legal reform was taken to be a serious project. Indeed, it was central to the liberal-imperial impulse that drove colonialism. A law commission was established and tasked with revising India's civil and criminal laws, and the Council of the Governor-General in Calcutta was recomposed to include a law member. The Benthamite project was visible in codifications of laws governing contract, property, evidence, and crime. The project had been so successful that, by the time the nineteenth century came to an end, scholars spoke of the Indian codification experiment with celebration, and identified still further areas where codification should be undertaken.[17]

A stark instance of revolution was the Indian Penal Code of 1860, which was "a self-conscious attempt to construct a code de novo."[18] The Code was a product of neither local nor foreign prevailing practices, and it was created, as Eric Stokes once observed, "ex nihilo by the disinterested philosophic intelligence."[19] The contrast with English law, which remained uncodified, was plain. "To compare the Indian Penal Code with English criminal law is," James Fitzjames Stephen felt, "like comparing cosmos with chaos."[20] While statutes relating to civil procedure or contract law were less radical than the Penal Code when assessed in the context of English law, they were nonetheless committed to the objectives of rationality and internal consistency. This commitment is nicely revealed by the formal structure the codes shared. Each legislation followed the identical framework and plan. They all used sections, clauses, short titles, definitions, illustrations, and so on in the same fashion, making the products seem like the outcome of one grand design.[21]

Beyond these statutory instruments, there was a third kind of codification during colonial rule. Statutes ranging from the Regulating Act of 1773 to the Government of India Act of 1935 possessed a kind of superior constitutional status.[22] These documents divided power among various officials and provided an overarching governance framework in India. In the early years of colonial rule, changes to such laws were motivated by the need to alter either the relationship between the Company and the Crown or the relationship among the Crown's officials in India. For example, the working of the Regulating Act had led to tensions on two fronts: first, between the governor-general and his council; and secondly, between the Supreme Court, on the one hand, and the governor-general and his council, on the other.[23] Subsequent legislation sought to remedy these tensions and restructure the relationship between the various actors. In the later years of colonial rule, statutory enactments were the product of negotiations with Indians, and were often shaped by local demands for political participation.[24] The Indian Councils Act of 1861 offered one nominated Indian a place in the provincial councils, and subsequent developments entailed a contest over the place and power that Indians would hold in representative posts. These reforms offered constitutional arrangements to accommodate different Indian stakeholders, such as granting Muslims separate electorates in 1909 or creating a federation with Indian princes in 1935. Regardless of the differences between the various legal instruments over the course of colonial rule, these laws were all essentially concerned with regulating public power and allocating responsibility among different and potentially quasi-sovereign actors.

These motivations for codification differed considerably from those underlying the Constitution. The 1950 text was not an attempt to either institutionalize extant social practices or rationally organize behavior. Prior codification efforts, such as those related to civil and penal laws, did, of course, aspire to bring legal clarity to social behavior, but they were not focused on ordering behavior to facilitate a collective political life. Codification at India's founding was also distinct from the third kind of codification during the colonial era—namely, the codification that we have just considered in the creation of statutes like the Government of India Act of 1935. These laws were long and weighty, to be sure, but they were aimed at forming pacts and maintaining the peace among different elite players and undemocratic power holders. They did not try to confront the realities of popularly authorized institutions.

Studies of the Indian founding, to the extent that they exist, have ignored the instinct that drove codification. Instead, such reflections have mirrored a broader contest in constitutional theory between limiting constitutions and enabling constitutions. For decades now, constitutional theory has been preoccupied—one might even say burdened—with two visions of constitutionalism. On one account, constitutions are tools that control state power. Their task is to identify the exercise of public power, and to keep that power in check. For theorists who hold this *constraining* view of constitutions, the obvious challenge lies in reconciling restrictions on state power with popular rule. Many solutions have been offered to this problem. One standard technique for legal constitutionalists, as they are called, lies in offering a conception of democracy that moves beyond majority rule. It is a conception that rejects, in Ronald Dworkin's notable phrase, "the majoritarian premise."[25] The focus is on the subordination of politics to law.

A second account regards constitutional documents as *enabling*. Here, the effort lies in instantiating rather than rejecting sovereignty. For those who hold such a viewpoint, often termed political constitutionalists, the emphasis is on the expression of popular sovereignty. The constraining view of constitutions is seen as mistaken.[26] Unlike legal constitutionalists, political constitutionalists emphasize the empowering features of constitutions: the establishment of institutions and the mechanisms for collective decision-making.[27] The challenge for political constitutionalists lies in explaining why majoritarian decision-making should carry moral legitimacy, and this challenge might be met in numerous ways, such as by taking seriously the right to participation and the phenomenon of political disagreement.[28] The emphasis for such scholars is on the right to self-rule. They turn away from the Platonic question of what might be correct to the Hobbesian worry about which body ought to be the legitimate decision-maker.

As constitutional scholars are well aware, the difference between legal and political constitutionalists is often played out in the context of judicial review.[29] Those who view constitutions as limiting devices are almost invariably defenders of the authority of courts to invalidate duly enacted legislation. The internal procedures of advocacy and principles of adjudication are seen to be counterbalancing rules to those that inform politics. Political constitutionalists, on the other hand, question the special legitimacy of judges, and bemoan the disregard that judicial review displays toward the practices of representative institutions. What we can see is that the contest between political and legal constitutionalism nearly always turns into a contest over constitutional codification: Should there be a single canonical constitutional text that recognizes rights and guarantees their enforcement by an independent judiciary?[30]

Much has been said about these positions and their relative strengths and weaknesses. But whichever corner of the ring we are partial toward, we can observe how both schools of thought proceed on assumptions that do not obtain in many parts of the world. The case for political constitutionalism rests on well-functioning legislative institutions; it is based on practices and norms that relate to lawmaking and the enactment of legislation. Similarly, the case for legal constitutionalism is developed in the context of prevailing canons of reasoning, principles that determine legal meaning, and interpretive techniques and approaches. For some nations in the West, it is not unnatural to ask whether judicial review is legitimate in a milieu of well-performing legislatures and courts. But for many other countries, the more pressing question is how they might arrive at such legislatures and courts. Their primary task, in situations like India's founding, is to establish the apparatus that can make the debate over legitimacy even possible—and the position on legitimacy that they ultimately adopt may well turn on which institutions are able to perform better. This result is not one in which theory is sacrificed to empirical realities. On the contrary, it is one that invites the deepest questions over the relationship between constitutional theory and constitutional politics.

It is, to be sure, tempting to see India's founding as falling within the standard contest over constitutional codification. For instance, one might explain several choices through the lens of legal constitutionalism. The document's size might encourage one to suppose—as Carl Schmitt did—an extreme attempt to limit political action. Schmitt saw the Indian Constitution as a device that did not merely create a legislature but went further and effectively enacted laws. There is some truth to this perspective. Several provisions in the text were based on the belief that their protection needed to be guaranteed in some special way. Provisions relating to the Election Commission—an independent institution entrusted with the running of elections—are a notable example. There was a concern that the powers relating to the conduct of elections, such as the transfer of electoral officers, might be abused by the executive. B. R. Ambedkar felt that "the greatest safeguard for purity of election, for fairness in election, was to take away the matter from the hands of the executive authority and to hand it over to some independent authority."[31] Another example is judicial independence. A number of conditions meant to secure such independence, like the salaries of judges, were codified into the constitutional text. While Parliament was empowered to change such salaries, the Constitution specified that this power was applicable only to new judges and that the terms of service of sitting members of the judiciary could not be adversely affected.[32]

The effort to insulate legal rules from ordinary politics was also seen in the determination of the powers of specific institutions. Consider the power granted to the judiciary to issue prerogative writs. Ambedkar noted that such writs were not new to India's existing legal framework. The writs of *habeas corpus* and *mandamus* had, for example, already been recognized by the Code of Criminal Procedure of 1861 and the Specific Relief Act of 1877, respectively. But they were recognized by statutes, and mere statutory recognition meant that the protection these writs promised was "at the mercy of the legislature."[33] The fact that these writs were now recognized by a constitutional text rather than a statute meant that their removal was more difficult, and the guarantee was therefore more secure. As Ambedkar put it, they could not "be taken away by any legislature merely because it happens to have a majority."[34] When decisions of this sort were taken, they were often accompanied by an open acknowledgment of the distrust of politics. For instance, in a discussion on the civil service—whose independence was secured constitutionally rather than by statute—one member candidly admitted that he "had no faith in adult franchise."[35] "I do not know," he exclaimed, "what kind of people will come in the future Parliament of India. In the heat of extremism or at the altar of some radical ideology, they may like to do away with the provision that we have made in . . . favor of the services."[36]

We can therefore appreciate why the Indian founding has been seen by some as a case of legal constitutionalism. Interestingly enough, there has also been an effort to interpret the episode in contrasting terms—that is, to see it as an exercise that entrenched state power. The recognition of rights alongside explicit limitations, the creation of an executive government with sweeping emergency powers, the unitary character of the federal design, the range and depth of state responsibilities imposed by the text, and so on, have been underlined to make the argument that Indian Constitution is a statist document.[37] This contemporary scholarly perspective was shared by several members in the Constituent Assembly. As one participant noted, in comparing the new legal regime with the old colonial one: "None of the existing provisions of the powers of the executive has been done away with; rather, in some respects, those powers are sought to be increased."[38] Instead of restricting state power, this camp feared that the constitutional moment paid tribute to the authority and necessity of the state.

Each of these explanations possesses some degree of accuracy. Some provisions were included in the Constitution to make it harder for legislators to amend them. Similarly, the Constitution recognized the importance of the state, and granted it a great many powers. Yet neither of these accounts quite captures the animating sentiment behind codification. An emphasis on legality conflates codification with justiciability, and it cannot explain why the exercise of judicial power itself evoked concern. The error in its interpretation follows from a narrow conception of the constitutional mechanisms for depoliticization. A state-centered reading commits the opposite mistake. It offers a thin analysis of the rules in the text and thereby disregards the many constraints on legislative and executive authority. Such a reading is also hard to reconcile with the persistent fear of state power expressed by Indian nationalists. The horror of colonial rule was that it represented, as Jawaharlal Nehru noted in his autobiography, "the ideal police state."[39] The struggle for Indian independence was not simply a struggle for freedom from alien rule. It was a shift away from an administration of law and order centered on despotism—where despotism shared a key relationship with state authority.[40]

The neat distinction between constitutions as enabling and constitutions as limiting has set the terms for contemporary studies on India's constitution-making effort.[41] But the fear of uncertainty that drove the codification exercise at India's creation captured instead the choice between an open-ended and an explicit text. The primary question was not whether the legislature or judiciary should have more power but instead whether the text could be silent on the underlying norms of democratic constitutionalism. Codification could provide common meaning to a set of principles relating to democracy in a land without such meaning. Familiar constitution-making endeavors, whether they aimed to limit the exercise of power or to enable it, had already presupposed a great deal of shared understanding. But the Indian context offered no such joint consensus. Codification was an effort to explicate such a consensus.

This theory of codification is captured by a series of interventions in the Constituent Assembly over the purpose behind constitution-making. Before we turn to those interventions, it is worth noting that in the years prior to the formal constitution-making process, numerous written texts had been produced. Some aimed at engaging with the colonial state and articulating the terms of freedom. Some, like the Motilal Nehru Report of 1928, offered indications of future commitments. They revealed, for example, the place that social and economic welfare occupied within the nationalist imagination. There was also the endorsement of several constitutional principles. From its second session onward, for example, the Indian National Congress spoke of the separation of executive and judicial functions.[42] The Sapru Committee Report of 1945 also stressed the significance of judicial independence.[43] But beyond mentioning basic freedoms and the importance of the rule of law, the particulars of India's future governing document were a relatively open matter when the Constituent Assembly met in the winter of 1946.

In the Assembly, considerable debate ensued over the form that written constitutions should take. Jawaharlal Nehru prominently expressed concern over excessive codification. He feared that a thick constitutional text would be inflexible. It would make the Constitution unadaptable to social and economic change, and thereby make it less likely to endure. It was important, he felt, to not lose sight of the distinction between constitutions and ordinary legislation. To codify liberally would mean to confuse higher principles with quotidian matters of administration. A constitution overwhelmed with detail would lose its character. He held that

> so far as the basic nature of the Constitution is concerned, it must deal with the fundamental aspects of the political, the social, the economic and other spheres, and not with the details which are matters for legislation. You will find that if you go into too great detail and mix up the really basic and fundamental things with the important but nevertheless secondary things, you bring the basic things to the level of the secondary things too. You lose them in a forest of detail. The great trees that you should like to plant and wait for them to grow and to be seen are hidden in a forest of detail and smaller trees. I have felt that we are spending a great deal of time on undoubtedly important matters, but nevertheless secondary matters—matters which are for legislation, not for a Constitution.[44]

Nehru's position was far from unreasonable. Constitutional elasticity was a matter of some interest to scholars at the time. James Bryce's *Studies in History and Jurisprudence,* published in 1901, had encouraged scholars to categorize constitutions as being either rigid or flexible rather than as written or unwritten. Flexible constitutions, Bryce observed, were those that had developed over time and that carried the same status as ordinary laws. The term "constitution" did not refer to a single document but to the laws and customs that structured the political system. In the case of a rigid constitution, however, the "instrument (or instruments) in which such a constitution is embodied proceeds from a source different from that whence spring the other laws, is repealable in a different way, exerts a superior force."[45] Flexible constitutions, for Bryce, did not result in unstable political regimes. Their key feature was not disorder but malleability: "They can be stretched or bent so as to meet emergencies, without breaking their framework; and when the emergency has passed, they slip back into their old form, like a tree whose outer branches have been pulled on one side to let a vehicle pass."[46] The virtue of such constitutions was their capacity to absorb revolutionary challenges. They could adapt themselves to new demands.

Nehru did not resist the idea of a single written constitutional text, but he placed a premium on constitutional elasticity. For him, a longer document would effectively mean greater rigidity, a point that Ivor Jennings would later make to criticize the Indian Constitution.[47] Perhaps the best-known articulation of Nehru's sentiment—that constitutions should operate at a certain level of generality (and, resultantly, be brief)—was Chief Justice Marshall's opinion in the United States Supreme Court decision *M'Culloch v. State* (1819).[48] An exhaustive constitution, Chief Justice Marshall had observed, "could scarcely be embraced by the human mind" and "would, probably, never be understood by the public."[49] What was required from a constitutional text was, he noted, "that only its great outlines should be marked, its important objects designated, and the minor ingredients which compose those objects, be deduced from the nature of the objects themselves."[50] Marshall, like Nehru, did not offer an argument against written constitutions *in toto;* it was an argument about the kind of writing that a constitution should adopt.

Nehru's concern with extreme legalism was not new. In the battle against colonial rule, he made clear his disagreement with those who sought constitutional means for gaining power. Rather than drafting "paper constitutions," Nehru desired radical structural change.[51] It was the dependence on precedent that especially aggravated him. "Too much reliance on past practice," Nehru felt, "has somehow succeeded in twisting the lawyer's head backward and he seems to be incapable of looking ahead."[52] His concern with rigidity was apparent even in his early reflections on the colonial project of codifying India's religious laws. For Nehru, the customs and rules of Hindu society had shown remarkable adaptability until British intervention. But putting pen to paper had changed everything. Through codifying "customs and flexible laws on very conservative principles . . . it became impossible to change these customs and laws except by fresh legislation."[53]

The apprehension was that India's radical democratization could lead to situations so unforeseen that rules based on past knowledge would stymie necessary action. That rules promote stable decision-making is a point that Nehru would have readily conceded. Moreover, he remained committed to institutional processes and norms, and acknowledged their value as such. Indeed, it was his fidelity to procedure and civil liberties that separated him from the communists, whose economic sentiments he largely shared. His opposition was neither to the formal stability that legal rules promised nor to the need for some canonical legal text that protected democratic principles and regulated state power. It was instead related to the character that codification should take. An approach to written constitutionalism that went beyond the basic principles required by democracy and the rule of law would be incapable of managing social and political pressures. This seemed especially worrisome in India's context, where an unpredictable future suggested a need for greater legal flexibility.[54]

Nehru saw the risk of being bound to intricate, extensive canonical rules in India's circumstances as greater than the risk of providing some leeway to actors and institutions. By posing matters in this way, he approached the question of written constitutionalism in traditional terms—namely, as a choice between authorizing political action and restraining it. This perspective had support within the Assembly. When such a large document was eventually produced, it became clear to all concerned that the text bore little resemblance to standard practice. One member noted, "We have not been able to keep clear in our mind the distinction between an act of the legislature and the provisions of a constitution."[55] Another observed with sarcasm, "I congratulate Dr. Ambedkar, the Chairman of the Drafting Committee, and the members thereof for producing such a voluminous Constitution in which nothing has been left out . . . I venture to think that if they had the time, they would have even prescribed a code of life in this Constitution."[56]

Yet codification had its advocates—their views eventually succeeded, and it is crucial to ask why. Such participants were, after all, well aware of the distinction between constitution-making and ordinary lawmaking—the Constituent Assembly acted in both roles and carefully divided its time in performing each. For the supporters of codification, the flexibility of the constitutional text was a valid concern, but it could be met, as it was, by way of a relaxed amendment procedure. Those who defended the text, like Rajendra Prasad, claimed that the "Constitution should be self-contained as far as possible."[57] "We should not," he observed, "depend on the interpretation of clauses in other constitutions, as it may lead us to any amount of confusion."[58] When Ambedkar was questioned on the Constitution's length and content, he conceded that the decision to incorporate provisions that might otherwise have been left to statutory law was atypical. In explaining the rationale for such incorporation, he turned to George Grote's *A History of Greece.* In his study of Athenian democracy, Grote had used the term "constitutional morality" to depict fidelity to constitutional forms and practices. The presence of constitutional morality, Grote had argued, meant the commitment to constitutional means, to its processes and structures, alongside a commitment to free speech, scrutiny of public action, legal limitations on the exercise of power, and so on. In this way, constitutional morality signified the combined existence of the ethic of self-restraint as well as the flourishing of freedom. It signified a kind of respect that transcended disagreements and disappointments.[59] Because it functioned so quietly, almost invisibly behind the daily drama of individuals and institutions, one might suppose that constitutional morality was a normal, expected feature of constitutional systems. But Grote regarded such an assumption as mistaken. The attitude was hard to create and sustain, and it was one that was crucial for the endurance of a constitutional order.

Ambedkar was sympathetic to Grote's account and to the place that it accorded constitutional morality in the success of Athenian democracy. But he saw the account as incomplete. It provided only a partial theory of constitutional failure:

> While everybody recognises the necessity of the diffusion of constitutional morality for the peaceful working of a democratic constitution, there are two things interconnected with it which are not, unfortunately, generally recognised. One is that the form of administration has a close connection with the form of the constitution. The form of the administration must be appropriate to and in the same sense as the form of the constitution. The other is that it is perfectly possible to pervert the constitution, without changing its form by merely changing the form of the administration and to make it inconsistent and opposed to the spirit of the Constitution. It follows that it is only where people are saturated with constitu-

tional morality, such as the one described by Grote the historian, that one can take the risk of omitting from the constitution details of administration and leaving it for the legislature to prescribe them. The question is, can we presume such a diffusion of constitutional morality? Constitutional morality is not a natural sentiment. It has to be cultivated. We must realize that our people have yet to learn it. Democracy in India is only a top-dressing on an Indian soil, which is essentially undemocratic.[60]

Ambedkar feared that the perversion of a constitutional order could occur even without the overturning of formal constitutional principles. The reason for this was that legislatures enjoyed considerable discretion regarding the administration of law, and consequently ordinary legal measures like statutes could be used to dramatic effect. A constitutional order could thereby be destroyed even if the overall formal structure of the order remained intact. The only way to guard against this was to provide content to the powers that legislatures enjoyed. Matters that were typically left to legislatures needed to be filled out—they needed to be codified in the constitutional text itself.

Only a few years earlier Ambedkar had thought that the constitution-making task in India had few new questions before it. The American founders, he had then observed, "had to evolve ideas, suitable for the constitution of a free people."[61] There were "no constitutional patterns before them to draw upon."[62] In the Indian case, however, constitutional models were "ready at hand" with minimal "room for variety."[63] He saw the Indian enterprise as being largely derivative. The only outstanding issue, Ambedkar had then declared, was the relationship between Hindus and Muslims. But a few years later, in his new role as the chairman of the Drafting Committee of the Constituent Assembly, he had come to have a broader outlook. The novelty of the Indian experiment had become clear. The undemocratic character of modern Indian society was a reality that required negotiation. It presented circumstances in which it was "wiser not to trust the legislature to prescribe forms of administration."[64] Through codification, the actions of Indians could be structured by specific forms of knowledge. The constitutional text would allow them to deliberate and exercise authority in ways that were suitable to a free society with a shared consensus over the principles of self-government. Codification would, in other words, make Indians democrats.

Social and Economic Welfare

The provisions contained in this Part shall not be enforceable by any court, but the principles therein laid down are nevertheless fundamental in the governance of the country and it shall be the duty of the State to apply these principles in making laws.

—*Article 37, Constitution of India, 1950*

The State shall, within the limits of its economic capacity and development, make effective provision for securing the right to work, to education and to public assistance in cases of unemployment, old age, sickness and disablement, and in other cases of undeserved want.

—*Article 41, Constitution of India, 1950*

The State shall regard the raising of the level of nutrition and the standard of living of its people and the improvement of public health as among its primary duties and, in particular, the State shall endeavour to bring about prohibition of the consumption except for medicinal purposes of intoxicating drinks and of drugs which are injurious to health.

—*Article 47, Constitution of India, 1950*

The impulse toward codification is captured by considering specific choices that lay before the Constituent Assembly. One might begin with a question at the heart of Indian political thought in the first half of the twentieth century: the relationship between political independence and socioeconomic liberty. The promise of democracy was in part the promise of the life that it would produce. A system of self-government held the potential to generate conditions where freedom could be realized. In the absence of democratic norms, however, much uncertainty loomed over the outcomes that the practices of self-authorization would engender. In imagining possible futures, India's leaders searched for an understanding of the relationship between popular rule and substantive justice. This quest culminated in an interesting, if curious, feature in the Constitution: a set of socioeconomic goals—the "Directive Principles of State Policy"—that were binding on the government but were judicially unenforceable. The text stated that the directive principles "shall not be enforceable by any court," while specifying that they were "nevertheless fundamental in the governance of the country" and that "it shall be the duty of the state to

44

apply [them] in making laws."[65] This was a crucial instance of the codification project at the heart of the Indian Constitution.[66]

In the last few decades of colonial rule, a number of Indian thinkers addressed the relationship between political and socioeconomic freedom. Some, most conspicuously Mohandas Gandhi, had taken the radical view that socioeconomic transformation required decentering the state. His idea of a collective life departed from conventional models of modern politics. It was structured around local bodies, where no single authority could claim sovereignty. Jawaharlal Nehru was one the most significant figures to offer a different perspective. He resisted the idea that the domain of politics was at odds with other domains of freedom. Mainstream Indian nationalism of the 1920s and 1930s had disappointed him. He had seen it as unduly narrow and unambitious.[67] The attainment of political liberty from alien rule was surely worthy, but Nehru felt that its ultimate worth must depend on tangible improvements in ordinary life.[68]

For him, British rule was problematic not only because it had deprived Indians of political agency but also because it had failed on its own terms. In putting forth an internal critique of the Raj, Nehru considered how it had ignored education, health, and working conditions, and had led to little material improvement.[69] The British had access to India's tremendous resources and were given "a century and a half of unchecked despotism."[70] Yet all that they had produced for India, he asserted, was "grinding poverty, and widespread illiteracy, and general absence of sanitation and medical relief, and a lack of all the good things of life."[71] Even though the world saw shifts in public finance norms—there had been far greater attention to "free and universal education, improvement of public health, care of the poor and feeble-minded, insurance of workers against illness, old age and unemployment"—the British poured all the revenue that the state generated into the perpetuation of a coercive order.[72]

Colonialism had famously been justified on consequentialist grounds. In Britain's imagination, only foreigners could maintain harmony on Indian soil. Nehru took this argument head-on, responding on the same terms. He was not the first to challenge the internal logic of imperialism. In the early years of the twentieth century, economic nationalists such as Dadabhai Naoroji and R. C. Dutt had described India's economic downfall under colonial rule.[73] They emphasized the exploitative character of the foreign regime. Nehru shared Naoroji's and Dutt's argumentative framework, but he went one step further in reflecting on the colonial experience to consider the future of freedom in an independent India. For any constitutional order to be meaningful, it would have to be a vehicle for a better life.[74] Nehru found little satisfaction in the constitutional proposals that emerged during the struggle for self-rule. He saw these proposals as preoccupied with matters of administration and felt that they ignored systemic questions, such as patterns in land distribution. Such proposals failed to see that, as far as India's masses were concerned, "it was not a matter of a fine constitution drawn up in London or elsewhere, but of a basic change in the land system, especially in the *zamindari* areas."[75] Laws like the Government of India Act of 1935 did "not touch a single problem of India."[76] Nehru expressed anguish over the Act's silence on "the economic problems—of grinding poverty, of immense unemployment of the middle classes, of the industrial workers, and chiefly of the rural population."[77]

At a time when others were largely focused on political agency, Nehru uttered the bold claim that poverty, rather than foreign rule, lay at the heart of the Indian tragedy.[78] "The Indian problem" was to be viewed "in terms of relieving the poverty and raising the mass of peasants and workers to a human level."[79] This landscape emerged against the backdrop of democratic failure in Europe. In reviewing Bertrand Russell's *Roads to Freedom* in 1919, Nehru reminded his readers that "representative institutions and democracy as prevalent in Western countries at present have proved failures."[80] It was a view that Nehru consistently held over the next two decades. Throughout the 1930s he felt that "the old style of democratic form has ceased to exist" and that "the so-called democratic countries in the West are democratic only in a political sense."[81] It was "not enough to give a vote to a hungry man"; the "failure of democracy in Europe [was] the failure of the one-sided and partial democracy."[82] The exclusive emphasis on political arrangements had proven to be an inadequate answer to the problems of the world.

By 1936 Nehru had come to understand that only two models for state-building were on offer: either some version of fascism or some version of socialism or communism.[83] Given this choice, Soviet Russia became a natural source of guidance. One had to acknowledge both its "unpleasant aspects" and its tremendous possibility.[84] Even if the Soviet experiment failed, Nehru felt that it would be "partly because Russia was a very backward country and partly maybe because of wrong methods" but not for any fault with the overall ambition.[85] Yet, even though the Soviet experience had many lessons to offer, Nehru warned against blindly copying its methods. A scientific approach to socialism was one in which "the socialist tries to solve the problems of each country in relation to its varied background and stage of economic development, and also in relation to the world."[86] What India required was an adaptation of the Soviet experiment— a commitment to socioeconomic transformation without violence to civil rights. Nehru's faith that such adaptation could be possible was based on the character of the anticolonial struggle: "During the past few years in India, ever since the idea of radical social changes has assumed importance here, it has often been stated that such change necessarily involves the use of violence and cannot therefore be advocated . . . But, in theory, if it is possible to bring about a great political change by a non-violent technique, why should it not be equally possible to effect a radical social change by this method?"[87]

Thus, the ends of the Soviet experiment could be severed from their means. A nonviolent route that was sensitive to civil rights and the broader landscape of liberal constitutionalism could arrive at the same destination. But Nehru asserted that to make this possible, a new understanding of democratic constitutionalism would have to emerge—an understanding that offered a flexible state, burdened only by basic legal rules. Legislatures would have to "confine themselves to laying down general principles and policies."[88] The details of policies were to be left to experts.[89] The constitutional order needed to do less rather than more. A constitution, Nehru posited, should make possible "the socialization of society."[90] To achieve such change, it should be a document with "no restrictions."[91]

Though Nehru was committed to effecting socioeconomic change through the means of democratic constitutionalism, he did not present very many further details of the precise legal form by which this change might occur. The major statements on rights prior to India's independence appear to share this quality. Indeed, it would be a mistake to confuse the widespread support for a state-centered economic vision with support for judicially enforceable socioeconomic rights. The sentiments that were prevalent lacked institutional specificity. We can form only a minimal, if telling, sense of how rights were understood. Consider, for example, the Motilal Nehru Report of 1928. Even though the report drew no formal distinction between rights, and recognized both civil-political and socioeconomic rights, it used a different language for the enforcement of the latter. Clause 4(v) of the report, for example, provided that "citizens in the Commonwealth of India shall have the right to free elementary education . . . and such right shall be enforceable as soon as due arrangements shall have been made by competent authority."[92] No such qualifying statement was made with respect to civil-political rights, indicating that they would be enforceable with immediate effect. Similarly, clause 4(xvii) declared that "Parliament shall make suitable laws for the maintenance of health and fitness for work of all citizens, securing of a living wage for every worker."[93] This clause empowered Parliament to enact certain welfare legislation, but it did not in itself recognize any socioeconomic right, such as a right to health or a right to work.

The phrasing of the Indian National Congress's Karachi Resolution of 1931 is equally interesting. The resolution declared that "political freedom must include real economic freedom of the starving millions."[94] In furtherance of this goal, it committed the Congress party to a list of twenty items which a future constitution was to incorporate. The items in this list ranged widely, from adult suffrage to a graduated inheritance tax. The first item in this list contained the "fundamental rights of the people."[95] But the nine rights under this entry did not include any socioeconomic guarantee. Such guarantees, like free primary education, were mentioned in other items as individual heads. One should not put too fine a point on the resolution, not least because it never concerned itself with institutional details like justiciability and enforcement mechanisms. Nonetheless, its textual form reveals some understanding of how freedom was conceptualized. It discloses the belief that "fundamental rights" were in some way different from social and economic protections. What was significant about the resolution, as Nehru recognized in his *Autobiography*, is that it moved beyond previous resolutions which had focused exclusively on political freedom.[96] Gandhi too saw the resolution as primarily serving a signaling role. He estimated that it would "make it clear to the world and to our own people what we propose to do as soon as we come into power."[97]

Somewhat remarkably, genuine debate over socioeconomic rights arose only during the process of the drafting of the Constitution, from 1946 onward. The distinguished lawyer Alladi Krishnaswami Ayyar's note in the Sub-Committee on Fundamental Rights is a crucial document in this context. It saw the distinction between enforceable civil-political rights and unenforceable socioeconomic rights as natural. As far as Ayyar was concerned, a distinction had "necessarily to be drawn between rights which are justiciable and rights which are merely intended as a guide and directing objectives to state policy."[98] But Ayyar also felt, as he made clear in the proceedings of the Sub-Committee, that the inclusion of unenforceable rights in a constitutional document was pointless.[99]

It remains unclear whether the upshot of this was that the directive principles should be excluded altogether or that they be made enforceable, and Ayyar's inclination to exclude primary education as a justiciable right, in a subsequent meeting of the Sub-Committee, does not fully clarify matters.[100]

The notes by K. M. Munshi and K. T. Shah, two active and influential players in the constitution-making process, offer more definite opinions. Munshi and Shah were ideologically dissimilar figures, veering toward the right and the left, respectively, but both offered unambiguous objections to the unenforceable character of the directive principles. Munshi was skeptical of "mere precepts" and felt that "most of the general declarations found in national constitutions and international documents have proved ineffective to check the growing power of the modern state."[101] In India it was all the more likely that such declarations would be ignored: "General precepts which may be considered less than necessary by an advanced thinker on socialistic lines will not be looked at, much less understood, or applied in some parts of the country where feudal notions still are deeply engrained."[102] Munshi's comparative survey further encouraged him to support judicially enforceable rights. Even in Britain, where Parliament was sovereign, "prerogative writs have become part of the positive law to such an extent that the Parliament would never dream of overriding or abrogating them."[103] Although Munshi did not provide any specific example of a case where socioeconomic rights had been enforceable, he relied on rights-based instruments to make a broader claim about enforcement. "The existence of a legal right in the constitution must," he asserted, "necessarily imply a right in the individual to intervene in order to make the legal right effective."[104]

K. T. Shah put the matter in even stronger terms, fearing that nonjusticiability would reduce the directive principles to "pious wishes."[105] The state would feel no pressure to deliver on the promise of these principles. Their inclusion in the Constitution would be somewhat misleading without a mechanism for their enforcement. The fact that the directive principles included socioeconomic goals, whose realization was a complex matter, was often taken to be an argument against justiciability. Shah turned this argument on its head. The very fact that "many rights in this category . . . may not be practicable all at once to give effect to" meant that the state could "avail themselves of every excuse to justify their own inactivity in the matter, indifference, or worse."[106] Alternatively, if the Constitution was to provide for the enforcement of such rights, "those responsible for giving effect to it would have to bestir themselves to find ways and means to give effect to it."[107]

In contrast to Munshi and Shah, whose views are relatively clear, B. R. Ambedkar's thoughts on this matter have invited some reflection. A recent study has characterized Ambedkar's Memorandum and Draft Articles on the Rights of States and Minorities of 1947 as "the strongest articulation of social and economic rights."[108] The memorandum made an impassioned case for a socialist economic outlook. Its message, it has been suggested, sits uneasily with Ambedkar's subsequent speech before the Constituent Assembly in November 1948. This thesis—that Ambedkar's memorandum and his subsequent speech are at odds with one another—merits greater attention. Article 2 of the memorandum dealt with fundamental rights. The list of rights mentioned was wide-ranging, and Ambedkar made it clear that their judicial enforcement was guaranteed.[109] Equality before the law, access to public spaces, protection against unreasonable searches and seizures, and religious freedom all found a place in the text. Not a single socioeconomic right was mentioned, however.

A different set of provisions outlined an economic philosophy structured around the state—"industries which are key industries or which may be declared to be key industries shall be owned or run by the state"; agriculture must be a state industry; the state was empowered to "determine how and when the debenture holder shall be entitled to claim cash payment"; and so on.[110] In an explanatory appendix to the memorandum, Ambedkar justified the inclusion of such provisions. He felt that it was imperative "to put an obligation on the state to plan the economic life of the people on lines which would lead to the highest point of productivity without closing every avenue to private enterprise, and also provide for the equitable distribution of wealth."[111] India could rapidly industrialize only through some version of "state socialism."[112] The private sector, he feared, lacked the capacity for major industrialization, and even if such industrialization were possible, it would come at the cost of wealth inequality.

Ambedkar proceeded to draw a relationship between his economic vision and rights. Rights were meaningless without certain background social and economic conditions: "The fear of starvation, the fear of losing a house, the fear of losing savings, if any, the fear of being compelled to take children away from school, the fear of having to be a burden on public charity, the fear of having to be burned or buried at public cost are factors too strong to permit a man to stand out for his fundamental rights. The unemployed are thus compelled to relinquish their fundamental rights for the sake of securing the privilege to work and to subsist."[113] Ambedkar rejected the standard practice where constitutional provisions were used exclusively to constrain state power and positive actions like the protection of the poor were placed within the ambit of legislative discretion. He felt that legislative institutions were vulnerable to both interest group capture and political change. One needed to moderate the enthusiasm for parliamentary democracy, keeping in mind that an "essential condition for the success of a planned economy is that it must not be liable to suspension or abandonment."[114] For constitutions to enable freedom in all its forms, they needed to address both political liberty and the structure of economic life.

As I have noted, scholars have tried to reconcile Ambedkar's Memorandum and Draft Articles on the Rights of States and Minorities with a speech that he subsequently made in the Constituent Assembly. In this speech, Ambedkar defended the status of the directive principles, asserting that the Constitution "only provides a machinery for the government of the country. It is not a contrivance to install any particular party in power."[115] Three possible reasons have been offered to explain Ambedkar's shift in position: his revisiting of the question through legal rather than political eyes; his effort to reconcile socialism with parliamentary sovereignty; and his strategic emphasis on other concerns like the rights of the lower castes.[116] Each of these explanations carries a degree of plausibility, but the shift in Ambedkar's position deserves interrogation.

In his transition, Ambedkar did not downgrade his support for enforceable socioeconomic rights into support for unenforceable socioeconomic rights. Even though it had been suggested that Ambedkar's memorandum "challenged constitutional lawyers to think differently about the possibility of incorporating social and economic rights,"[117] at no point did he argue for enforceable socioeconomic rights.[118] The focus was instead on whether a constitution could be silent on the question of welfare and thereby limit itself to the right to self-rule. To understand Ambedkar's position, our emphasis should not be on why the directive principles were not made enforceable in the same manner as the fundamental rights. The bulk of historical analysis has mistakenly focused on this inquiry.[119] It has tried to uncover why socioeconomic rights allegedly went out of fashion at India's founding, and it has presented reasons for the seemingly secondary status of the directive principles.[120] With regard to Ambedkar, the "puzzle" is made out to be that "he gave strong support to the project of incorporating such rights . . . [but subsequently] provided a reasoned defense of the eventual outcome without acknowledging that this implied any sort of withdrawal or retraction."[121] But the reason Ambedkar made no such acknowledgment is that he did not substantially change his position. In fact, his original position continued to be a commonly held view. Barely months after India acquired independence, the All India Congress Committee refused to rest on the achievement of political freedom and declared that "the establishment of real democracy . . . can only be realized when democracy extends from the political to the social and economic spheres."[122] Rather than analyze a dilution in standing that never occurred, we must ask what possible purpose the directive principles were meant to serve, given their unenforceability. To put the question crudely: What point did these principles have?[123] This question matters if only for the elementary reason that the inclusion of a meaningless set of provisions would undercut the force of other provisions in the text.[124]

The directive principles emerged out of a worry over the outcomes that the use of legislative power would generate. The principles were based on reservations about the behavior of newly elected representatives. At the core of both Ambedkar's memorandum and his speech in November 1948 was an argument against constitutional silence on the subject of welfare. What is notable about the speech, in comparison with the earlier memorandum, is the working out of the commitment to welfare. The speech was an effort to give this commitment institutional expression, and to determine its place within the broader vision of self-government. It was also an attempt to negotiate the relationship between the pledge to welfare and other commitments like the right to property, as Ambedkar later acknowledged.[125] The right to property might be diluted by later generations (as indeed it was), but for the moment the Constitution had rejected the state's "freedom to nationalize or socialize all private property without payment of compensation."[126]

Ambedkar's speech in November 1948 is not special because it offers us a rationale for the unenforceability of the directive principles. The Sub-Committee on Fundamental Rights already presented us with that. In explaining the reason for unenforceable directive principles, it noted that it was "as impossible for a worker to prove, as for a court to find, that a general right [such as the rights of workers to decent conditions] has been infringed in a given case."[127] Ambedkar himself, only a month after his speech of November 1948, registered his preference for using the language of rights for situations involving an enforceable remedy.[128] The Constitutional Adviser to the Constituent Assembly, B. N. Rau, had also regarded the distinction between the directive principles and fundamental rights as one between positive and negative rights, respectively. For him, it was "obvious that rights of the first type are normally not either capable of, or suitable for, enforcement by legal action, while those of the second type may be so enforced."[129] He pointed to the Irish Constitution and to H. Lauterpacht's 1945 text *An International Bill of the Rights of Man,* both of which had distinguished between the two kinds of rights.[130]

H. Lauterpacht's work is worth noting, given its significance in the international postwar recognition of rights. Lauterpacht offered a theoretical and historical framework for thinking about a bill of rights, a study of the relationship between the law of nature, natural rights, and the law of nations, as well as a carefully scripted model along the lines of which a bill of rights might be conceived. Lauterpacht's draft law distinguished two kinds of rights. (The model bill also contained a third part, focused on enforcement.) The first part on rights contained familiar civil and political liberties. The second part included, though it was not limited to, socioeconomic rights. For example, Article 13 of the draft law dealt with the right to work, the right to education, and such, and Article 14 dealt with the conditions of work. To recognize such rights, Lauterpacht maintained, was to admit the "connection between political freedom and economic freedom, between legal equality and economic and social equality of opportunity."[131]

Lauterpacht did not perceive any difference in the relative importance of the rights in parts I and II of his draft. Indeed, the two sets of rights were to be regarded as complementary to one another. Without the rights in part II, those in part I would "tend to become purely theoretical."[132] Yet the protection of these rights was to be "different in form and less definite in degree" than part I rights.[133] Individual nations, he observed, had taken different approaches to part II rights, like the right to work. Despite variations in approaches, however, a general trend was discernible: such rights were typically framed as policy prescriptions to guide legislation. Lauterpacht wondered if such prescriptions were fitting as rules of international law in a context where such rules had been instantiated in a variety of ways and lacked a rule-like character within domestic legal regimes. To make such rights enforceable would be to undertake at an international level a project that had not even been undertaken at a national level. It would instead be more suitable for such rights to function, not as judicially enforceable in a typical fashion, but as a source of inspiration and pressure in other ways.

An International Bill of the Rights of Man is a reminder of the climate of global opinion surrounding welfare rights, and a theory of historical and social change, that made the unenforceable character of the directive principles a relatively uncontroversial matter. Ambedkar did not need to defend that decision in any major fashion. But he did need to offer some understanding of the value of the directive principles given their lack of enforceability. This is the reason Ambedkar's intervention in November 1948 is important. The speech is significant not for reasons that have hitherto been supposed—that it marks some transition in Ambedkar's thought—but because Ambedkar therein gives us a positive account for the directive principles. It is at this moment that he articulates a reason for their codification. The directive principles mattered because although the rules of democracy mandated that the people must elect those who will hold power, the principles confirmed that "whoever captures power will not be free to do what he likes with it."[134] The directive principles, Ambedkar contended, were akin to the Instruments of Instructions under colonial legislation like the Government of India Act of 1935. The "only difference" between the two was that the principles were instructions to the legislature and executive rather than to the governor-general and governors.[135] The inclusion of such instructions in a constitution was "to be welcomed," for when "there is a grant of power in general terms for peace, order, and good government, it is necessary that it should be accompanied by instructions regulating its exercise."[136] Even though the principles might lack "legal force" and those in power "may not have to answer for their breach in a court of law," they would "certainly have to answer for them before the electorate at election time."[137]

The analogy between the directive principles and the Instrument of Instructions is a telling one. Before the Simon Commission—a British contingent in charge of constitutional reform in the late 1920s—Ambedkar had launched into a searing critique of the dyarchy under the Government of India Act of 1919. The Instrument contributed greatly to the reduction of ministries to nonentities. For example, the Instrument called on the governors to safeguard the interests of civil servants. But this instruction was interpreted with great freedom, and the governors "insisted that all matters relating to the services including the question of their appointments, posting, and promotions in the Minister's department should be under [their] charge."[138] For Ambedkar, history suggested that the Instrument expanded the authority of those to whom it was directed. It was a mistake to regard the Instrument—as it would be a mistake to regard the directive principles—as meaningless.

One way to read Ambedkar's speech in the Constituent Assembly, as scholars have done, is to see him as offering a democratic justification for the unenforceability of the directive principles.[139] But another, as I have suggested, is to understand his intervention as making a case against the sufficiency of political democracy. Indeed, this sentiment had long been a feature of Ambedkar's thought. In a 1943 speech on the nineteenth-century Congress party leader and social activist Mahadev Govind Ranade, Ambedkar observed that the "formal framework of democracy is of no value and would indeed be a misfit if there was no social democracy."[140] Ambedkar's focus may have been somewhat different from Nehru's on this point, but the faith that egalitarianism extended beyond one man, one vote, was shared by both. This was not simply a matter of principle. It was crucial to the survival of democracy. As Ambedkar noted on another occasion in the same year, the reason for democracy's collapse in Italy, Germany, and Russia and its survival in England and America was "a greater degree of economic and social democracy in the latter countries than it existed in the former."[141] The speech on Ranade revealed a further facet of Ambedkar's thinking: his emphasis on the effectiveness of rights. He challenged the "unwarranted assumption" that "once rights are enacted in a law then they are safeguarded," indicating that the limitations of political constitutionalism could not be resolved by legal constitutionalism.[142] Without the directive principles, legislators might be entirely at sea, and—more dangerously—might exercise power without an overarching conception of socioeconomic welfare. The codification of the directive principles would expose both the ruler and the ruled to the proper exercise of power. The pedagogical promise of the Constitution would thus be furthered, for directive principles would have, as Rau put it, "an educative value."[143]

Rights and Limitations

(1) All citizens shall have the right—
    (a) to freedom of speech and expression

   . . .

> (2) Nothing in sub-clause (a) of clause (1) shall affect the operation of any existing law in so far as it relates to, or prevent the State from making any law relating to, libel, slander, defamation, contempt of court or any matter which offends against decency or morality or which undermines the security of, or tends to overthrow, the State.
>
> —*Article 19, Constitution of India, 1950*

The directive principles were not the only peculiar feature in the Indian Constitution. The text also adopted an unusual approach to enforceable rights. In several cases where the text recognized rights and guaranteed their enforcement—as in the case of the right to freedom of speech and expression—it also limited such rights. A reading of the Constitution is therefore a somewhat dissonant experience. On the one hand, there is a grand proclamation in favor of a right. On the other hand, there is a strong statement enumerating the exceptions to the realization of the concerned right. Should we regard this textual reality as embodying a lack of commitment to rights? What purpose was such a drafting strategy meant to achieve?

Rights, which often are seen as central to a liberal constitutional order, were only marginally in focus during the Indian nationalist movement. Mohandas Gandhi's vision was arranged around duties rather than entitlements. The energy of those like Jawaharlal Nehru was spent on the structure of economic life. In the immediate years preceding the end of alien rule, constitutional debates were almost invariably focused on the question of minorities and representation.[144] In spite of being sidelined during the public life of India's freedom struggle, however, rights did make an appearance in more than a few documents and resolutions. In 1918 a special session of the Indian National Congress called for equal treatment before the law, the right to bear arms, the freedom of the press, and so forth.[145] A year later, Motilal Nehru's presidential address to the Congress party included the bold assertion that "no constitution can meet our needs unless it is accompanied with a guarantee and a clear declaration of our elementary rights."[146] Civil-political rights found endorsement in subsequent Congress party resolutions.[147] In the same vein, the suppression of civil liberties was condemned.[148]

In 1931 the Congress party, in its well-known Karachi session, went further and committed itself to a range of social and economic goals. For the younger Nehru, writing at the end of the 1930s, it was a settled fact that "there are certain fundamental rights guaranteeing the freedom of the individual which we would like to ensure and to be incorporated in the constitution."[149] His list included equal protection, religious liberty, and free expression. The Sapru Committee Report of 1945 acknowledged that enforceable rights were at odds with the British principle of parliamentary sovereignty, but it proceeded to note that "the peculiar circumstances of India" made such rights "necessary not only for giving assurances and guarantees to the minorities but also for prescribing a standard of conduct for the legislatures, government, and the courts."[150]

Political leader V. S. Srinivasa Sastri placed rights at the center of attention in his 1926 Kamala lectures. Rights, he contended, were distinguishable by three characteristics. First, they were "an arrangement, rule, or practice sanctioned by the law of the community and conducive to . . . the moral good of the citizen."[151] Second, they were guaranteed by law. That is, they were enforceable in a court of law and their violation resulted in remedial action. Third, no person had a monopoly on rights. They "must be open to all citizens."[152] Even though Britain had rejected the idea of a written constitution with a bill of rights, Sastri defended the codification of rights. The textual recognition of rights served an instructive purpose. It was a reminder of the principles on which political action was to be based: "In the distractions of public life, in the busy interactions and conflict of diverse interests, an uninstructed person, concerned only with his own minute aspect of affairs, is apt to forget, even if he knew the fundamentals of political action, the proprieties which may not be violated, the guarantees of justice and fair play which must never be brought into jeopardy."[153]

As we have seen, rights did appear in the Indian Constitution, but many were explicitly limited in some fashion. The thought that rights might be restricted was not new; it had been expressed in texts like the 1928 Nehru Report.[154] It was only during the making of the Constitution, though, that the issue of limitations on rights became an aspect of drafting strategy. The question was not whether rights were absolute. It was whether the grounds on which they were limited ought to be codified in the constitutional text.

A number of participants in the Constituent Assembly saw such codification as a mark of skepticism toward rights. One member put the matter directly: "Many of [the] fundamental rights have been framed from the point of view of a police constable."[155] "Very minimum rights," he argued, "have been conceded and those too very grudgingly and these so-called rights are almost invariably followed by a proviso."[156] The concern was that the limitations on rights would ultimately hinder the development of democratic norms. For instance, the right to freedom of speech and expression was central to the emergence of political opposition and public opinion. If India's founders "lay down fundamental rights and then insert provisions in every clause for taking away those rights," they would become "a laughing stock before the whole democratic world."[157]

Numerous others shared this sentiment. K. T. Shah claimed that the attitude to rights confirmed a lack of faith in India's capacity for self-government. He criticized the Assembly for being "still unable to trust, in full, the people."[158] The codification of exceptions meant that the constitutional statements of rights were merely a "verbal promise" rather than provisions that had "any hope for actual performance."[159] "Almost in every case, in every clause, and in every sentence of each clause," he found, "the right given, conferred, or declared is either restricted, conditioned, or made dependent upon certain contingencies that may or may not happen."[160] Another member felt that "the freedom of assembling, freedom of the press, and other freedoms have been made so precarious and entirely left at the mercy of the legislature that the whole beauty and the charm has been taken away."[161] It was feared that the restrictions would limit the power of judicial review. The courts would only be able to examine the bona fides of the legislature. The "actual provisions and the extent of the restrictions imposed would be out of the scope of judicial determination."[162] The "right will in practice," one member dreaded, "cease to be justiciable."[163] The provisos seemed to effectively nullify the very purpose of recognizing the rights. The member Kazi Syed Karimuddin noted with respect to the restrictions on the right to peaceful assembly, "the very purpose of this fundamental right is being defeated."[164] Such claims often drew strength from comparative studies. Karimuddin, for example, observed that the American Constitution had chosen a different textual approach. Unlike in the Indian case, rights in the United States had "been entrusted to the judiciary."[165]

Members of the Constituent Assembly who supported the codification of the limitations on rights understood the matter rather differently. They thought that it was a mistake to see such codification as placing a limitation on rights in any special way. Codification, it was argued, was an effort to elaborate the concept underlying the right—it did not change the concept of the right. To show the necessity for such elaboration, defenders of codification also turned to the American experience, although for them it was important to first clarify the nature of this experience. It was an error, B. R. Ambedkar argued, to regard rights under the Constitution of the United States as absolute. The difference between the American and Indian approach was simply "one of form and not of substance."[166] To substantiate this claim, Ambedkar turned to the revered free speech guarantee, and showed that even here American law had established limitations. He cited the U. S. Supreme Court's holding in *Gitlow* (1925) that the right to free expression "does not confer an absolute right to speak or publish, without responsibility, whatever one may choose, or an unrestrained and unbridled license that gives immunity for every possible use of language and prevents the punishment of those who abuse this freedom."[167]

Ambedkar's larger point was that rights had been limited in the United States by the Supreme Court's recognition of the state's inherent police power. The problem before India's founders was that there was no guarantee that the Indian judiciary would similarly recognize this power on behalf of the state. Drafting the rights in absolute terms would mean "depending on our Supreme Court to come to the rescue of Parliament by inventing the doctrine of police power."[168] By empowering the state directly to restrict rights, the same outcome had been achieved. "What one does directly, the other does indirectly. In both cases," he observed, "the fundamental rights are not absolute."[169]

One notices that the contest over rights and the textual incorporation of limitations was not a contest over the content of the individual rights themselves. For the most part, all parties agreed that rights were not absolute. It was accepted that rights were necessarily limited. There was also no serious disagreement on the character of the specific restrictions. The real disagreement was over the theory of constitution-making. Critics of codification feared that putting restrictions into writing would give the state an undesirable degree of presumptive power, whereas supporters of codification felt that it would provide a stronger guarantee because the character of the right would be better described. Indeed, the incorporation of restrictions might well enable more rather than less freedom, for it meant that the rights could be limited only on those grounds that had been explicitly recognized. Codification was not focused on enabling or limiting the state. It was motivated by the sense that if a reasonable set of restrictions were available at hand, it was wiser to incorporate them within the text rather than to leave the matter unsettled. In drawing the contours of a right, one was furthering the prospect that the right in question would be guaranteed, rather than opening the door to the specification of the right by legislators and judges, who might well end up misunderstanding the concept at hand.

This fear of an open-ended constitutional text took place against the backdrop of a perceived failure of legal constitutionalism. There was "a danger," Alladi Krishnaswami Ayyar noted, "in leaving the courts, by judicial legislation so to speak, to read the necessary limitations, according to idiosyncrasies and prejudices it may be of individual judges."[170] In a later speech while reviewing the draft constitution, Ayyar described the attack on codification as "entirely without foundation."[171] "The exceptions and qualifications introduced into the articles reproduce in statutory form the well-recognized exceptions and limitations on the fundamental rights dealt with in the article. Similar restrictions have been read by the U. S. Supreme Court into the United States Constitution which in general terms provides for these rights. Our Constitution, instead of leaving it to the courts to read the necessary limitations and exceptions, seeks to express in a compendious form the limitations and exceptions."[172]

The danger of giving courts the power to restrict rights was mapped out by B. N. Rau in 1946. In a careful note Rau put forth a study of American constitutional doctrine to demonstrate how judicial discretion had failed to provide clarity.[173] The equal protection guarantee afforded an example. In *Connolly* (1902), the U. S. Supreme Court had refused to draw a distinction between trusts and combinations in agricultural products and livestock and in other goods and commodities.[174] It held that both could be detrimental to the public interest, and therefore an antitrust statute that exempted the former could not be upheld. But nearly four decades later, in *Tigner* (1940), the Court permitted a distinction between agriculture and other activities.[175] Rau sharply noted that "the same classes of persons that appeared to the courts in 1902 to be manifestly equal in fact were found in 1940 to be, in truth, unequal," and the Court's turn in *Tigner* revealed that the equal protection guarantee had "worn very thin."[176]

A reading of these cases suggests less judicial capriciousness than Rau's note suggests. In *Connolly*, an Illinois antitrust statute of 1893 was challenged as being repugnant to the American Constitution. A provision in the law rendered it inapplicable "to agricultural products or livestock while in the hands of the producer or raiser."[177] The Supreme Court found no basis for this classification and upheld the challenge. It could see no reason for blocking "combinations of capital, skill or acts, in respect of the sale or purchase of goods, merchandise or commodities" that dictated prices and harmed the public interest, without the suppression of "like combinations in respect of agricultural products and livestock" that similarly caused harm.[178] In *Tigner,* a Texas antitrust law that too exempted agricultural products and livestock was challenged by relying on the *Connolly* decision. On this occasion, the Court noticed a shift in public policy toward agriculture in the interim period. Legislators, focusing on free market legislation, had come to see farmers as different from industrialists. In the four decades following *Connolly,* the Court found that the "states as well as the United States have sanctioned cooperative action by farmers; have restricted their amenability to the antitrust laws; have relieved their organizations for taxation."[179] These measures, which had been upheld, evidenced a legislative understanding that agriculture played a role that was different from that of other industries. The agricultural sector might pose threats and dangers, the Court noted, but such threats and dangers had been judged to be of a different nature. Given that the equal protection guarantee did not prohibit classification, *Tigner* chose to defer to elected representatives, declaring that "to write into law the differences between agriculture and other economic pursuits was within the power of the Texas legislature."[180]

While *Connolly* and *Tigner* delivered somewhat different outcomes, as Rau noticed, underlying the varying levels of judicial scrutiny in both cases were varying degrees of leeway afforded to the legislature. In other words, the American approach toward codification failed to constrain or guide the relevant actors in a meaningful fashion. This concern is further brought out by Rau's study of a second set of cases. These pertained to graduated taxation measures. Here Rau noted that even though the U. S. Supreme Court upheld a graduated tax scheme in *Fox* (1935),[181] barely a few months later, in *Stewart Dry Goods* (1935), it invalidated a law that imposed a variable tax scheme.[182] Moreover, five years later, in *Madden* (1940), the Court upheld a tax statute that imposed differential rates depending on where one's money was deposited.[183]

Yet again, these cases are more distinguishable than Rau's note implies. Although the U. S. Supreme Court did uphold a graduated tax scheme in *Fox,* it treated chain stores and separately owned stores differently. The validity of this classification was central to the upholding of the impugned measure. In *Stewart Dry Goods,* by contrast, the variable tax measure taxed the sales of a merchant. A major reason this measure failed is because of the complex relationship between sales and profits: an increase in sales

THE GRAMMAR OF CONSTITUTIONALISM

need not indicate an increase in profits, and thereby need not reflect a greater capacity to pay. As the Court noted, a "merchant having a gross business of $1,000,000, but a net loss, must pay a greater tax than one who has a gross of $400,000, and realizes a substantial net profit."[184] While referencing *Fox,* the Court was careful to mention that it had no objection to graduated taxation schemes per se. The problem was the classification in the instant case, which failed because the statute disregarded "the form of organization and method of conducting business."[185] As the Court put it, "The taxable class is retail merchants, whether individuals, partnerships or corporations; those who sell in one store or many; those who offer but one sort of goods and those who through departments deal in many lines of merchandise. The law arbitrarily classifies these vendors for the imposition of a varying rate of taxation, solely by reference to the volume of their transactions . . . It exacts from two persons different amounts for the privilege of doing exactly similar acts because one has performed the act oftener than the other."[186]

Similarly, in *Madden* the decision turned on the validity of the classification. A state law that imposed a differential rate of taxation depending on whether one's bank deposits were within or outside the state was upheld on the basis that tax collection imposed different burdens for accounts outside the state. Again, what we notice is not so much the instability of legal doctrine arising from confused or poor judicial reasoning but instead the inability of the rights-based clauses to provide the required instruction.

Rau's study taught him that blanket constitutional guarantees were too open-ended. The danger that he identified was not the danger of excessive and unrestrained judicial power. It was the danger of uncertainty. Textual precision was vital under a system that recognized judicial review, for the absence of limitations could be interpreted positively and courts may be regarded as not having the power to develop the appropriate meaning of the right. As Rau noted elsewhere: "It may be asked why we cannot trust our courts to impose any necessary limitations instead of specifying them in the constitution itself. The explanation is that, unlike the American Constitution, the draft constitution of India contains an article which in terms states that any law inconsistent with the fundamental rights conferred by the constitution shall be void; unless, therefore, the constitution itself lays down precisely the qualifications subject to which the rights are conferred, the courts may be powerless in the matter."[187] The standard approach in constitutional texts is to avoid specifying the limitations on rights. A lack of specification leaves rights incomplete. Their formulation is bequeathed to future political actors, who, in resolving the understanding of the right, continue the task of constitution-making.[188] At India's founding, however, a theory of language and the rule of law led to a more ambitious effort at constitution-making. The worry was that giving courts and other actors broad powers of interpretation would provide direction to neither judges nor legislatures. The rules would lack the attribute of enabling actors to evaluate the action that was being performed. Put differently, the result would mean not providing for any rights at all.

Due Process

> No person shall be deprived of his life or personal liberty except according to procedure established by law.
>
> —*Article 21, Constitution of India, 1950*

Thus far, we have studied the theory of codification in the context of two specific textual choices: the choice to include the unenforceable directive principles, and the choice to incorporate rights alongside specific limitations on those rights. In each of these instances we have seen the instructive role that codification was meant to play. We now turn to a final case study that clarifies the character of constitution-making at India's founding. This dealt with the choice between two concepts of due process—procedural due process and substantive due process—that applied to the right to life and personal liberty. Under the procedural due process standard, if an action by the state was challenged as violating the right to life or personal liberty, courts would have the power to review the action and examine whether it conformed to the applicable statute that the legislature had enacted. Thus, the judiciary would assess whether the action fell within the boundaries of the legislative enactment. Any deprivation of the right to life and personal liberty would, as per this standard, be evaluated on the basis of the procedure required by the legislation. To offer a concrete example, an enactment might require a warrant to allow the police to search someone's home. A search without a warrant would violate the procedure specified in the law, and it would therefore be an invalid application of the law.

In the case of substantive due process, however, the standard was different. Here, courts were empowered to go beyond merely evaluating whether the action by the state fell within the rules established by the applicable statute. In addition to making this assessment, they had the power to consider the validity of the legislative enactment itself. Thus, in a case involving the right to life and personal liberty, courts could not only examine whether the impugned action violated the parent statute, but they could also examine whether the parent statute itself violated the right to life and personal liberty. To return to our example, under a substantive due process standard, courts would have the authority to ask whether the very idea of a law that permitted the searching of one's home was valid. Such an inquiry would typically focus on whether such a law could be considered fair and reasonable, and over time judges would develop criteria to facilitate such an inquiry. Substantive due process rested on the idea that for something to count as "law," it must possess certain characteristics. For example, a statute that targeted only a single individual would lack generality; it would resemble a judicial verdict rather than an act of legislation. Judges may, in such an instance, see the law as invalid.

Thus, whereas procedural due process allowed judges to review the executive application of a law but disallowed the review of the law when it came to the right to life and personal liberty, substantive due process permitted this additional layer of review. Not every statute enacted by a legislature could count as *law*. One standard provided a check on executive action; the other imposed limits not only on executive action but also on legislative action. We can therefore see that the choice between procedural and substantive due process in the context of the right to life and personal liberty would have major consequences for the power that the judiciary would enjoy. The choice between both options would turn on one's theory of the location of rationality.

The clause that was eventually chosen by the Constituent Assembly protected only procedural due process. The additional layer of protection against the legislature provided by substantive due process was rejected. A number of Constituent Assembly members, such as K. M. Munshi, were disappointed by this result. They saw the guarantee of procedural due process as having "no meaning at all."[189] For Munshi, the guarantee would be meaningful if courts had been empowered to "examine not merely that the conviction has been according to law or according to proper procedure, but that the procedure as well as the substantive part of the law are such as would be proper and justified by the circumstances of the case."[190]

The decision to choose procedural due process over a more substantive standard was interpreted by many Assembly members as marking a preference for state power. Members sensitive to civil rights saw the rejection of substantive due process as "the crown of our failures."[191] One participant sensed that the Constitution had taken away the presumption of innocence and made it "competent for the legislature to lay down a provision that in the matter of detention of persons whether for political or other reasons, the jurisdiction of the courts is ousted."[192] Another took the outcome to express support for preventive detention. It meant that "the legislature is all-powerful and whatever procedure is deemed proper under the circumstances will be binding upon the courts."[193]

These feelings were genuine, but they were off the mark. It is true that substantive due process provided for greater rights-based scrutiny by courts than the scrutiny provided by procedural due process. It would be a mistake, however, to suggest that the choice of the latter was based on statism. To better understand the choice, one must examine the controversial history of substantive due process in the United States.[194] The historical experience of this guarantee in America had left B. N. Rau with much cause for worry. Under the American Constitution, due process was recognized by the Fifth and Fourteenth Amendments. Over time, the protection offered by these provisions had shifted from being procedural to substantive in nature. For Rau, the phrase "due process of law" had become "synonymous with 'without just cause,' the court being the judge of what is just cause."[195] This change, he feared, posed a problem for welfare legislation. Any progressive measure aimed at improving the collective good would involve some regulation of property rights and other liberties. With the standard of substantive due process, such laws would fall within the purview of judicial review. The concern was that they would thereby become hostage to an individual judge's view on the matter.[196]

Rau's views were partly shaped by a visit to America. Justice Felix Frankfurter of the U. S. Supreme Court had informed him that substantive due process "is not only undemocratic (because it gives too few judges the power of vetoing legislation enacted by representatives of the nation) but also throws an unfair burden on the judiciary."[197] For Rau, the American experience indicated that lawmaking under conditions of substantive due process would be difficult, because legislators would struggle to predict how courts would subsequently act. He was further concerned that enforceable rights, cast "in general terms," would create "a vast mass of litigation about the validity of laws, and the same law that was held valid at one time may be held invalid at another or vice versa; the law will therefore become uncertain."[198] The problem would only grow worse as irremovable judges would be insensitive "to public needs in the social and economic sphere" in comparison with "the representatives of a periodically-elected legislative body," and would effectively "have a veto on legislation exercisable at any time at the instance of any litigant."[199]

Thus, the concern was that the substantive due process standard—which gave courts the power to review laws themselves, and not only the application of a law—could limit legislatures and thereby result in the obstruction of welfare legislation. For Rau, the potential for a substantive due process standard to adversely impact welfare legislation had been illustrated by the U. S. Supreme Court's decision in *Louisville Joint Stock Land Bank* (1935).[200] He noted that even though in this case the Court had accepted certain propositions in defense of the impugned law, it had found the taking of private property without just compensation to be dispositive, and the law was therefore declared to be unconstitutional.[201] To demonstrate the danger posed by judicial uncertainty, Rau performed a study of labor legislation in the United States. He observed that whereas *Lochner* (1905) struck down a New York law that forbade work hours that exceeded sixty hours per week or an average of more than ten hours per day in bakeries/confectionaries, twelve years later a ten-hour law for factories was upheld in *Bunting* (1917).[202] He located a similar story in the case of minimum wage legislation. *Adkins* (1923) had struck down a minimum wage for women and children, but in *West Coast Hotel* (1937) the fixing of minimum wages was found permissible.[203]

As we observed when considering Rau's study of American jurisprudence on rights, these cases could have been placed in a different narrative. *West Coast Hotel* may have been read reassuringly, for it marked the U. S. Supreme Court's abandonment of substantive due process. After 1937 the doctrine was jettisoned, and a host of economic regulations were upheld in the years following the decision. Justice Hugo Black stated some years later in *Ferguson* (1963), "We have returned to the original constitutional proposition that courts do not substitute their social and economic beliefs for the judgment of legislative bodies, who are elected to pass laws."[204] It has been correctly pointed out, with some measure of curiosity, that Rau's study draws on U. S. Supreme Court decisions from the early years of the twentieth century and omits later decisions.[205] Rau never mentioned the turn in American jurisprudence. This would have been strange except that—as in the case of codifying the limitations to rights—it was judicial uncertainty rather than judicial power that led to the adoption of procedural due process. Seen through this lens, the rejection of substantive due process only confirmed the fact of uncertainty. Rau's omission raises no puzzles. The mentioning of later decisions would only have strengthened Rau's point.

The record of the American judiciary was repeated in the Indian Constituent Assembly. "The United States Supreme Court," Alladi Krishnaswami Ayyar stated, "has not adopted a consistent view at all and the decisions are conflicting."[206] To sample the spectacle, one only needed to "take the index in the Law Reports Annotated Edition for fifteen years and compare the decisions of one year with the decisions of another year and he will come to the conclusion that it has no definite import. It all depended upon the particular judges that presided on the occasion. Justice Holmes took a view favorable to social control. There were other judges of a Tory complexion who took a strong view in favor of individual liberty and private property."[207] Ayyar believed that it was wiser to jettison substantive due process than to allow judges to adapt American decisions "according to their conservative or radical instincts as the case may be."[208] He identified a lack of consistency across America's due process jurisprudence. Ever since the U. S. Supreme Court had incorporated substantive due process and reasonableness had become a matter of judicial determination, "a conflict was always noticeable between the police power of the state and the due process clause and the judicial decisions themselves were not uniform on the import of the due process clause."[209] He found that, in the process of "drawing the line between personal liberty and the need for social control," the Court had "created new limitations upon social control and has put new limitations upon personal liberty."[210]

Dissenters in the Constituent Assembly, who felt that procedural due process could "do great mischief in a country which is the storm center of political parties and where discipline is unknown," found little traction.[211] Every single amendment that tried to replace the phrase "procedure established by law" with phrases such as "save in accordance with law" or "except in accordance with law" was rejected. What should we make of the rejection of substantive due process? It is tempting to see the choice between procedural and substantive due process as a choice between welfare legislation and civil liberties, respectively, which was precisely the manner in which several members in the Assembly saw the choice. But the case in favor of procedural due process was not based on a more permissive view of matters like preventive detention.[212] Instead it was driven by a concern over whether substantive due process would be fully intelligible to the legislature and judiciary. For B. R. Ambedkar, it was a mistake to characterize the due process debate as a debate about state power—for example, as a debate about the validity of preventive detention. Instead, the issue was the relationship between the power of the legislature and the power of courts. Where one stood on procedural and substantive due process depended on which institution one had more trust in:

> For myself I cannot altogether omit the possibility of a legislature packed by party men making laws which may abrogate or violate what we regard as certain fundamental principles affecting the life and liberty of an individual. At the same time, I do not see how five or six gentlemen sitting in the Federal or Supreme Court examining laws made by the legislature and by dint of their own individual conscience or their bias or their prejudices be trusted to determine which law is good and which law is bad. It is rather a case where a man has to sail between Charybdis and Scylla and I therefore would not say anything.[213]

Both options that were before the Assembly had costs. The risk with substantive due process was that it might disallow welfare legislation through judicial overreach. The risk with procedural due process was that it might enable draconian criminal enactments through legislative hubris. What was missing was any real debate over the nature of substantive and procedural due process per se. Both sides in the contest over due process were equally committed to welfare legislation and civil liberties. That is, the choice of clause did not reflect divergent views on the character of state power. For both sides, laws would have to satisfy rule-of-law characteristics; that is, they would have to be fair and reasonable, and possess the form of *law*. Instead, what split the camps was the concern over how different institutional actors were likely to behave when awarded power. Would judges become superlegislatures while performing the review of legislative action? Would legislatures move beyond lawmaking and enter the realms of law application and law enforcement?

The Constituent Assembly eventually opted for procedural due process. As we have seen, the decision was driven by concerns of intelligibility and uncertainty. It is interesting to note—for it nicely confirms the impulse toward codification—that the dilemma between procedural and substantive due process was additionally tackled through further codification. Ambedkar came to feel that the Assembly, in prescribing that an arrest must only conform to the procedure that had been laid down, "had not given sufficient attention to the safety and security of individual freedom."[214] Seeing the need for "compensation" for rejection of substantive due process, he introduced a new set of provisions that constitutionalized criminal law guarantees.[215] Targeting arbitrary arrests, Ambedkar felt that the new category of provisions "saves a great deal which had been lost by the non-introduction of the words 'due process of law.'"[216] Insofar as uncertainty could be minimized, it could be minimized through further constitution-writing.

Conclusion

It is sometimes observed that the specific character of constitutional texts is of limited importance in well-functioning modern constitutional democracies. There is some truth to this observation. The codification of a rule by itself can carry a political community only so far. What ultimately determines the success of any constitutional project is not the creation of rules but their reception. The text of constitutional provisions, however settled they may be, will invariably need greater meaning supplied to them.[217] Over time, the practices and traditions that come to be established are what shape the behavior of political actors in constitutional states.[218] Yet the enterprise of reception and assignment, the reliance on practices and traditions, can occur only in the context of some form of common knowledge. In this chapter I have focused on one mechanism by which common knowledge was sought to be created at India's founding.

Western constitutional theory has frequently taken constitutional open-endedness to be a virtue. Law, it is suggested, offers a special means to respond to the problem of diversity and disagreement. By enabling low-level agreement on a range of matters, it can reduce social conflict and avoid radical choices on contentious questions.[219] Recently, open-endedness has been studied in the specific context of constitution-making. Scholars have considered how drafters might strategically choose to defer matters of controversy to future legislators and courts to resolve. Deferral is a way for constitution-makers to postpone divisive issues that can threaten the success of the drafting process. It can allow different stakeholders to come together by avoiding the taking of sides. In addition to its legal consequences for the subsequent interpretation of the constitutional text, silence may also serve expressive and signaling goals about the trust that is bestowed on future actors.[220]

What is missing in such accounts, whether in constitutional theory as a general matter or in specific studies of constitution-making, is that incomplete theorizing can only occur against the background of a common language. The idea of deferral already presupposes practices that exist in institutional and individual behavior. To be able to agree to put something off the table, participants must have a shared understanding. Taking an adjournment on politically contentious matters does not depict the absence of consensus. It is the product of a consensus. It cannot exist without the existence of intersubjective meaning.[221] Incomplete theorizing places faith in the practices of popular decision-making—faith that is possible only in the presence of norms that inform such practices. That is, it is possible only in a context where such rules are present, have meaning, and therefore can guide behavior by making judgments possible.[222] In other words, the open-ended character of a constitutional text was not a concern for India's founders simply because it might lead to greater dependence on arbitrary will. More fundamentally, it would offer no possibility for the exercise of one's will.

The contest between political and legal constitutionalism has framed the debate over constitutional codification for some decades now. But as we can see, that debate has already taken much for granted. The questions faced by much of the world are not whether judicial review might be legitimate in the context of well-functioning legislatures or whether reasoning by judges might provide an independent form of legitimacy. Instead they are questions of how to arrive at well-functioning legislatures in the first place; or how to create the background understanding that can enable a contest in judicial reasoning. For many countries in the world, constitutions must do more than merely allocate power. They must be pedagogical devices that can create a constitutional culture. The various textual choices at India's founding—from unenforceable socioeconomic goals to rights that were explicitly limited—were attempts to direct the actions of popular representatives, law-applying officials, and the people. In addition to the standard benefits associated with rules—their impersonality, their predictability, their solution to information problems—rules were thought to make agency possible. Indians would be able to relate to one another in new ways.

In the final days of the Constituent Assembly, B. R. Ambedkar warned against the "grammar of anarchy."[223] To embrace constitutionalism was to subject disagreement to distinct forms of decision-making. The codification project explicated these forms. It made available the grammar of constitutionalism, and it aimed to depoliticize behavior in a manner that is not quite captured by crude contests over institutional power. The shared knowledge and common understanding that a democratically oriented polity would have formed was missing in India. There was no precommitment that could have been recorded in the Constitution.[224] And without the rules of constitutional grammar, there could be no legitimization of conduct and no realization of freedom. It was impossible, say, to protect a right without some determinate understanding of what the right in question meant. Both codification and democratization were thus seen as linked, in the same way that a democracy cannot exist without general rules because this would not be a form of rule at all.[225] The Indian context was without a shared understanding of the practices that constituted self-rule. The act of codification proceeded on the assumption that the practices that we engage in are at least partly constituted by the vocabulary we employ. The words in the constitutional text are not only ways to mold action and deliberation. They also hold the potential to bring into being the actors and concepts that can make action and deliberation possible. In the Indian case, the consensus that is ordinarily present in precommitment would have to be provided—codification was an effort to supply that consensus.

2

The Location of Power

A striking fact of the twentieth century was the triumph of the nation-state over competing possibilities. Though the end of the Second World War witnessed the proliferation of nation-states, actors and theorists had explored other alternatives for some years. A diverse set of federal proposals appeared in the first half of the twentieth century, and they came to be associated with a disparate set of political projects. Some tried to maintain the imperial world order and provide a new framework for the British empire; some sought to build an inclusive global community in the aftermath of imperialism; some attempted to control the excesses of state power, especially with regard to ethnic minorities; some hoped to secure weak postcolonial states in a world of unequally distributed power; some were focused on a new economic order, where growth and welfare were conceptualized in universal terms; and some were based on the idea of free trade and the flow of capital.[1] These proposals offered distinct paths to determining a world order where empires were in decline and the domain of the political was being redefined.

In the face of such proposals, the victory of the nation-state is a remarkable feature of modern history. The Indian state, with its centralized framework, is a crucial, if neglected, part of this story. In a strictly legal sense, the Constitution of India is federal in character. B. R. Ambedkar defended this characterization by noting the formal partitioning of power between the central and regional units.[2] Both sets of authorities have exclusive powers of legislation. Yet even though Ambedkar minimized the Constitution's centralized apparatus, commentators at the time understood that the text was not straightforwardly federal. K. C. Wheare, the Oxford scholar of government and a leading authority on federalism, for example, underlined the fact that the regional units had not been granted independent political identity and could be territorially altered without their consent. Parliament was empowered to create new entities and abolish existing ones.[3] In light of such features, as well as others like strong emergency provisions that effectively enabled a unitary state, Wheare resisted seeing India's framework as federal. He instead referred to it as "quasi-federal."[4]

C. H. Alexandrowicz, another theorist of modern legal forms, similarly found India's federal model hard to define.[5] Alexandrowicz, a Polish-British intellectual who taught at the University of Madras and studied the evolution of international law and transnational relations, was intimately acquainted with India's legal setup. He rejected Wheare's characterization as being unhelpful and instead drew a distinction between contractual and administrative federations. In contrast to familiar federal arrangements, India did not contain sovereign units that joined together to form a new political identity.[6] No region of British India had been sovereign. The territory had been populated by princely states, which were governed with varying degrees of internal autonomy through treaties with the British, and by provinces, which the colonial state administered directly. By way of a different reading of the Constitution's provisions, Alexandrowicz did find some meaning in seeing India as federal but acknowledged that the text was *sui generis*. He appreciated that the text did not acknowledge the autonomy of regional units and described it as "a constitution imposed from above."[7]

In this chapter I focus on the turn to centralization at India's creation and the founding commitment to an overarching state.[8] Such a state, I shall argue, promised a distinct form of political mediation. It was not merely an effort to prevent secession through the concentration of authority.[9] More fundamentally, the existence of a centralized state involved a turn to modernity—including the power dimension associated with modern institutions—and enabled a new kind of intersubjectivity. India's founders saw localism as burdened by a set of practices that disabled individual agency. Simply put, natives were seen to be without a politics that could enable self-rule. The founders sought to liberate Indians from localism—to rescue them from villages and kings—in order to grant them collective agency. The centralized state could mobilize allegiances and thereby pave the way for a form of deliberation appropriate to popular government. It could be a vehicle for development and industrialization, and it could avert capitalist exploitation and undertake modernization. This was not solely a point about institutional efficacy. The state was the body that could reconstitute interpersonal relationships by placing all individuals under its aegis. By situating all Indians within its orbit, the state could alter relations and practices and the forms of meaning that they entailed. As a result, Indians would come to have a new understanding of authority. They would be liberated through submission to an impersonal force that saw them as equal agents, and that liberated spirit would make possible socioeconomic transformation.

This chapter brings to light this perspective. Before we study the idea of centralization, however, we must reflect on other paths that might have been taken. In the first part of this chapter, I consider an alternative local government tradition that fell out of favor at India's founding. Referred to as political pluralism—for the reason that it involved a dispersion of power and did not entail a singular political authority such as the state—this tradition departed from the statist perspective. The differences between the two perspectives ranged over matters including the reality of localism, the locus of social change, the meaning of political participation, and the relationship between modernity and freedom. A study of the local government tradition shows that the nation-state was not the only imagined anticolonial outcome.[10] Moreover, the rejection of this tradition reveals the premises behind the choice to centralize. I then examine the centralization and modernization drive in the years prior to Indian independence, underlining the relationship between radicalism and state power as it evolved within Indian political thought. After this I turn to the Constituent Assembly's decision to centralize authority. I suggest that the decision was not a contingent fallout of the partition of British India, and I set out the link between democratization and centralization that influenced the Assembly's deliberations. I conclude this chapter by bringing this link into sharper focus, suggesting that the variance between the different institutional conceptions at India's founding rested on fundamentally contrasting notions of the state and society.

Political Pluralism

In the early years of the twentieth century, Indian political thought underwent a shift in emphasis. The predominant intellectual inquiry of the previous century—namely, explaining why India had fallen prey to for-

eign rulers—faded away. In the nineteenth century, this inquiry had motivated Indians to scrutinize their social practices and had contributed to
a kind of Indian renaissance.[11] In time, however, attention turned to a
more forward-looking set of concerns, which were centered on the meaning
of independence and ways to achieve it.[12] Mohandas Gandhi's 1909 tract
Hind Swaraj (Indian Home Rule) marked a crucial moment in this transition. Although the text considered the colonization of India—chapter 7
was titled "Why Was India Lost?"—its emphasis was on liberation. In
Hind Swaraj, Gandhi claimed that Indians were "impatient to obtain
Swaraj, but . . . certainly not decided as to what it is."[13] They were enthu-
siastic about the removal of foreign rule but had failed to reflect on what
this outcome might achieve. To desire the same form of government with
different personnel, to seek similar models of statehood with more participation, was, Gandhi asserted, the pursuit of "English rule without the
Englishman."[14] It was akin to wanting "the tiger's nature, but not the
tiger."[15] For Gandhi, such an aspiration would merely result in a new form
of confinement. It was a version of *swaraj* that was "not truly *swaraj.*"[16]

Gandhi's claim rested on a critique of Western political institutions.
He began by considering their efficacy. The British Parliament he branded
"a sterile woman and a prostitute."[17] Its "natural condition" was "such,
that, without outside pressure, it can do nothing."[18] He compared it to "a
prostitute" on the ground that it was "under the control of ministers who
change from time to time."[19] Gandhi could locate no institutional reason
for Parliament's failures. Legislators worked without a salary to maintain commitment to the public good, and a broad level of literacy existed
among the voters. Given these factors, Parliament should in theory be effective. And yet, Gandhi observed, "it is generally acknowledged that the
members are hypocritical and selfish."[20] It was well known that they
voted on party lines without independent thought, that their decisions
lacked finality, and that the institution remained riddled with indiscipline.
The prime minister was invested in entrenching his own power rather than
furthering public welfare. Political leaders under such a system might not
give in to bribery, but they were "open to subtler influences."[21]

A study of these institutional failures was followed by a wholesale attack on Western civilization. Gandhi condemned, for example, the privileging of physical comfort and making "bodily welfare the object of life."[22]
This point was borne out by numerous illustrations—the improvement
in homes and conditions of living, the change in clothing from skins to
modern apparel like trousers, the replacement of manual labor by machines,

the birth of the steam engine, and so on. Civilization was the story of progress along such lines. This continual improvement in our worldly condition would result in diminishment of our capabilities—the capacity to travel across the world in only a few hours, for instance, Gandhi hypothesized, would eventually result in our not even requiring the use of our limbs. He understood such changes as exemplifying newer forms of bondage. "Formerly," he observed, "men were made slaves under physical compulsion, now they are enslaved by temptation of money and of the luxuries that money can buy."[23]

Hind Swaraj offered many reasons to reject such worldliness. To begin with, Gandhi observed that the so-called progress in civilization was in reality the provision of remedies for symptoms. Diseases emerged that had never previously existed, but improvement was seen as an increase in medical care rather than the absence of such conditions. The test of civilization was not a decrease in desires, but the satisfaction of wants as they grew. Alleged improvements were not solutions to our problems—they were instead a deepening of the problem. Civilization, in other words, failed on its own terms: "Civilization seeks to increase bodily comforts, and it fails miserably even in doing so."[24] This attack was linked to civilization's indifference toward morality and religion, though *Hind Swaraj* did not expand on either term. Gandhi did clarify that his use of the term "religion" was associated with no particular form of organized religion and related to "that religion which underlies all religions."[25] He wanted to underline the mental and physical unrest that civilization had engendered— that people in the civilized world "appear to be half mad," are without "real physical strength or courage," are sustained by "intoxication," and cannot "be happy in solitude."[26]

Gandhi saw a natural link between the modern state and imperial rule, and he explored this relationship in two respects. The first was on behalf of Indians themselves. The British, Gandhi argued, had not "taken India"— Indians had "given it to them."[27] The introduction of foreign rule and its persistence had been made possible only through domestic consent. The surrender to foreign rule, as it were, occurred because of material desires. Indians welcomed the East India Company in the hope that they would acquire wealth. Their internal conflicts were motivated by a search for money and power, but such conflicts only served to give the Company more control. He compared Indians to addicts. The person supplying the drug may carry some responsibility, but ultimately it was the addict who was to blame for his condition.

Second, Gandhi claimed that the imperatives of modern civilization had led the British to colonize India. Their motivation was commerce. In seeing colonialism as a consequence of modern civilization, Gandhi presented the British in a sympathetic light. They were no longer uncomplicated oppressors, as much of Indian nationalism had suggested, but instead victims of modernity. In the preface to *Hind Swaraj*, Gandhi registered his surprise at the banning of the text. He saw *Hind Swaraj* less as an attack on the British government, for which a ban may have made sense, and more as a defense of ancient forms of social ordering. He regarded the Indian belief that "they should adopt modern civilization and modern methods of violence to drive out the English" as "a suicidal policy," and instead called on Indians to "revert to their own glorious civilization."[28] In the first chapter of the text, Gandhi defended figures like Dadabhai Naoroji and Gopal Krishna Gokhale. Both men were prominent nationalists who fought for Indian causes but had close links with the British. Gandhi argued that their proximity to the Raj should not reduce their historical stature. Here again, the underlying impulse was the same. The colonizers were not the enemy. Colonialism did not occur because of "any peculiar fault of the English people."[29] On the contrary, India's foreign rulers were so deeply seduced by modern civilization that they "deserve our sympathy."[30] Thus, Gandhi believed, the link between imperialism and the modern state showed that the rejection of the former must involve a rejection of the latter.[31]

For Gandhi, *Hind Swaraj* articulated a set of universal truths. Its arguments were not limited to the Indian situation. The crisis of Western institutions was, after all, a crisis being experienced in the West. As sources of inspiration, Gandhi listed a range of Western thinkers. The preface to *Hind Swaraj* mentioned Ralph Waldo Emerson, John Ruskin, Henry David Thoreau, and Leo Tolstoy as writers he had "endeavored humbly to follow."[32] He claimed that the book's message was accepted not only "by many Indians not touched by what is known as civilization" but also "by thousands of Europeans."[33] He saw his remarks as resting on the shoulders of Western theorists. His attack on Parliament, for example, had already been voiced by "great English thinkers."[34]

The study of civilization in chapter 6 of *Hind Swaraj* commenced with a reference to Edward Carpenter's *Civilization: Its Cause and Cure*.[35] Carpenter had perceived the pessimism surrounding civilization—the lurking feeling that it may be "some kind of disease that the various races of man have to pass through."[36] Civilization was, for him, a historical phase littered with troubling features. In our physical life, medicine had advanced alongside rising ill health and an increase in doctors. In society, individuals were involved in endless competition, classes were embattled in conflict, and the success of one person came at the cost of another. Our mental health was victim to a similar narrative. Carpenter was concerned not by the growth in asylums but by the "strange sense of mental unrest which marks our populations."[37] Individuals were overwhelmed by internal conflicts, a striking departure from the "naïve insouciance of the pagan and primitive world."[38] Each of these domains—the mind, the body, and society—was without harmony. For him, disease marked the absence of unity. In the premodern world, health had been understood positively. But in modern times it had been understood in purely negative terms. It was regarded as the absence of a condition rather than a form of positive anchoring. Carpenter saw private property as bearing ultimate responsibility for these changes. The institution had fundamentally altered the ordering of society. In *Civilization: Its Cause and Cure,* he imagined in poetic, nostalgic terms a different world, marked by leisure, natural beauty, and a sense of community—a world without the modern institutions of government. For Carpenter, the very need for government was, after all, "evidence in social life that man has lost his inner and central control and therefore must resort to an outward one."[39]

The idea of the state as an external figure animated much of Gandhi's thought. He saw it as a foreign body mediating social relationships, thereby likening it to another form of alien rule. For him, internal tensions should find their own resolution, and such resolution was indeed possible. The understanding of Hindu–Muslim conflict in *Hind Swaraj* recorded this belief:

> I do not suggest that the Hindus and Mahomedans will never fight. Two brothers living together often do so. We shall sometimes have our heads broken. Such a thing ought not to be necessary, but all men are not equi-minded. When people are in a rage, they do many foolish things. These we have to put up with. But, when we do quarrel, we certainly do not want to engage counsel and to resort to English or any other law courts. Two men fight; both have their heads broken, or one only. How shall a third party distribute justice amongst them? Those who might may expect to be injured.[40]

In *Hind Swaraj* Gandhi employed the external-internal lens in contexts ranging from foreign rule to local political institutions to modern professions. Lawyers, for instance, "advance quarrels, instead of repressing them."[41] They only cause and further social conflict, and in the process increase their own material wealth. Similarly, doctors prescribe medicines to remedy "negligence or indulgence," but such treatment only legitimizes the condition.[42] Such examples revealed the absence of freedom: "A continuance of a course of medicine must . . . result in loss of control over the mind."[43] The ultimate impact of modern devices was that they made humans live as if they were different beings.

In this narrative, machines bore responsibility. One consequence of the arrival of machines had been the creation of social divisions. Railways, for example, had prevented a shared experience under the British: "It was after the advent of railways that we began to believe in distinctions."[44] The emphasis here was on the *unnatural* way of being that modernity involved. Our body parts were meant to limit our physical movements, and the railways were an attempt to reject these natural limitations. The belief in external solutions had enabled British rule, and a belief in Western political institutions would be a mistake of the same kind. For Gandhi, the only path to genuine self-rule was to resist outside authority. The alternative world in *Hind Swaraj* recalled a life with villages, hand looms, manual labor, agricultural practices, few professionals, and, above all, no machinery—"the chief symbol of modern civilization."[45] Such forms of living did have shortcomings, of course, but such shortcomings were not internal to the system.

Gandhi's interest in India's premodern institutions had been apparent from his earliest writings. In South Africa, his efforts drew on Henry Maine to document India's long history with institutions of governance.[46] Indians had grasped the idea of representation since the ancient era.[47] The place of the panchayat was similarly affirmed. It was a body that "guides all the actions of an Indian."[48] Gandhi viewed Maine's descriptions as far from fanciful. In 1905 he considered a set of administrative reforms that the economist R. C. Dutt was bringing to the State of Baroda. Dutt's proposals for decentralization, Gandhi noted, had "endowed the villages with control of their own management . . . given certain powers to the headman, revived the village school-master," and had succeeded in enabling "real elective representation."[49] He felt that if South African readers studied the Baroda experiment, they might come to acknowledge the seriousness of such possibilities.[50]

This admiration for the past came alongside fierce criticism of the present. The turn away from agriculture, the rejection of rural life, the devotion to modern science, and so on, were all causes for worry. Gandhi feared that Indians, in their "impatience of English rule," would simply "replace one evil by another and worse."[51] He dreaded the day when India would go through "the process of civilization," imitating the "gun factories and hateful industrialism" that had "reduced the people of Europe to a state of slavery and all but stifled among them the best instincts."[52] This critique of modern civilization found its most powerful articulation in *Hind Swaraj,* but in the years following the publication of this tract, Gandhi often returned to its themes with a more focused reappraisal of village life.[53] The people of Europe, he remarked, had no political power. They had no real freedom, no *swaraj.*[54] In 1945 he wrote to Nehru affirming the model of governance outlined in *Hind Swaraj:*

> I believe that if India, and through India the world, is to achieve real freedom, then sooner or later we shall have to go and live in the villages—in huts, not in palaces. Millions of people can never live in cities and palaces in comfort and peace. Nor can they do so by killing one another, that is, by resorting to violence and untruth. I have not the slightest doubt that, but for the pair, truth and non-violence, mankind will be doomed. We can have the vision of that truth and non-violence only in the simplicity of the villages. That simplicity resides in the spinning-wheel and what is implied by the spinning-wheel. It does not frighten me at all that the world seems to be going in the opposite direction.[55]

In his account of bottom-up constitutionalism, each village was to have autonomy in its own affairs. He sketched the following, somewhat fantastic, image: "In this structure composed of innumerable villages, there will be ever-widening, never-ascending circles. Life will not be a pyramid with the apex sustained by the bottom. But it will be an oceanic circle whose center will be the individual always ready to perish for the village, the latter ready to perish for the circle of villages, till at last the whole becomes one life composed of individuals, never aggressive in their arrogance but ever humble, sharing the majesty of the oceanic circle of which they are integral units."[56] This harmonious universe would rely on consent rather than coercion. Panchayats, as he conceived of them, would not impose their authority on others. Instead, the undertaking of public functions and "constructive work" would organically invite respect.[57] This form of democracy lacked the violence associated with centralized, representative alternatives.[58] For him, such alternatives were impossible to maintain without the use of force.

During these years Mohandas Gandhi was not alone in his attack on the modern state. As scholars have recently reminded us, a major figure in the tradition of pluralism—a conception of politics where power is scattered across groups and associations—was the economist and sociologist Radhakamal Mukerjee.[59] In a 1916 study of the Indian rural economy, Mukerjee critiqued Western industrialism for its fixation on the division of labor, its difference toward community bonds, and its rejection of transcendentalism. For him, the Indian village community offered a different, self-contained image:

> The village is still almost self-sufficing, and is in itself an economic unit. The village agriculturist grows all the food necessary for the inhabitants of the village. The smith makes the ploughshares for the cultivator, and the few iron utensils required for the household. He supplies these to the people, but does not get money in return. He is recompensed by mutual services from his fellow villagers. The potter supplies him with pots, the weaver with cloth, and the oilman with oil. From the cultivator each of these artisans receives his traditional share of grain. Thus almost all the economic transactions are carried on without the use of money . . . village communities are the most complete and the most contented in the world. Within their self-sufficing confines trade is no vulgar source of profit for which men scheme and thrive, but a calling, often a holy calling, handed down from father to son through generations, each with its own unchanging ideals, its zealously-guarded crafts.[60]

In subsequent years Mukerjee developed these themes into an ambitious study of organization beyond the modern centralized state.[61] This new work, titled *Democracies of the East,* was motivated by lessons from the West. The First World War had revealed the moral shortcomings of the modern statist vision. Economic conflicts could no longer be explained and resolved by simplistic sovereignty-based accounts. The importance of regional autonomy, administrative decentralization, and group life was increasingly being acknowledged. But Mukerjee was less interested in the reshaping of Western political thought. His emphasis was instead on the implications of these developments for India's future. He feared the cementing of Western laws—the indifference toward local conditions—on Indian soil. Western institutions, for instance, had no solution to the problem of ethnicity. For Mukerjee, the "solution for the poly-ethnic masses of Eastern Asia, like that of Eastern Europe after the war" lay in decentralization, which was "the old Eastern tradition."[62] This tradition spoke of separate regions, associations, and cities, each functioning with autonomy and some degree of interdependence. Small self-governing communities were easier to imagine as laboratories of freedom than the totalizing centralized state. Political pluralism offered a way of life that went beyond "that unfortunate dualism between the state and the individual which has been the overgrowth of the mechanical state of the nineteenth century."[63] It was the need of the hour: "Humanity all over the world is imprisoned in the bleak institutional orderliness of a mechanical and exploitative type of state. And nothing is more needed today than a new principle of social constitution which will once again orient man and his allegiances in natural and elastic groups for a freer expression of his gifts and instincts."[64]

For Mukerjee, the defining characteristics of modern governance—centralization, representation, delegation—had "made politics mechanical and barren."[65] What India required was another vision of participation. Cautionary tales could be found in the experiences of Japan and China. Both nations had long traditions of social organization and stability, and both had been harmed by the brutal imposition of foreign ideals. The recovery of communal life could prevent similar errors at home, and such recovery could thereby rewrite the rules of comparative politics. Mukerjee felt that such an experiment would be not only "more adaptive and life-giving than the imitation of Western political methods" but also "a distinctively Eastern contribution to the political history of man."[66] For him, the decision to choose monism or pluralism should be context-specific. It should turn on matters such as social differentiation, religious doctrine, and historical burdens.

Democracies of the East considered the communal character of Indian and Chinese life to illustrate their departure from Western society. Here Mukerjee stressed the example of property in China. Property had historically been freehold and divided among male family members. There were no permanent estates as seen in the West, and thus no landed aristocracy. As a result, the crucial Western distinction between the nobility and common people, which had major implications for the development of feudalism, was absent in China. The arrival of feudalism in Western

Europe encouraged the turn to individual leaders rather than community groups—power became structured around particular figures, such as a bishop or a major landowner. In China, however, empires were composed not of feudal arrangements but instead of communities and associations. These networks of groups coexisted peacefully, in sharp contrast to the aggression and violence in Western societies.

The state, as imagined by Mukerjee, would not supplant social groups but respect their spheres of operation. It would exist as "a supplementary organ . . . to secure for the groups the general conditions under which each can pursue its own interests and functions without coming into mutual conflict."[67] Whereas groups in the West were organized in professional or functional terms, in the East they were also vested with administrative powers. The hallmark of such an organizational reality was the breakdown of centralized sovereignty. This kind of federalism was more ambitious than, and conceptually distinct from, the single division of land into different territorial units. It involved a novel notion of authority, where power was overlapping and coordination arose organically.[68] Where sovereignty was the goal of Western politics, "the search for social unity" was the ambition of the East.[69] In polities like India and China, the state was not an absolutist entity; it worked alongside local government. Individuals were bound by an inner moral code, and village communities self-regulated their actions.[70] As an example Mukerjee cited an ancient Indian code for merchants, the *Vaisya Dharma*. The code regulated the group, limited their earnings, and prescribed conformity to certain principles of fairness.[71] The principle of communalism was an alternative to the principle of representation—the dominant mode of political organization in the West. In pluralist arrangements, the large degree of autonomy enjoyed by local groups came alongside an imprecise notion of citizenship. Indeed, the animating theme here was "sociality rather than . . . political citizenship."[72]

Like Mohandas Gandhi, Radhakamal Mukerjee believed that a recovery of pluralism was necessary for the achievement of freedom. The parliamentary system had shown itself to be incapable of resolving ongoing challenges, whether these related to the problem of ethnic diversity or economic conflict. For both thinkers there was no small irony in the fact that the imitation of such institutions was occurring in India, a land whose history was rich in other possibilities. A communal form of organization, built layer upon layer, was far more democratic than a parliamentary system whose leaders were "out of touch, necessarily, with their enormous constituencies, and too much dependent on agents, reporters, and even on the press."[73] In fact, even though Russia's revolutionary experiment was different from the pluralistic hope, Mukerjee praised it for challenging the status quo.[74]

Mukerjee's claims rested on the premise that the Indian village experiment *could* be revived. While he admitted that British legal institutions had produced radical, perverse consequences in India, he suggested that several parts of India were still organized around village communities. Indeed, a remarkable feature of the village had been its resilience over centuries. To underscore this, Mukerjee turned to the text *Local Government in Ancient India,* authored by his brother and leading historian Radhakumud Mookerji.[75] A defining feature of India's ancient civilization, Mookerji had argued, was the separation of the state and society. Each operated as a distinct entity, and noninterference was the animating theme of state policy. Such an orientation was at odds with Western ideals, where state power was sovereign and where decentralized units, insofar as they existed, were creations of the state. The autonomous character of Indian society had enabled it to withstand political transformations and remain unaffected during the sharp vicissitudes of politics. Regimes like the Mauryan Empire had been successful because they had never aspired to a single centralized governing authority. Their success lay in a capacity for federalism.[76] In Mookerji's account, Muslim rulers had often been hostile to Hindu cultural and intellectual life. Yet the latter had nonetheless survived because it had rested on "a system of organization which had an independent existence and life of its own and was impenetrable to the foreign political powers who were unable to touch it for good or evil."[77]

Apart from its historical contribution, *Local Government in Ancient India* aimed to make a practical intervention in an ongoing contest between two schools of political reform. One school sought "to introduce self-government 'from above'; the other aimed to achieve this 'from below.'"[78] Mookerji hoped that a study of ancient institutions could show the participatory and functional value of the latter approach. It could confirm the capacity for local self-government to facilitate collective life and secure the stability of society. One of Mookerji's chief arguments was that ancient Indian local self-government was not a primitive tribal form of association but instead involved an astounding degree of sophistication— with considerable specialization of functions and occupations, and well-organized industrial and commercial bodies as well as administrative

THE LOCATION OF POWER

organizations. To repeat but one of Mookerji's many examples of rural administration in ancient India, temple inscriptions dating back to the tenth century offered elaborate details of different governance committees, their respective roles, their composition and selection, and so forth.[79]

By relying on *Local Government in Ancient India*, Radhakamal Mukerjee was suggesting that Indian village communities were capable of meeting modern challenges. This argument pervaded *Democracies of the East*. One of the noteworthy claims in the text pertained to the creation and development of legal rules. The law operated differently in pluralistic states, but such states were not lawless—their public law emerged, not from private legal norms or conflicts with state action, but instead from local traditions and practices that were manifest in customary behavior. In monistic states, the law was imposed on the people. A conqueror used it to shape the conquered people in specific ways.[80] The sovereign authority was the source of all law, and the law was an expression of a single will. In pluralistic states, in contrast, the process was inductive—the law arose from an expression of tradition and custom. To illustrate this, Mukerjee presented a study of the nature and evolution of Hindu law, from the norms of marriage and property to the principles of administration and governance.[81]

The resilience of the Indian village and its remoteness from politics had been acknowledged in colonial works. An 1812 report of a committee of the British House of Commons had considered the structure and composition of the Indian village. In the description offered, village members ranged from a *curnum,* an accountant in charge of matters relating to cultivation, to a cowkeeper, who took care of cattle. This organizational framework, the report noted, had survived the passage of time. Villages had suffered disasters, "war, famine, and disease," but they had nonetheless managed to maintain their character and makeup.[82] Political transitions left little impression on village life. A regime may come and go but "the *potail* is still the head inhabitant, and still acts as the petty judge and magistrate, and collector or renter of the village."[83] Only a few years prior to this report, Charles Metcalfe's minutes on revenue collection had warned against revenue settlements with individual cultivators. Such a system, in contrast to one that involved settlements with village communities, would disturb the structure of village constitutions. Village communities, he had noted, "seem to last where nothing else lasts."[84] They were untouched by political revolutions, undisturbed by external developments, and secure in their group identity. Metcalfe felt that it would be a mistake to encourage individual interests in such an established form of community life. In subsequent decades, the major contribution to this subject was, of course, offered by Henry Maine, whose work would be a source of ideas and inspiration for Indian pluralists.[85]

Radhakamal Mukerjee acknowledged these references but felt that even if Indian village communities had sometimes been recognized, such communities had been portrayed as primitive and backward. Even a scholar as sensitive as Maine, Mukerjee lamented, had understood the shift from status to contract to be a universal one, thereby influencing others to see the transition from communal to individual forms of life as a sign of progress.[86] Mukerjee felt that Maine's book *Ancient Law* had remained hostage to Western paradigms and was simply "a presentment of Roman legal history."[87] Mukerjee sought to provide a new narrative. The Indian village needed to be given a new past and a new future.

Mukerjee's *Democracies of the East* is best seen as a work of historical sociology. It examined themes ranging from judicial administration to property rights to economic policy. India's many regions and races were considered and distinguished. Time periods were identified and evaluated. From the sources of revenue to the intricacies of governance to the varieties of hierarchy, the Indian village was carefully deconstructed—and painted as vibrant, peaceful, and stable. Alternatively, the monistic state was presented as an idea whose time had passed. As recent work has shown, Mohandas Gandhi and Radhakamal Mukerjee were part of a global tradition of political pluralism whose members included the distinguished British intellectuals and activists Harold Laski and G. D. H. Cole.[88] The closing pages of *Democracies of the East* reveal the reach of this tradition. Mukerjee relied on, for example, a contribution by the American philosopher George H. Sabine.[89] Sabine had argued that the historical conditions under which state power was conceived were no longer present. Initially power had been divided among the Church, the Holy Roman Empire, and feudal lords. The realm of the political had acquired independence only gradually. The advent of royal absolutism, the unrestrained power of the king, had opened the door to the idea of a sovereign state, and the relationship between the sovereign and the subject became the framework for modern politics. Yet the eventual abstraction of sovereign authority and the theory of parliamentary sovereignty were unable to match the fluid reality of power. A wide variety of bodies such as courts, executive officers, and governmental agencies created law and operated with degrees of independence, thereby making it hard to view the state as a single, unitary law-creating body. For Sabine, the idea of sovereignty had become only formal. It bore little resemblance to the actual functioning of modern politics.

Mukerjee's other references included Laski. He relied on Laski's 1917 *Harvard Law Review* note on Léon Duguit, which had commenced with the grand declaration: "We seem on the threshold of a new epoch in the history of the state."[90] For Laski, the emphasis on state coercion had been a philosophical and sociological error. It had presented a model of power that failed to pay due attention to the reality of consent. A parliamentary statute that prohibited Englishmen from being Roman Catholics would, for example, fail to have any effect.[91] Mukerjee also cited Duguit directly, along with additional thinkers like Roscoe Pound, showing both the range of his sources and the burgeoning support for his agenda. He felt that communalism had special potential in the East, for it represented "a principle of social grouping in which the including group stands not for partial, hypostasized interests of the segmented man, but for the concrete interest and representing the whole personality."[92] The West, in contrast, faced a greater challenge with competing group identities and the absence of local structures. For India to embark on this transformative political project, it merely needed to return to its own history. It needed to see that the "future belongs not to imperialism but to federalism," and to recognize that "the secret of the federal spirit is the group principle."[93]

Both Mohandas Gandhi and Radhakamal Mukerjee did more than challenge the inevitability of the transition from empire to statehood. Each put forth plans for realizing the pluralist vision. For them, the village would be the center of political activity and the singular location for direct elections. Mukerjee envisioned a harmonious model of pluralism, with quasi-autonomous bodies functioning together. He imagined a "peasant democracy rising layer upon layer from the old and essential local and functional groupings" that would gradually federate into a national assembly.[94] The schema would recover a "democratic process that begins, not in parliament, but right from the bottom in myriads of local bodies and assemblies."[95] Gandhi, somewhat differently, viewed the village as a secluded space and a classroom for perfecting individual self-discipline. His conception of the village as a freestanding, isolated entity entailed an anti-statist edge. It meant that his version of pluralism was effectively a form of anarchism. The violent commanding state was replaced by non-hierarchical internal forms of authority.[96]

On the other hand, one could see a cooperative stance in Mukerjee's account. This was visible in the contrast he drew between the pluralist and traditional sovereignty-based perspectives: "In the monistic state-type a constitution expressing the undivided will of the community is created, and then a magistracy is established in connection with the constitution, which represents the original, unlimited, and central ratifying will or fiat imposed upon all persons, associations, and things within its jurisdiction. In the pluralistic state-type the constitution differentiates the particular spheres of the diverse organs of the body-politic from one another as well as from the State, and creates a divided, multicellular political control, maintained by custom or voluntary co-operation."[97] Mukerjee viewed prior attempts at decentralization, such as the Local Self-Government Act of 1885, as too modest. They did not involve any restructuring of power. The unions and *taluka* boards were still part of the overall centralized bureaucratic apparatus. Such attempts did not recover the community. For them, "the community ceases to exist in the eyes of the law."[98] Yet Mukerjee did believe that change could occur through radical legislation. To inaugurate a "new track of modern constitutionalism,"[99] he proposed that a "detailed code should be drawn up to show the limits of jurisdiction and the nature of the cases for which no appeal will lie from the decision of the *panchayat.*"[100]

The daily experience of politics would be very different under such conditions. In *Hind Swaraj,* Gandhi had observed that modern politics had collapsed into a struggle for power. Mukerjee lamented the same reality, seeing the centrality of political parties as a major failure of Western parliamentarianism. The majority in a legislative chamber was no longer representative of the majority of the population. It was instead an unworkable collection of different minorities. All of its attention was devoted to acquiring positions of office rather than to addressing matters of principle. A turn to localism could prevent this kind of capture. In the schema that Mukerjee sketched, small units would not have "limited and qualified powers delegated to them from above"—"a half-measure" that he referred to as "discouraging and demoralizing."[101] Further, the units would recognize various kinds of diversity, including regional and functional diversity, and thereby disable conflict. He allowed "ample room for experiments as regards the electorate and franchise basis . . . to counteract such disadvantages as the narrow and sectional outlook of functionally organized units or the crude majority rule and lack of local attachment of the population franchise."[102] The institutions of Indian civilization—its "noblest products" like temples and academies and town halls—had been built by local participation.[103] These institutions had enabled the evolution of Indian law through the exercise of careful judgment. Mukerjee's plan would take inspiration from this past and shift the focus from "checks and balances" to "the organization of social and personal values and primary satisfactions."[104] The power of bottom-up constitutionalism was that its rules were not imposed rigidly and universally. The scheme would liberate local units from the control of other authorities.

In 1946 Shriman Narayan Agarwal, an economist and self-proclaimed Gandhian, put forth a constitutional proposal for translating the pluralist image into concrete terms.[105] In a previous text, Agarwal had noted Gandhi's concerns with modern civilization.[106] The context for that work had been the growing support for national planning, and Agarwal warned against "imposing a rigid and elaborate plan on a nation."[107] India's ancient economy, with its cottage industries, nonviolent path to economic equality, and respect for manual labor held greater promise for the development of a fulfilling life. In a comment on the text, Gandhi spoke of "70,000 villages of India dominating the center with its few towns required in the interest of the villages."[108]

In his *Gandhian Constitution for Free India,* Agarwal turned his attention to constitutions. He viewed such texts as "always in the nature of organic growth" and felt that it was "most unscientific to foist on a country a system of administration foreign to its own genius."[109] Indians would "betray gross ignorance of sociological sense" in impersonating Western frameworks.[110] Agarwal regarded Western democracy as being in a state of profound disarray. It had experienced widespread malfunction and collapse and had often paved the way for totalitarian regimes—with its tendency to concentrate power, succumb to the influence of capital, and ignore the common person. Small institutional changes could not resolve these failures. Ongoing experiments, like Soviet Russia's effort at a planned economy, had "reduced individuals to, more or less, non-entities and automatons."[111]

The solution to the extant crisis was to be found in a new form of association structured around the village. Village communities would enable citizen participation, and cooperative agriculture and industry would prevent economic exploitation. For Agarwal, the village was not an isolated entity. In terms more reminiscent of Mukerjee's thought than Gandhi's, Agarwal spoke of a coordinated framework with "rural republics gradually [passing] into larger political organizations on a federal basis rising layer upon layer from the lower rural stratifications on the broad basis of popular self-government."[112] Village panchayats would be chosen via direct elections, and they would enjoy wide powers of security, industry, and public welfare. They would also have the power to administer justice. The British judicial system had, Agarwal lamented, "worked havoc in the socio-economic life of the country."[113] The system had led to exploitative lawyers and unaffordable procedures, and its working resulted in a thorough neglect of the truth. A judicial order operated by panchayats would "not only be simple, prompt and cheap but also 'just' because the details of civil and criminal cases will be, more or less, open secrets in the village and there shall be hardly any scope for fraud and legal juggleries."[114] Higher bodies (*talukas* and district panchayats) would be indirectly elected and possess advisory rather than coercive powers.

In this proposal of bottom-up constitutionalism, where "the whole system will be turned upside down," the state was viewed as both problematic and unnecessary.[115] It was problematic for its violent, indifferent, and corrupt ways of functioning. It was unnecessary because Indian society, in and of itself, had the internal resources for solving the problems that the state was meant to fix. Indian society had been self-sustaining in the past, and it had the potential to be self-sustaining in the future. Rather than hoping to collectivize agency, the political pluralists sought to internalize it. Instead of a state, they offered a landscape of group networks that could make possible the practice of individual self-discipline. As we shall see, this vision was decisively rejected—and, in holding a very different view of the Indian state, the critics of this vision held a very different view of Indian society.

Centralization and Modernization

In the years when pluralist thought flourished, a parallel discourse emerged around centralization and modernization.[116] An early contribution to this conversation was M. Visvesvaraya's 1920 text *Reconstructing India*.[117] Visvesvaraya was a prominent engineer who had served as the Dewan of Mysore. Seeing the end of alien rule as imminent, he turned to the task of Indian nation-building. For him, such an inquiry was critical. India had appalling standards of living. The condition of primary and higher education, the inattention to local industry, the premodern modes of agricultural production, and so on had led to dire economic circumstances. India's performance was miserable across indicators ranging from health and literacy to infrastructure capacity and industrial production.[118] Visvesvaraya held the colonial state responsible for this situation. He also felt that Indians had only made matters worse by subscribing to ancient customs. But, for all its severity, Visvesvaraya did not see this situation as permanent. He believed that change was possible, though it would require Indians to embrace modern ways of thinking. He called this challenge "The Indian Problem."[119]

Visvesvaraya's text was among the first serious manifestos on Indian development. During the 1930s and 1940s a broad-ranging dialogue flourished on India's transition to an industrial society. The relationship between science and technology, the connection between pure and applied science, the implications of colonialism for scientific advancement, and the institutional environment needed for industrial research were all integral elements in this conversation.[120] Participants in this remarkable conversation included the notable physicist Meghnad Saha, whose interest in socioeconomic concerns and planning was sparked by the problem of flood management, and forums that encompassed the magazine *Science and Culture,* which provided a space for reflection on the role of science and planning in social change.[121] Among political leaders, a critical role was played by Subhas Chandra Bose. As president of the Indian National Congress in 1938, he expressed a commitment to industrialization and put together a National Planning Committee.[122]

Jawaharlal Nehru's embrace of the modernization project would have the most significant long-term consequences.[123] In Nehru's view, only some form of state control could end poverty, reduce unemployment, and improve material conditions. He saw socialism as "the inevitable step to social and economic change."[124] *Khadi* and village industries—the hallmarks of Gandhi's unconventional vision—were only "temporary expedients of a transition stage rather than as solutions of our vital problems." Only through "the rapid industrialization of the country" could "the standards of the people rise substantially and poverty be combated."[125] Nehru's writings on his 1927 trip to the Soviet Union capture his curiosity regarding the transition from an agricultural to an industrial society. He was sensitive to the political structure of the Soviet Union—from its focus on economic units in representation to its curbing of political dissent to the centrality of the Communist Party—but felt that the Soviet experience could not be ignored.[126]

By the 1940s the work of the National Planning Committee and its subcommittees had cast considerable light on the nature of planning. Nehru's role in this regard was significant.[127] His note to the Committee in 1939 is worth highlighting. In the note he claimed that "economic regeneration" required industrialization.[128] Drawing on the Congress party's Karachi Resolution, which had declared that the state should have control over major services, Nehru argued that all large-scale enterprises must be regulated, if not owned, by the state.[129] Nehru's note appealed to a particular vision of democracy—one that entailed equality and a certain standard of living. This vision was linked to the planning agenda: "The ideal of the Congress is the establishment of a free and democratic state in India. Such a full democratic state involves an egalitarian society, in which equal opportunities are provided for every member for self-expression and self-fulfillment, and an adequate minimum of a civilized standard of life is assured to each member so as to make the attainment of this equal opportunity a reality. This should be the background or foundation of our plan."[130] Both here and in other writings, Nehru argued that industrialization was essential to the realization of freedom.[131] Initially he indicated that industrialization could occur alongside a commitment to the village economy. He underplayed, even denied, any conflict between Gandhi's vision and his own. The problems of India were so severe that they could not be solved by any one approach. Village industries could, for example, play a part in reducing unemployment even if they could not improve production.[132]

In time, however, Nehru confronted the Gandhian alternative more seriously. In a letter to Gandhi in 1945, he rejected the supposed link between nonviolence and village life. For Nehru, villages were "backward intellectually and culturally and no progress can be made from a backward environment."[133] Such an environment led to the birth of narrow-minded individuals, and such persons were "much more likely to be untruthful and violent."[134] Nehru reiterated the importance of material needs—food, clothing, shelter—and the belief that only heavy industrialization could enable their provision.[135] India's "immediate problem" was "appalling poverty and unemployment."[136] The solution was "a rapid growth of industry, scientific agriculture and the social services, all coordinated together, under more or less state control, and directed towards the betterment of the people as a whole."[137] In making his case, Nehru highlighted the importance of scientific advancement. For a country to retain independence in the modern world, it would have to control the tools of science.[138] The ideas in *Hind Swaraj,* Nehru proclaimed, were "completely unreal."[139]

As we have observed, Gandhi viewed modernization as foreign rule by another name. Nehru resisted this characterization of the modernization agenda and framed it in more ambitious terms. He desired, as he put it in *An Autobiography,* "a new state and not just a new administration."[140] It was not large-scale industrialization that had brought about violence or injustice but instead private capital. The problem was capitalism rather than industrialization: "It is essentially private ownership and the acquisitive form of society that encourage a competitive violence. Under a socialist society this evil should go, at the same time leaving us the good which the big machine has brought."[141] Western democratic institutions had indeed failed. But Nehru argued that it was wrong to read this failure as a failure of representative democracy. Instead, he understood the problem to be "the unholy alliance of capitalism, property, militarism and an overgrown bureaucracy, and assisted by a capitalist press."[142] Economic power had become all too easy to translate into political power. The solution lay not in rejecting Western democracy but in freeing democracy from such "malign influences."[143]

The turn to centralization entailed a rejection of the imperial premise in two respects. It denied the proposition that modernization was a prerequisite for self-government, and it dismissed the idea that the colonial state had improved material conditions. The colonial government had been an authoritarian police state. In his autobiography, Nehru charged it with creating fear among the people and being indifferent to education, health, working conditions, and so forth.[144] He would reiterate this charge in later years, attacking the Raj's inattention to social development. Nehru felt that a democratic government would be committed to welfare because it would rest on consent.[145] The people would be attentive to their own well-being.[146]

A centralized state made possible a planned economy—and it held the promise of the equal advancement of India's different units.[147] In a country whose regions lacked the capacity and resources for industrial activity, experimentation, and initiative, no other option seemed viable. As the 1940s progressed, the case for modernization continued to gain momentum. In the early years of this decade, Visvesvaraya delivered another book— *Prosperity through Industry*—that captured the sentiment at the time.[148]

He reiterated his previously expressed horror at India's poverty and declared that the "promotion of industries is the one development which, if vigorously pursued and persisted in, promises to give rich results in the way of improved living conditions to the average citizen in an appreciably short time."[149] He lamented the "many defects in outlook and behavior" left behind by India's traditions and the "host of factors in our social system which militate against progress."[150] As before, he placed particular emphasis on mass education. Without a literate and trained population, India would fail to industrialize. *Prosperity through Industry* explored how industries might be established and run, on matters ranging from initial market research to the proper maintenance of accounts, and how they should be classified; and considered central and regional organizations for their promotion. Visvesvaraya called on leaders to rouse the people and enlist them in the industrialization mission. He hoped to create a cooperative spirit that could carry India into a new age of modern civilization.

Texts such as *Prosperity through Industry* were noteworthy, but the leading document of the decade was the *Memorandum Outlining a Plan of Economic Development for India,* authored by a coterie of influential industry leaders in 1944.[151] The Bombay Plan, as it was called, sought to double per capita income in a period of fifteen years. It called for massive increases in output from industry, services, and agriculture, with industrial output carrying the bulk of this transformation. The plan highlighted the significance of social services, especially education; it offered proposals for the sourcing of capital; and it made India, in the words of an early commentator, "planning-conscious."[152] Above all, it placed centralized state control at the heart of the country's economic future. In the week before India became a republic, a resolution by the Congress party's Working Committee affirmed this agenda with great force and proposed the creation of a planning commission for the independent nation.[153]

It is crucial to see that modernization was not driven by merely a desire for material progress. Underlying the search for equal standards of living, as revealed in Nehru's abovementioned reply to Gandhi, was the search for a different kind of citizenship. By displacing the local, a centralized state promised a new form of political association. It would allow natives to transcend their narrow fields of vision and coexist under a single authority, thereby placing them in a different relationship with one another. For Nehru, local government simply could not enable a politics that was fit for the modern world:

Our local bodies are not, as a rule, shining examples of success and efficiency, though they might, even so, compare with some municipalities in advanced democratic countries. They are not usually corrupt; they are just inefficient, and their weak point is nepotism, and their perspectives are all wrong. All this is natural enough; for democracy, to be successful, must have a background of informed public opinion and a sense of responsibility. Instead, we have an all-pervading atmosphere of authoritarianism, and the accompaniments of democracy are lacking. There is no mass educational system, no effort to build up public opinion based on knowledge. Inevitably public attention turns on personal or communal or other petty issues.[154]

Nehru had long spoken similarly of India's other hidden pocket—the princely kingdoms. He saw these units as independent fiefdoms. They were not only apathetic toward the struggle against self-rule, but moreover represented a mode of collective life that was a thing of the past. "The states," he wrote, "are dark and wholesome corners in India where strange things happen, and people disappear leaving no trace behind."[155] They were identifiable by "their backwardness and their semi-feudal conditions" and were "personal autocracies, devoid even of competence or benevolence."[156]

That a centralized state could inaugurate a new form of citizenship is a familiar notion. The contractarian suggestion was, after all, that the state not only provides certain conditions that make freedom possible, but in fact constitutes individuals. By providing for a new form of political membership, it re-creates them, and thereby re-creates the relationship they share with one another. The very existence of this new relationship is itself a form of freedom. This conception of the state found expression not merely in Nehru's writings, but also in B. R. Ambedkar's. Like Nehru, Ambedkar registered the widespread discontent with parliamentary democracy.[157] Even among countries that were opposed to authoritarian rule, the support for democracy was fast declining. For Ambedkar, this situation was an outcome of the freedom of contract. Political democracy had been encouraged without social and economic democracy. In other words, liberty had been promoted but equality had been ignored.[158] Gandhi's response to this reality, Ambedkar alleged, was primitive and flawed.[159] In the same vein as Nehru, Ambedkar asserted that the problem was not modern civilization, but the importance granted to institutions like private property and the power wielded by private capital. "If machinery and civilization have not benefitted everybody," Ambedkar contended, "the remedy is not to condemn machinery and civilization but to alter the organization of society so that the benefits will not be usurped by the few but will accrue to all."[160] He went so far as to suggest that the Gandhian solution was incompatible with democracy:

> Gandhism may be well suited to a society which does not accept democracy as its ideal. A society which does not believe in democracy may be indifferent to machinery and the civilization based upon it. But a democratic society cannot. The former may well content itself with [a] life of leisure and culture for the few and a life of toil and drudgery for the many. But a democratic society must assure a life of leisure and culture to each one of its citizens. If the above analysis is correct then the slogan of a democratic society must be machinery and machinery, and civilization and more civilization. Under Gandhism, the common man must keep on toiling ceaselessly for a pittance and remain a brute. In short, Gandhism with its call back to nature, means back to nakedness, back to squalor, back to poverty and back to ignorance for the vast mass of the people.[161]

As far as Gandhi was concerned, centralized industries were a problem even if they were owned by the state. In fact, he observed that "the obligation to increase wants will not only not decrease but may be strengthened where such industries are owned by the state."[162] As we have seen, Gandhi felt that ending Western rule without ending Western institutions would simply replace one form of domination by another. Ambedkar turned this argument on its head. The removal of Western rule alongside the preservation of Indian society, he suggested, meant retaining a social structure that legitimized domination.[163] Earlier, as a member of the Bombay legislature, Ambedkar had identified the village system as the sole reason for the absence of Indian nationalism. The village, for him, "made all people saturated with local particularism, with local patriotism. It left no room for larger civic spirit."[164]

Centralization promised the creation of this civic spirit. The idea that federalism was a conservative force in politics had emerged in the aftermath of the Government of India Act of 1935. The statute recognized the princely states and envisaged a federation between them and the rest of

India. Indians complained bitterly about this support for nondemocratic rule and saw the pact as an impediment to achieving independence.[165] Importantly, the experience with provincial autonomy had allowed Nehru to draw a relationship between citizenship and welfare: "The working of provincial autonomy, restricted as it was, had many dangers for us. It tended to emphasize, as it was no doubt meant to, provincialism and diverted our anti-imperialist struggle into narrower channels. Because of this, internal conflicts grew—communal, social, and organizational. The major problems of poverty, unemployment, the land, industry, clamoured for solution, and yet they could not be solved within the framework of the existing constitution and economic structure."[166]

Nehru and Ambedkar thus came to believe that radicalism was possible only with distance. What the pluralists saw as participation, they saw as localism. The lower one went in choosing the location of power, the more society would infiltrate the state. As a result, both Nehru and Ambedkar felt that proximity to the exercise of power did not necessarily further democracy. And they also believed that democracy, as an idea, meant more than just shared practices of participation—it meant carrying India's millions out of poverty. Nehru and Ambedkar spent much of their lives occupied with somewhat separate concerns. Nehru was more attentive to the promise of economic transformation; Ambedkar displayed greater interest in the afflictions of caste. But they shared an understanding of power that went beyond formal, legal conceptions and entailed a deeper sociology. To determine where to locate power, one would have to detect where societal constraints were minimal. One would have to invent a force that could dismantle the structures of influence that pervaded India's provincial villages and feudal havens. That force was the centralized state.

The Decision to Centralize

This new political sociology found expression in the sessions of the Constituent Assembly. In its early meetings, however, the Constituent Assembly conceived of regional units that would have considerable autonomy. The Aims and Objectives Resolution, for instance, acknowledged the independent character of regional entities.[167] This was only to be expected, for at that time the Assembly was operating under the terms of the Cabinet Mission Plan of 1946, which had proposed a formula to prevent the division of British India. Among other things, the scheme placed severe limitations on the power of the federal government and left matters such as the status of the princely states unaddressed. In coming to accept the conditions of the Plan, the Assembly acknowledged the functional attractions of federalism. In its inaugural session, for instance, one member drew on James Bryce's *The American Commonwealth* to stress the accommodative character of American federalism. He wished that "in some such scheme, skillfully adapted to our own requirements," "a satisfactory solution may be found" to meet competing demands.[168] It was hoped that a weak center might also tempt the princely states to accede to the Indian Union. Even though the Assembly never countenanced any form of government other than a republic, its initial meetings expressed the possibility of monarchical arrangements in these states. Jawaharlal Nehru, in relying on the distinction between sovereignty and government, felt it was "quite possible that the people may like to have their *rajas*."[169] He found no "incongruity or impossibility about a certain definite form of administration in the states, provided there is complete freedom and responsible government there, and the people really are in-charge."[170] Other members were similarly willing to accept monarchy as long as it was rooted in popular consent.[171]

At this initial stage, some participants were more open in their opposition to regional autonomy. Even though they accepted the framework set out by the Cabinet Mission Plan in the hope that such acceptance would please the Muslim League and prevent the division of territory, they nonetheless expressed concern with local autonomy.[172] Such autonomy was not, in one member's words, in India's "best interests."[173] During these early days, B. R. Ambedkar candidly revealed a sense of disappointment at the absence of a strong center. He felt that an independent India required a central government that was even stronger than that envisioned in the Government of India Act of 1935.[174] It is clear that, for Ambedkar and others, support for regionalism at this time was directly linked to limitations imposed by the Cabinet Mission Plan. One member observed, "If a free vote is taken in this House or in the country, they will oppose residuary powers being vested in the provinces. But simply because we want to allay the fears of the Muslim League, imaginary or real, we respect their feeling and accepted that residuary powers shall vest in the provinces."[175]

It is no surprise, then, that all of this was to change with the Plan's failure and the subsequent partition of British India. The event liberated the Assembly from the framework under which it was operating. "I feel— thank God—that we got out of this bag at last," a member exclaimed.[176] We are, he said, "free to form a federation of our choice, a federation with a Centre as strong as we can make it."[177] "We are relieved," said another, "of the shackles which we had imposed on ourselves on account of the acceptance of the Cabinet Mission Plan."[178] Jawaharlal Nehru put the matter in simple terms as chairman of the Union Powers Committee:

> The severe limitation on the scope of central authority in the Cabinet Mission's plan was a compromise accepted by the Assembly much, we think, against its judgment of the administrative needs of the country, in order to accommodate the Muslim League. Now that partition is a settled fact, we are unanimously of the view that it would be injurious to the interests of the country to provide for a weak central authority which would be incapable of ensuring peace, of coordinating vital matters of common concern and of speaking effectively for the whole country in the international sphere.[179]

The Committee, Nehru proceeded to note, had chosen a federation with a strong center. Legislative power would be demarcated in three lists, following the 1935 Act, and residuary power would lie with the federal government. As these reflections confirm, the turn to centralization was not a reaction to the partition of British India. Although it was indeed feared that a weak center might encourage the Balkanization of India and "lead to the establishment of innumerable Pakistans," the more significant outcome of partition was that it freed the Assembly and allowed for a fresh debate on the federal question.[180] On the question of centralization, partition mattered not because it forced a new way of thinking but because it validated prior beliefs. The drama and horror that it involved confirmed previously held understandings of Indian society. Much the same might be said of other traumatic historical episodes. Take, for example, the Bengal famine of 1943. The famine was seen to reveal the sheer incapacity of provincial governments, not only administratively but also in terms of their outlook. Without outside support, regional units would simply unravel. As one member from Bengal observed, "If the center cannot interfere in cases where there is communal disturbance or there is famine, then we will have to consider what will happen to the people of those provinces."[181] It was felt that the tragedy would have been prevented had the federal government been able to intervene in local administration.[182]

With the constraints imposed by the Cabinet Mission Plan out of the way, the major themes that had shaped the discourse around centralization and modernization in the period prior to Indian independence acquired prominence in the Constituent Assembly. Members spoke of the need for industrial development.[183] They feared that India's units would be in constant battle unless they were moderated by strong central authority.[184] The reason for "the unity of public life," it was declared, had been the overarching administrative structure in place from the Charter Act of 1833 to the Government of India Act of 1935.[185] The real danger, one member observed, was not excessive central power. It was that "fissiparous tendencies may gather momentum and, as in the past they have led to the downfall of empires and kingdoms, may lead to the same fate."[186] Underlying these observations, and intricate contests over the legal division of power, were divergent ideas of the state and society. Ultimately the Constitution conferred extraordinary powers on the central government. These included powers that operated in ordinary times, such as the residuary power of legislation, as well as emergency powers targeted at specific crises. Notable among the latter was the authority to dismiss regional governments and control their administration in the case of a "failure of constitutional machinery."[187]

Strong emergency provisions were viewed as essential in a new democracy.[188] The power to terminate regional governments was regarded as "the responsibility of the federation."[189] It was a way to offer stability in administration. The clause allowing for the removal of regional governments had been modeled on Section 93 of the Government of India Act of 1935—a controversial provision that had in its time been severely attacked by Indian nationalists, who saw it as exemplifying "the distrust of the Indian politician."[190] But the Constituent Assembly rejected the analogy between the 1935 Act and the Constitution. The latter was based on representative government. As a result, any action taken under it would be an action having popular support. Moreover, the existing circumstances required such a provision:

> We are in grave and difficult times. The units are of different dimensions and responsible government has not been at work, in some of the units at any rate, for a very long time. Even suffrage is unknown in certain states, and we have introduced responsible government into the states not all of which are like the advanced units of what might be called the old British Indian provinces. Under those circumstances, in the interest of the sound and healthy functioning of the Constitution itself, it is necessary that there should be some check from the Centre so that people might realize their responsibility and work responsible government properly.[191]

The situation was worse in the princely states. These entities operated with varying but considerable internal autonomy. The 1935 Act had taken the emerging political recognition of the princely states forward, creating an all-India federation between the states and provinces. The Act, it was hoped, would weaken the Congress party and secure the colonial state.[192] This institutional framework never came into effect, but it did invite harsh criticism from Indian political leaders. Over the next decade or so, the princely states lost whatever political capital they may have once enjoyed. This is not the place to explore the reasons for their remarkably sudden decline and fall.[193] What is notable is the widespread consensus among India's political elite that the princely states lacked the ideological orientation and executive apparatus necessary for self-rule. They were described as units of "pure autocracy" that did not possess the political development required for immediate empowerment.[194] One member who visited several kingdoms termed their condition as "most miserable" and found that the people lacked any knowledge of electoral politics.[195] Their condition was seen to hold little promise.

Though centralization had its supporters, it also had its critics. Those who opposed a strong center feared that it "would result in the center becoming very oppressive and would result in the crushing, so to speak, of the liberties and privileges of the people living in component units."[196] The regional units, several members lamented, had been reduced to bodies with little power or identity.[197] The emergency provisions were analogized to those present in the Weimar Constitution of the Third Reich.[198] One member sharply asked whether the enemy was Pakistan, the Soviet Union, or the people of India itself.[199] Another compared the center's power to redraw regional boundaries to the Earl of Dalhousie's annexation policy.[200] This parallel was sketched out in a deeper way, with supporters of regional autonomy comparing arguments for centralization with those for imperialism. "The old British argument that they must intervene in petty provisional matters," one member noted, "is again being revived and adopted by the very opponents of that argument."[201] Another member put the allegation plainly: "In the place of foreign imperialism, we are now having an Indian imperialism."[202]

If democracy was to be valued, the argument ran, regional units ought to be empowered and allowed to learn from their mistakes.[203] It was through the act of self-government that self-government could be furthered.[204] The claim was that the concentration of control would result in bureaucratic rule rather than representative government.[205] It would take democracy away from regional units and separate the people from those in power.[206] In sum, critics of centralization alleged that the supporters of concentrated state power viewed universal suffrage "not only with grave suspicion but as a matter of grave danger."[207] This was also the feeling among advocates of village republics, who formed a distinct bloc. These members posited variants of political pluralism, lamenting the rejection of a constitutional framework "built from the bottom."[208] Ambedkar, one member mourned, knew considerable global history but little about the history of his own nation. To reject the village was to reject a rich democratic tradition.[209] It was claimed that the village had been a site of freedom and peace for centuries.[210]

In its rejection of these perspectives, the Constituent Assembly offered a dark image of the inner corners of the Indian nation. To turn a blind eye to the reality of the regional units was to be "guilty of a grave dereliction of duty."[211] Ongoing events demonstrated the incapacity of the regional units. Mired in their petty political battles and administratively handicapped, they were unable to handle the business of government. Consider the frustration expressed by Nehru in a note to Lord Wavell in October 1946, focusing on violence in East Bengal:

> There was the famine three years ago. There was the Calcutta killing two months ago, and there is now this mass slaughter, etc., in Noakhali and the surrounding districts which, if reports are correct, is far worse than the Calcutta killing. Law and special and other responsibilities have no meaning when they become completely incapable of controlling such a situation. But it is also a terrible responsibility for us and we too have to answer before the people of India. What is the good of our forming the Interim Government of India if all that we can do is to watch helplessly and do nothing else when thousands of people are being butchered and subjected to infinitely worse treatment?[212]

If one attends to such perspectives, the call for centralization is no surprise. In his defense of emergency powers, Ambedkar posited that "only the center . . . can work for the common end and for the general interests of the country as a whole."[213] Local units would, as it were, think locally. To centralize was to rise above the bounded sphere of the local. It was to commit to a kind of standardization that could rescue Indians from their native confinement. Such reasoning involved the coming together of two analytically distinct ideas: *uniformity* and *coercion*. A centralized state could achieve both objectives—and their interaction is illustrated by Ambedkar's defense of a unified, integrated judiciary:

> A federation being a dual polity based on divided authority with separate legislative, executive and judicial powers for each of the two polities is bound to produce diversity in laws, in administration and in judicial protection. Up to a certain point this diversity does not matter. It may be welcomed as being an attempt to accommodate the powers of government to local needs and local circumstances. But this very diversity when it goes beyond a certain point is capable of producing chaos and has produced chaos in many federal states. One has only to imagine twenty different laws—if we have twenty states in the union—of marriage, of divorce, of inheritance of property, family relations, contracts, torts, crimes, weights and measures, of bills and checks, banking and commerce, of procedures for obtaining justice and in the standards and methods of administration. Such a state of affairs not only weakens the state but becomes intolerant to the citizen who moves from state to state only to find that what is lawful in one state is not lawful in another.[214]

For Ambedkar, India's villages had supporters "largely due to the fulsome praise bestowed upon it by [Charles] Metcalfe, who described them as little republics having nearly everything that they want within themselves and almost independent of any foreign relations."[215] Such communities may well have lasted, Ambedkar conceded, but their longevity was hardly indicative of their virtue. He called them "the ruination of India" and referred to the village as "a sink of localism, a den of ignorance, narrow-mindedness, and communalism."[216] "I am glad," he remarked, "that the Draft Constitution has discarded the village and adopted the individual as its unit."[217] Centralization enabled the *individual* to become the unit of organization.

The fears over regional passions are borne out by the Constituent Assembly's deliberations on December 30, 1948. On this date, an intense debate ensued over the center's powers regarding the concurrent list in Schedule VII to the Constitution. This record contained the items that would fall under the joint jurisdiction of the center and regional governments. The contest was over whether the center's powers were limited to the power of legislation or went further and included executive power. By giving the center not just legislative but also executive power, many argued, the regional governments would have no power at all. Further, it would mean that those impacted by the laws, situated as they might be in far and remote corners, would have to engage with the center rather than with authorities on the ground.[218]

Such concerns were noted but rejected. The Congress party leader T. T. Krishnamachari denied that the inclusion of executive powers would make India a unitary state. Federalism, he observed, had many interpretations, and much would turn on the working of the document.[219] The Constitution, he predicted, would "either become fully federal or partially federal in actual practice over a period of time."[220] More to the point, Krishnamachari argued that experiences under colonial legislation showed that regional governments often evaded their responsibility to execute the laws.[221] The opposition to federal power was "political opposition," by which Krishnamachari meant that it was not based on a principled disagreement with any feature of the constitutional framework but was instead an attempt by different entities to gain power.[222] He went so far as to assert that "the opposition . . . has its origin in the fact that the Muslim League never wanted India to be a strong country, with a strong government."[223]

Ambedkar endorsed this historical narrative. For him, the conflict over regional autonomy dated back to the first Roundtable Conference in London in 1930–1931, where the center's powers had been limited to accommodate the Muslim League. The League had feared that it would be dominated by Hindu forces at the center, and regional autonomy was an attempt at power-sharing. Ambedkar characterized the acceptance of the Muslim League's position as a "concession" rather than "an acceptance of the principle that the center should have no authority to administer a law passed in the concurrent field."[224] The context for this debate was a provision in the Government of India Act of 1935 that placed certain limitations on the powers of the central government.[225] These limitations, Ambedkar argued, were not based on any principled rationale. It was therefore improper to rely on them to oppose central authority. Ambedkar felt that members in the Assembly were merely echoing arguments of the Muslim League without being attentive to changed circumstances. He pointed out that the colonial state itself had given up its support of such a schema by enacting a new provision in the 1935 Act.[226] This new provision, introduced as a result of the Second World War, allowed the central government to take over the administration of not only concurrent subjects but also of items in the provincial list. Even though the provision had been introduced for emergency situations, Ambedkar found it to be equally fitting in ordinary times.[227] India's constitutional arrangement required concentrated authority that could be modulated depending on the circumstances.[228]

Whether or not we find this argument persuasive, the examples that Ambedkar used to support his case for centralized control over the administration of law are telling. His first illustration was a central legislation that banned untouchability and imposed penalties on its practice. There might be regions, Ambedkar contended, where such a law would find resistance. Without central force, such a law would remain unexecuted. Similarly, he offered the example of child marriage, where reform would be impossible without the center's power to enforce radical legislation. His third example was labor legislation:

> Is it desirable that the labor legislation of the central government should be mere paper legislation with no effect being given to them? How can effect be given to them unless the centre has got some authority to make good the administration of laws which it makes? I therefore submit that having regard to the cases which I have cited—and I have no doubt honourable members will remember many more cases after their own experience—that a large part of legislation which the centre makes in the concurrent field remains merely a paper legislation, for the simple reason that the center cannot execute its own laws.[229]

By locating authority at the center, one could therefore oppose the tendencies of a backward society. To distance power from local actors meant that power could be exercised progressively. The state itself, it was almost assumed, would have no ideological predisposition to satisfy, and it would commit itself to the welfare of its citizens. To accept such a model of statehood, it was moreover suggested, was to be on the side of the future. Global trends, the Assembly claimed, favored centralization. Despite the appearance that Soviet Russia empowered local units, in truth it was a state "maintained through the rigid and ruthless discipline of the communist party."[230] In the United States, the Supreme Court had come to interpret the general welfare and trade and commerce clauses widely, thereby strengthening the center.[231] After the Great Depression, American law had slowly brought agriculture, education, and industry all under centralized control.[232] In both Canada and Australia, governmental commissions had underlined the importance of increased central power.[233] In late

1949 Deputy Prime Minister Vallabhbhai Patel wrote to the province premiers, encouraging them to accept this new state of affairs. Prior notions of regional autonomy, he observed, "have become out of date."[234] The world had become a smaller place, but its shrunken character was invisible to narrow, local eyes.

Conclusion

India's founders offered various arguments in support of a centralized state, and connected the idea of such a state with the idea of self-rule. When framed as a contest between the state and society, one can see the underlying orientations that fashioned the call for the concentration of authority. Supporters of centralization saw their opponents as sharing a faith in Indian society. Even those who desired state-centered regional governments rather than political pluralism were seen to carry this conviction, for the boundary between the state and society became porous as political authority traveled downward. The equivalence between regional state authority and pluralism is a matter of some importance.[235] To understand this equivalence, we cannot simply record the support for a state over other kinds of associations. This inquiry must be followed by a subsequent one— namely, an understanding of which entities were regarded as appropriate for *becoming a state*. A critical factor in determining the structure of a political entity is the capacity of its central and constituent parts.[236] There are key judgments to be made in such inquiries, including those relating to questions of freedom, intersubjectivity, and transformation—a fact that should caution us against seeing debates on federalism in purely pragmatic terms.[237] To view the matter practically is to ignore the harsh reality faced by a great many nations in the world, where one must determine the kind of power that a particular body is equal to exercising. An account of *how* to make a state is less a question of political theory and more a matter of political sociology. It rests on an account of which bodies are capable of existing as states in the first place. For India's founders, regional territories simply could not become states—they could not construct a force that could counteract the tenacity of local cultural forms.[238] This is neither a trivial point of political sociology nor an odd fact limited to India. It is grounded in the notion that subordination itself dictates certain attitudes.

India's political pluralists were part of a global movement that either decentered the state or rejected it altogether, although there were some notable differences in the Indian tradition. The global trend veered toward functionalism, whereas its Indian counterpart focused on localism. In this regard Radhakamal Mukerjee's stance was more in sync with worldwide trends than Mohandas Gandhi's localist position was, because it incorporated some aspects of functionalism to undermine territory as a basis for association. For our purposes, however, the distinction between functionalism and localism has limited significance. What is important is that both were focused on non-state associations. In the ultimate analysis, the Indian pluralists shared a great deal with their foreign counterparts—they denied the sovereignty of the state, and they offered historical and sociological rather than logical explanations for the meaning of authority.[239] They also shared the same fate as pluralists elsewhere. Despite its astonishing reach, the effort to reject state sovereignty was a momentous failure, and the story of the twentieth century in many ways became the story of the victory of the nation-state. The failure of Indian political pluralism was neither a contingent consequence of Indian politics nor a result of factors unique to the Indian brand of this ideology. It was an outcome shaped by the internal logic of pluralism. Advocates for nonhierarchical arrangements struggled to elucidate how authority would be coordinated in such settings, and similarly struggled to show how the conditions for freedom would emerge.[240]

As scholars of pluralist thought have observed, this struggle exposed the internal limitations of its conceptual structure. The entire pluralist point was that the terms of order should emerge organically as a matter of history and sociology rather than be determined *ex ante* as a matter of logic.[241] But for figures like Jawaharlal Nehru and B. R. Ambedkar, as was the case with Thomas Hobbes, this prospect was terrifying. Hobbes had famously argued that society lacked any unity that preceded the existence of the state. It was precisely for this reason that Hugo Grotius's double contract theory, where society created an association prior to the institution of government, was seen to be mistaken. Ambedkar and Nehru did not always fear cycles of violence—their concerns were broader than the bare preservation of order—but they were consistently doubtful of society's internal capacity to reconstitute interpersonal relations. The pluralist schema may not necessarily have resulted in disarray, but it was seen to purchase stability at the price of individual freedom. Pluralism did not wholeheartedly defend the structures of social life, but it had no conceptual resources to explain how such structures might change. Similarly, it did not support unmitigated conflict, but it had no thesis to explain social preservation.[242]

In Gandhi's anti-statist stance, there was no rational account of how to preserve the peace. In Mukerjee's imagery of the state as one actor among many, little light was shed on how the boundary between the state and other actors would be policed. Both men simply observed—as a fact of historical sociology—that the Indian village had usually managed to resolve its problems. The past was a marker of harmony rather than antagonism.

Nehru and Ambedkar spoke of a different past, of course, but fundamental to their contrasting mural was a different conceptual story. Unlike what many alleged, the point made by Nehru and Ambedkar was hardly that India should imitate Western industrialization and casually embrace foreign frameworks for state formation. The pluralists, both in India and elsewhere, presented a powerful critique of Western modernity. But the pluralist failure lay in a theoretical incapacity to offer alternative institutional models that could solve the problems for which the state, an impersonal authority with its own logic, had been constructed. This was partly because they supposed that there was no such problem to solve— they had a contrasting notion of society and the freedom that it allowed—and partly because they thought that the domain of the social could resolve whatever flaws it had. The social could be a site of agency. For Ambedkar and Nehru, however, Indian society was in desperate need of change, and the change that was required was too severe to take place from within. Their critique of Indian society is what, above all, makes them radical. As far as they were concerned, one could not respond to the drama and tragedy of the social world by suggesting, in either historical or sociological terms, that it might sort itself out. Instead, one needed some account of how reform would occur. The chaos and violence in the final years of colonial rule offered very little promise for civility and reinforced fears about the structures of domination and layers of prejudice that pervaded society. Those years delivered facts that were in search of a theory. The only *theory* on offer was the theory of the state.

In understanding the case for the state, one must note the defeat of not only political pluralism but also communism. The sidelining of the communist agenda draws attention to the noninstrumentalist facet of Nehru's and Ambedkar's statist commitment and underlines the resistance to short-circuiting the path to modernity.[243] Both individuals cared a great deal about modernization but saw material advancement as insufficient for the realization of true independence. To live under conditions of freedom was as much about improving the conditions of life as it was about effectuating change through a set of procedures and practices that constituted the reality of self-rule. If the state were simply to be an instrument, and if its actions were not constituted in specific ways, the meaning of those actions would be different. To put the point crudely, such a situation would result in a different action being performed. Nehru and Ambedkar held that certain mechanisms mattered in and of themselves. As far as they were concerned, India needed democracy and it needed modernity—and democracy and modernity needed one another.

3

Identity and Representation

Our sense of self and our horizons are shaped by the political structures we inhabit. In previous chapters we have seen the role of legal
rules and the state in transcending local affiliations. If codification placed
Indians under a shared umbrella of understanding, centralization situated
them in an equal relationship to a common authority. In each instance,
one's self-conception and interpersonal stance were reordered to create a
democratic citizen who could be freed from prevailing forms of learning
and power. The path to self-rule was, however, burdened with one further matter to negotiate: the relationship between identity and representation. How were Indians to be classified, and how were their preferences
to be expressed?

Of the reasons that had been offered to justify colonial rule, few were
as boldly underlined as the challenge posed by India's fractured society. A
divided polity was seen to threaten collective political life. In *Considerations on Representative Government,* for instance, John Stuart Mill had
noted the dangers of mutual jealousy between different communities.[1]
From the contrasting historical efforts of James Mill and Mountstuart
Elphinstone to the ethnographic agenda of Herbert Hope Risley, the imperial mind had long imagined Indian society to be a constellation of groups.[2]
The individualized point of view integral to self-rule was seen as unavail-
able in a land so thoroughly constituted by communities. Freedom, as it
played out during the Raj, was a concept that did not gesture at individuals. The identity of groups had in fact assumed such profound meaning
during the final decades of British rule that the history of the period could

well be told through this lens. As Indian nationalism shifted its focus from greater political voice to complete independence from the colonial state, the negotiation of social cleavages marked a major theme in emerging constitutional proposals. The mechanics of representation was a serious problem facing Indian democratization, and it proved to be most challenging in the case of Muslims and the lower castes.[3] In this chapter I consider how India's founders addressed the challenge in each instance.

In mediating citizenship through community affiliation, the colonial state had embraced a static vision of participation where the interests of individuals were established in advance. The purpose of representation was articulation rather than transformation. Efforts at increasing participation, such as they were, saw participation as the negotiation and management of preset preferences. Different communities contended with one another under the auspices of their colonial masters, and each community was taken to have predetermined choices. The partition of British India marked a breakdown in constitutional negotiations and tore apart established modes of thinking. Its occurrence alongside the introduction of universal suffrage brought fresh attention to the question of representation. With the coming of democracy, the challenges posed by caste were also reexamined, which in turn revealed their own set of considerations. In both instances, the Constituent Assembly emphasized individual freedom. In the case of religion, the effort was to shift from fixed identities based on community membership to decisional ones that emerged from choices structured around democratic individualism. With regard to caste, we shall find that the solution was more complex, but it was equally focused on liberating individuals from the coercive power exercised by groups.

This chapter proceeds in three stages. First, I consider how a range of thinkers saw the problem of representation in the years prior to Indian independence. This excursion in intellectual history is necessary because it reveals the extent of the crisis of representation during this period. It provides the backdrop to the partition of British India, an event that threw into sharp relief the failure of an identity-based framework to provide for a fair and enduring solution to the problem of group diversity. Next I turn to the Constituent Assembly's proceedings, underlining the radicalism of the Assembly's approach, in particular its decision to move beyond a schema centered on identity and to discard communal representation in favor of the individualization of identity. Finally, I address the caste question, to identify the specific form of group recognition that was conceived and to situate the orientation toward caste within the overall conception of citizenship.

The task before India's founders was to understand the relationship between difference, inequality, and democracy. How did the cleavages within Indian society bear on the institution of self-rule? In the colonial era, the method of identification had classified society in a specific key, and the composition was found to be unsuitable for the institution of popular government. Once colonial rule came to an end, the challenge was to move beyond the extant model of recognition and to make representation possible in light of the new reality of universal suffrage. This called for an assessment of the attributes of democratic rule and the realities of Indian society. Our study of the performance of this task captures both the possibility of representation and the possibility of political change.

Representation before India

A conspicuous feature of Indian political thought in the last years of colonial rule was the absence of an account of representation that was free from communal affiliations. Whether one turns to major Muslim leaders, key actors within the Indian National Congress, or prominent Hindu nationalists, one encounters either resistance to the question of representation or little attempt to picture a polity centered on individual freedom. A great many thinkers appear to have been condemned to colonial categories in conceptualizing citizenship in a divided society. Others simply avoided the issue. In other words, they denied that representation posed any real problem. These failures, in which some of India's most serious minds were complicit, marked a profound crisis of representation. The crisis was brought into sharp focus by the partition of British India, an event that paved the way for noncommunal representation within India's constitutional imagination.

One might begin to study this crisis by considering the case of Muslim representation. Here historical attention has focused, understandably, on the partition of the Indian subcontinent in 1947. According to one strand of scholarship, the principal objective of the leader of the Muslim League, Mohammad Ali Jinnah, was authority at the center after the departure of the British.[4] His political competition, it has been observed, included not merely the Indian National Congress but also provincial Muslim leaders. A scheme with a weak center and strong provinces would have left Jinnah as a national leader without real power. In contrast, a strong central government would have kept Jinnah subordinate to the Congress party, whose strength lay in numbers. The suggestion is that it was in response to both of these possibilities that Jinnah sought a strong center where Muslims would be treated on a par with Hindus. The claim of parity, through the framing of Muslims as a separate nation, could move beyond the uncompromising logic of majority rule.

In this context, the Lahore Resolution of 1940—in which Jinnah notably expressed the demand for Pakistan—is viewed "as a bargaining counter."[5] This strand of reasoning sees the 1940 Resolution as having "the merit of being acceptable (on the face of it) to the majority-province Muslims, of being totally unacceptable to the Congress party and in the last resort to the British too."[6] Emphasis is placed on paragraph 4 of the Resolution. Here, the use of the word "constitution" rather than "treaty" is understood to capture Jinnah's commitment to a united India.[7] The statement, it is pointed out, mentioned neither "partition" nor "Pakistan."[8] A reading of this kind presents the Resolution as a *reductio ad absurdum* of the call for provincial autonomy by local Muslim leaders. It was a strategy by which the British and the Congress party would be forced to concede the demand for a strong center.

A different reading of the partition of British India underlines reasons that were internal to Islam.[9] Here the focus is on normative religious constraints that shaped Muslim political action. Even though colonial policies played a part in constructing Indian society along communal lines, Muslim leaders were, it is posited, limited in the forms of representation they could embrace. The supposition is that the idea of a *community* had salience within Islam, and this led numerous Muslim figures—from Syed Ahmed Khan and Amir Ali to Maulana Muhammad Ali, and Muhammad Iqbal to Mohammad Ali Jinnah—to draw a connection between political commitment and religious faith. Jinnah could claim to be the sole spokesman for India's Muslims "not only because therein lay the political secret of his and his party's undisputed claim to power," but also because doing otherwise would be to "reject the very sources of his own and his party's legitimation."[10] A Muslim consensus is therefore seen as having imposed divine considerations—it required more than legitimacy through numbers, and individual representation was rejected along with majority rule. The claim is that the special feature of separate electorates and the demand for parity was not merely that it treated Hindus and Muslims as groups with equal power, but that it embodied the idea of exclusivity.[11]

This contest has been performed in multiple iterations. A recent intervention, for example, has surveyed Muslim activity in the United Provinces of Agra and Oudh to challenge the thesis that Pakistan was an inchoate proposal that inadvertently succeeded. Rather than simply being a home for Indian Muslims, it is shown that Pakistan was imagined "as an Islamic utopia that would be the harbinger for renewal and rise of Islam in the modern world," as a place that would secure the Islamic global community and be "a worthy successor to the defunct Turkish Caliphate as the foremost Islamic power in the twentieth century."[12] It is sharply observed that if the proposal for Pakistan was indeed lacking in theorization—that is, if India's Muslims had not given much thought to the proposal—then the burden lies in showing how it led to a call for an independent sovereign state.

The scholarship on the 1947 partition is considerable in volume and detail. As we can discern from the abovementioned contributions, however, historians have by and large focused on *territoriality*. The matter of *representation* has simply been subsumed within and conflated with the study of territoriality. The political importance of partition—to say nothing of its drama and horror, and its stain on the imagination of South Asia—makes the interest in the event understandable. It is natural to ask why Britain ruled one territory only to leave behind two countries. But explicable as the conflation of both matters might be, territoriality and representation are analytically distinct concepts, and untying them is crucial for us to come to terms with the crisis of representation during India's early to mid-twentieth century.

By shifting our attention from territoriality to representation, we can see that the interpretive doubts over Mohammad Ali Jinnah's real intentions lose their relevance. Let us concede for a moment that "Jinnah was keeping his options open for a constitutional arrangement which would cover the whole of India" and that the Resolution of 1940 was an "incomplete and contradictory statement."[13] In other words, let us accept that Jinnah was agreeable to the idea of an undivided country. The fact remains that even if this is true, it is incontrovertible that he saw Hindus and Muslims differently. "The problem of India," he observed, "is not of an inter-communal character but manifestly of an international one."[14] For him, "the only course open ... [was] to allow the major nations separate homelands by dividing India into 'autonomous national states.'"[15] Whatever answer one may provide to the question of Jinnah's support for the territorial division of British India, he made his belief in the distinction between Hindus and Muslims clear:

> It is extremely difficult to appreciate why our Hindu friends fail to understand the real nature of Islam and Hinduism. They are not religions in the strict sense of the word, but, in fact, different and distinct social orders and it is a dream that the Hindus and Muslims can ever evolve a common nationality, and this misconception of one Indian nation has gone far beyond the limits and is the cause of most of our troubles and will lead India to destruction if we fail to revise our notions in time. The Hindus and Muslims belong to two different religious philosophies, social customs and literature. They neither intermarry, nor inter-dine together and, indeed, they belong to two different civilizations which are based mainly on conflicting ideas and conceptions. Their aspects on life and of life are different. It is quite clear that Hindus and Muslims derive their inspiration from different sources of history. They have different epics, their heroes are different, and different episodes. Very often the hero of one is a foe of the other and, likewise, their victories and defeats overlap. To yoke together such nations under a single state, one as a numerical minority and the other as a majority, must lead to growing discontent and final destruction of any fabric that may be so built up for the government of such a state.[16]

Even prior to his 1940 address, from which the above extract is drawn, Jinnah wrote to Mohandas Gandhi declaring India to be neither a nation nor a country.[17] He saw it as "a sub-continent composed of nationalities, Hindus and Muslims being the two major nations."[18] Jinnah's perspective is borne out by a volatile exchange he shared with Gandhi in 1944. Hindus and Muslims, he observed in the course of this dialogue, "are two major nations by any definition or test of a nation."[19] In matters ranging from "culture and civilization" to "art and architecture" to "customs and calendar," Muslims had their own "distinctive outlook on life and of life."[20] For Jinnah, it was incorrect to see the claim for a sovereign state as a form of "severance or secession from any existing Union."[21] Such an alleged "Union" was "*non est factum* in India"; the Muslim case was based on the fact that they were already a nation.[22]

If we focus on the theme of representation, we may in fact chart a reasonably consistent course of thinking that runs all the way back to Syed

Ahmed Khan, the most important Muslim intellectual in India in the nineteenth century. Khan is known for his commitment to the reconciliation of Islam with modernity.[23] His interest in politics emerged in the aftermath of the revolt of 1857. In his best-known work, *The Causes of the Indian Revolt,* he offered an explanation for the uprising.[24] Khan rejected a religious interpretation of the event, claiming instead that the dissatisfaction arose from the absence of Indian participation in governance and, in particular, the exclusion of Indians from the Legislative Council. For him, this singular fact was "the origin of all the troubles that have befallen Hindustan."[25]

Khan put forth a critique of the state's ignorance and apathy, and of the prevailing misapprehensions about its real intentions. In several contexts, there was the fear of state intervention. With regard to religion, for instance, the behavior of missionaries, who preached in public spaces and "attacked the followers and the holy places of other creeds," was at odds with local Hindustani practices where one "preaches and explains his views in his own mosque, or his own house."[26] Khan portrayed how local Indians responded anxiously to laws enacted without their involvement. From regulations relating to widow remarriage to the transfer of property to revenue collection, he observed how social norms had been upset by legal change. The case for greater Indian representation rested in part on cultural differences between the English and Indians. History was a reminder of the "differences and distinctions that have existed between the manners, and opinions, and the customs of the various races of men."[27] For Khan, it was "to these differences of thought and custom that the laws must be adapted, for they cannot be adapted to the laws."[28] It was a disregard of local customs and practices—a disregard for the peculiar practices of the Indian race—which had led to the 1857 revolt.

The Causes of the Indian Revolt was not a straightforwardly radical text. It did not put forth any significant claim pertaining to self-government. The interaction that Khan desired between the governing and governed was advisory in nature. Yet the text's emphasis on the Muslim community, on their unique predicament and condition, was noteworthy. Although parts of the book were written in general terms, where English rulers were compared to their Indian subjects, Khan repeatedly identified how the Muslim community had especially suffered. Interference in religious matters had, for example, impacted Muslims far more than Hindus. The was because "the Hindu faith consists rather in the practice of long established rites and forms, than in the study of doctrine."[29] In contrast to Hindus, who "recognize no canons and laws," Muslims regarded the "tenets of their creed as necessary to salvation."[30] Khan also noted that strict rules pertaining to employment were especially burdensome for Muslims. The Hindus, who were "original inhabitants" of the land, "were never in former days in the habit of taking service."[31] Rather, "they were engaged in such work as their forefathers had been engaged in before them."[32] The Muslims, on the other hand, "came in the train of former conquerors and gradually domesticated themselves in India."[33] This led to their dependency on service—that is, their reliance on being employed by others—and placed them at greater inconvenience than Hindus.[34] Another instance was the temper and lack of courtesy displayed by officials to natives, which was particularly offensive to Muslims, given their historical standing and the premium they placed on being shown respect. The "advancement of their honor in the eyes of the world" that they sought was further affected by local absence in high appointments.[35]

By way of such examples, Khan portrayed Muslims as a distinct group. In the intellectual life of the nineteenth century, he contributed considerably in challenging orthodox beliefs and furthering modern education. While his interventions were significant from the perspective of social reform, they had the additional consequence of politicizing Muslims. Khan himself, in later years, was "convinced that no part of India has yet arrived at the stage when the system of representation can be adopted, in its fullest scope, even in regard to local affairs."[36] He saw India as a land of many races, where larger communities would overrun smaller ones. It is thus hardly accidental that Khan received much tribute at the Muslim League's 1906 inaugural session, and his role in making India's Muslims aware of their separate interests was acknowledged.[37] Muslims were only a fifth of India's population. With the end of British rule, they would exist alongside a population four times their size. In such a situation, a speaker at the inaugural session feared, "our life, our property, our honor, and our faith will all be in great danger."[38]

The concerns expressed in Khan's writings did not take a specific institutional form. They pre-dated the phase in Indian political thought where arguments assumed a constitutional character. What is discernible, however, in texts such as *The Causes of the Indian Revolt* is a certain historical sensibility. The text displays an awareness that political conceptions were changing in some significant fashion. A shift was perceived from an aristocratic to a democratic model—a shift that led Khan to focus on the logic of a political community. His sense that the fate of Muslims was somehow separate from the fate of others proved to have astonishing staying power amid changing views on how best to secure Muslim interests. Interestingly enough, one might even enlist Abul Kalam Azad in the category of Muslims thinkers who adopted such a viewpoint. Azad, a prominent leader of the Indian National Congress and a minister in Jawaharlal Nehru's independent government, is typically cast as the mirror image of Mohammad Ali Jinnah. He is the Muslim figure who was committed to the Congress party and was keen to maintain an undivided India. But though his differences with Jinnah on the division of British India are well known, it is less certain whether he fully endorsed a theory of citizenship that was unmediated by religion.

As others have shown, Azad's early writings, such as those in the journal *Al-Hilal*, reveal that religion was central to his political thought. Religion was the reason for Muslim resistance to foreign rule. It was the foundation for a political community.[39] A recent exploration of Azad's thought has rightly characterized him as "a staunch Indian patriot and at the same time perhaps the most celebrated theorist of a trans-national *jihad*."[40] His call for Hindu–Muslim unity should not, we are reminded, be confused with secularism.[41] Azad broke with traditional Muslim opinion in two key respects. First, he challenged the ulama's interpretation of the sharia. For him, the ulama had been corrupted over time by a proximity to political power.[42] Second, his notion of a political community, founded on a shared commitment to Islam, had a place for non-Muslims and a vision for Muslim and non-Muslim cooperation.[43] In fact, the call for Hindu–Muslim unity in *Masla-i Khilafat* was explicitly based on a reading of the sharia, which Azad saw as sanctioning collaboration between the two communities.[44] Azad's move was to grant the sharia moral authority without insisting that this authority be backed by a coercive legal regime.[45]

In his 1940 presidential address to the Congress party, Azad delivered an impassioned plea for India's unity. "India's historic destiny" was "that many human races and cultures and religions should flow to her, finding a home in her hospitable soil, and that many a caravan should find rest there."[46] Yet this call for solidarity did not proceed alongside a common vision of citizenship. Azad referenced his writings in *Al-Hilal*, stating that there had been no change in his views over the course of nearly three decades. He asserted his "special interest in Islamic religion and culture" and declared that he "cannot tolerate any interference with them."[47] "The spirit of Islam," he contended, did not interfere with his political aspirations or support for "the indivisible unity that is Indian nationality."[48]

Azad acknowledged both the existence and significance of the communal problem. But he offered two reasons for assurance. The first reason was the Congress party's proposal for minority protection, which would offer "the fullest guarantee . . . for the rights and interests of minorities" and would empower minorities to "judge for themselves what safeguards are necessary for the protection of their rights and interests."[49] The second reason was specifically addressed to the Muslim community. The community, he lamented, had fallen prey to invidious colonial machinations and wrongly imagined itself to be a minority. In the world of politics, Azad argued, a minority could not be simplistically defined as a group that was numerically smaller than a larger group. More substantially, the idea of a minority related to a group "that is so small in number and so lacking in other qualities that give strength, that it has no confidence in its own capacity to protect itself from the much larger group that surrounds it."[50] India's Muslim population could not be regarded as a minority under such a definition. Its size was significant and its internal divisions were few. India's future constitutional schema would be based on provincial autonomy with a limited role for the central authority. He reiterated this federal proposal in later writings.[51] Such a scheme would give Muslims institutional freedom and thereby present them no cause for worry.

Azad's political thought does not disclose a neat theory of differentiated citizenship, but it is noteworthy that his composite nationalism and belief in a united India did not necessarily go alongside a theory of representation that transcended community lines. His vision of territorial unity proceeded together with his religious commitments. In 1946, for instance, he referred to the division of British India as "un-Islamic."[52] Azad's complex views highlight the importance of distinguishing between territoriality and representation and the need to differentiate between those who sought territorial unity/division and those who sought communal/noncommunal representation. In a departure from standard historical accounts, a similarity between Jinnah and Azad was once provocatively drawn, and it was suggested that both figures proposed to keep India's territory intact.[53] This historical claim with regard to Jinnah is controversial, but the comparison is telling. One may well approach the analogy from the opposite direction, to argue that neither Jinnah nor Azad offered a theory of representation centered on individual liberty. Azad's views confirm that the overwhelming focus on territoriality in contemporary scholarship is, in some sense, an intellectual distraction. Indeed, the claim for Pakistan was a kind of contradiction in terms, for it sought a separate homeland on the basis of a global religious movement that claimed to transcend the nation-state.[54]

If a theory of noncommunal representation was found missing among Muslim leaders, it does not appear that figures like Jawaharlal Nehru and Mohandas Gandhi quite offered a robust alternative. To be sure, both leaders—and the Indian National Congress more generally—rejected communalism and resisted the form of politics that it promoted. When the Congress party opposed separate electorates in 1909, for instance, it referred to the distinction between Muslims and non-Muslims as "unjust, invidious, and humiliating."[55] Yet Nehru's and Gandhi's rejection of communal politics and an identity-based framework for representation was not articulated alongside any positive theory. The rejection emerged from denial rather than engagement. Simply put, it failed to confront the problem of representation with the seriousness that was required.[56] In this sense, the painting of Nehru's and Gandhi's thought as universalistic may not be incorrect, but it does not quite record their orientation.[57]

In the late 1920s and early 1930s, when Jawaharlal Nehru started to comment on communal politics, he boldly declared that there was no place for a discussion of the Hindu–Muslim question.[58] Communalism was, for him, a "myth."[59] By denying Hindu–Muslim tension, Nehru was rejecting communal dissonance among India's masses.[60] Throughout the 1930s Nehru drew a link between communal forces, on the one hand, and foreign rulers and upper classes, on the other. As far as he was concerned, neither group had any solutions to India's economic problems, for any solution would necessarily "upset the present social structure and devest the vested interests."[61] The communal mind was apathetic to India's real difficulties—namely, the alleviation of hunger, the improvement of agriculture, the development of industry, and so on.[62]

In his 1936 autobiography Nehru similarly suggested that communalism was a colonial ploy "to preserve Indian vested interests against Indians themselves, against undiluted democracy, against an upsurge of the masses."[63] It had been *made* an issue during the Roundtable Conferences, a strategy deployed to frustrate political negotiations.[64] In charting the trajectory of Indian communalism, Nehru took note of Khan's efforts to advance the Muslim community. Though Khan had rightly addressed the education of Muslims and their economic progress, his narrow agenda had "cramping effects" and paved the way for the separation of Hindu and Muslim interests.[65] Muslim communalism was matched by its Hindu counterpart, and both sides had been exploited by the British with like prejudice. For Nehru, communal demands were ultimately economic and political demands that would benefit only a section of the upper middle class.[66] When Nehru delivered the presidential address to the Lucknow Congress party in the same year, he gestured at the incompatibility between communalism and democracy, though his chief interest lay in communalism's threat to economic transformation.[67] In 1938 he put the matter in clear terms on two separate occasions:

> There is no religious or cultural problem in India. What is called the religious or communal problem is really a dispute among upper-class people for a division of the spoils of office or of representation in a legislature.[68]

> The so-called Hindu–Muslim problem is not a genuine problem concerning the masses, but it is the creation of self-seekers, job-hunters and timid people, who believe in British rule in India till eternity . . . Whether Hindus or Muslims, poverty, unemployment and other hardships affect them alike; and it is nothing but playing a fraud with the country continuously to harp on the so-called Hindu–Muslim problem.[69]

Nehru characterized group-based thinking as "a medieval conception which has no place in the modern world."[70] The challenges that modernity posed were economic and political rather than religious, and the focus on the latter was an error.[71] Jinnah's politics was termed as the "politics of the Dark Ages."[72]

Nehru did recognize, on more than one occasion, the significance of the right to religious freedom.[73] He also made known that any future constitutional scheme would protect this right through judicially enforceable means.[74] But he did not explicate how modern citizenship could meet the problem of a divided society, for he did not believe in the existence of any such problem in the first place. If politics moved away from its elitism and spoke to the masses, he argued, we would notice the shared concerns that touched everyone equally. Every Hindu and Muslim farmer, for example, faced the same challenge of easing his or her debt.[75] The solution to the communal problem was, in other words, to focus on other (real) problems.[76] For Nehru, Jinnah's reluctance to widen the franchise confirmed that communalism had no appeal among India's Muslim population.[77] The Muslim League and the Hindu Mahasabha were two sides of the same coin. Neither had any "social basis in the masses," and both rested on "re-actionary and semi-feudal supporters in the princes and landlords."[78] The comparative advantage of both parties was linked to the support of such forces.

Nehru's outlook entailed the distracting away of religious difference. For him, the "communal problem [was] not a religious problem."[79] A study of the conflicts in Bengal, for example, revealed that the peasants were Muslims and the landlords were Hindus. On the face of it, a struggle between them might appear to be a religious conflict whereas in fact it was a tenant-landlord conflict.[80] In the United Provinces, the situation was the opposite, with the Muslims as the landlords. Here too the problem was often falsely characterized as religious.[81] The problem with a communal way of seeing was not only that it had missed the point and misconstrued such tussles. More fundamentally, Nehru argued, it was an active and invidious attempt "to take shelter behind the name of religion and prevent the people from joining the progressive forces, and consequently also to prevent the real problem—the economic problem—from being tackled."[82] In the epilogue to his autobiography, published five years later, Nehru described how communal demands had slowly become increasingly more absurd. He now saw the struggle against communalism as an additional battle in the war for freedom—a contest between those who sought independence and those who wanted to preserve the status quo.[83]

Nehru's thinking led him to treat Jinnah's call for a separate Muslim homeland with horror and shock. He expressed lament over the Muslim community's branding as an ordinary minority at risk of oppression, and over the shift away from what he saw as the questions that truly mattered.[84] But even in such times, even in face of intense political tension around the question of religion, he retained a belief in the economic origins of communalism.[85] Instead of scrutinizing the problem of political representation, Nehru's attention drifted instead to the irrationality of the proposal to dissect British India:

> You are aware of the Muslim League Resolution on Pakistan, that India should be split up into Muslim India and Hindu India, for which a propaganda has been going on for the last one year and a half. Nobody thinks what is happening today in the world . . . No small country can exist in the present-day world. Hitler has destroyed all the small countries of Europe. The small countries of

122

Asia are also gradually being swept out of existence. It means that if all these countries are to live in future they must live together.[86]

As the 1940s progressed, Nehru's engagement with the communal question showed some signs of change. In an interview in 1945 he suggested that India could either embrace modern democratic citizenship or adopt medieval forms of organization.[87] The fact that Nehru presented this as a genuine choice was indicative of the development of his thought, though the acknowledgment came alongside the reassertion that communalism had no purchase among India's masses.[88] In an address titled "The Absurdity of Partition," Nehru made several arguments against the division of India. The first was a reiteration of the unviability of small states. A partitioned nation would be akin to Iraq and Iran. That is, it would take the character of nations which were "not sovereign but just satellite powers, at the mercy of great nations."[89] He also argued that the idea of partitioning British India failed on its own terms. He observed that even if a division of British India occurred, the new territories would still contain minorities.[90] A better solution would be federalism: a united India with autonomous provinces that would secure minority freedom in cultural, linguistic, and religious matters.[91] He repeated these arguments in *The Discovery of India,* where he characterized the proposal for the division of territory as riddled with inconsistencies and as only furthering the minority problem.[92] Nehru struggled to understand the growing support for a proposal that he saw as senseless. In the end, he was left to acknowledge its evolving appeal in slow and partial terms, seeing it as a marker of the self-interest and prejudice that had consumed political life.[93]

On occasion, Mohandas Gandhi's response to religious difference seemed to take a similar form. Like Nehru, Gandhi characterized communalism as an elite affair. At a speech at Eton in 1931, for example, Gandhi remarked that the "bugbear of communalism is confined largely to the cities which are not India."[94] The British had infected Indian society, and "the moment the alien wedge is removed the divided communities are bound to unite."[95] In subsequent years he would often underplay Hindu–Muslim conflict. In an interview with the *New York Times* in 1939, he recognized certain tensions between the communities but predicted that they would resolve themselves in the face of shared political and economic challenges.[96] But Gandhi's answer to the Hindu–Muslim challenge was in fact altogether distinct from Nehru's. His solution lay in noninstitutional means, in political *practice*. It was the lived experience of toleration, acts of friendship and assistance, that could pacify communal tensions.[97]

When communalism was rising in the early decades of the twentieth century, Gandhi asked Hindus and Muslims to "pray to *Khuda-Ishwar* in mosques and in temples to grant that there might be an end to the disputes that frequently arise between our two communities."[98] Hindus and Muslims did not need to hold each other's beliefs in order to respect one another. A serious attempt at toleration would have to proceed on the basis of trust. It could not adopt suspicion as its starting point.[99] Hindus and Muslims would have to practice unity, through instances of helping and aiding each other, for unity to be achieved. This is why Gandhi viewed the Khilafat (Caliphate) movement, which sought to retain the sovereign religious power of the Turkish sultan, as such a fine opportunity to transcend differences.[100] For him, India's Muslims had a genuine fear, founded or unfounded, of Hindu majoritarian rule, and, as a general matter, Hindus had the responsibility to protect Muslims.[101] The Khilafat movement was a way for Hindus to relate to a Muslim demand as a religious demand. A sense of solidarity would not be forged out of institutional contracts and constitutional power-sharing mechanisms; it would emerge from examples of support. And there was no better way for the majority community to show support than by joining hands with the minority community in a cause that was special to them.

It is well known that Gandhi held a radical view of individual agency. He considered the practices that he proposed, even ones that appeared truly out of the ordinary, as possible to perform. This was because individuals could always change their ways; they could reimagine and reconstitute themselves. But even though he possessed this profoundly modern perspective on human nature, he denied that it could be realized via institutional means. At a theological level, Hindu–Muslim unity was a genuine possibility because many of the points of conflict between the communities related to nonessential aspects of their respective religious commitments.[102] Hindus who objected to the disturbance caused by music playing at a mosque might feel annoyed, but the music was not a challenge to their beliefs. Indeed, he suggested that Hinduism and Islam were versions of the same philosophy. A focus on particularities, fueled by foreign rulers and vested agendas, had obscured the shared faith that all religions captured. Gandhi made this point with great force in *Hind Swaraj*: "Is the God of the Mahomedan different from the God of the Hindu? Religions are different roads converging to the same point. What does it matter that we take different roads so long as we reach the same goal?"[103] All religions were paths to the same end point, and it was a mistake to identify variances among them. The introduction of British rule—and, in particular, the advent of modernity—had created such differences. Acknowledging shared outlooks behind the veneer of difference would enable joint action. For him, Hindus and Muslims did not have to reject religion in order to live in harmony.[104] One could have firm religious beliefs but still undertake practices to forge unity with those whose beliefs were different. In this way, Gandhi did have a solution to the Hindu–Muslim problem. The outcomes that he desired would be achieved through *actions*—the power of example would shape behavior.[105] This solution, however, did not belong to the realm of public rules. It was a noninstitutional solution that did not contain any *theory* of representation.

There is no small irony in the fact that one intellectual tradition that both acknowledged Hindu–Muslim difference and expressed some version of universalism was Hindu nationalism. The twist was that this universalism was predicated on all Indians being Hindu. In the 1920s, a growing concern for the preservation of Hinduism mutated into Hindu nationalism. V. D. Savarkar was the man behind this "qualitative leap" in ideology.[106] In his 1923 text *Hindutva: Who Is a Hindu?* Savarkar wove a thread of unity that tied Hindus together.[107] Hindutva, he claimed, was an all-encompassing idea, applicable to the entire Hindu race, and distinguishable from Hinduism, which was a narrower outlook that formed but one part of this grand vision. The origins of Hindutva were ancient and glorious, and Savarkar presented an evocative tale of Aryan settlement and expansion, consolidation and growth, and eventual nationhood. History was deployed to deemphasize familiar differences among Hindus. "We, Hindus," he boldly declared, "are all one and a nation, because chiefly of our common blood."[108] In challenging times, like invasions by foreigners, every kind of Hindu had suffered in the same way. As a term, "Hinduism" referred to "all the religious beliefs that the different communities of the Hindu people hold" and applied across the diverse practices and beliefs that Hindus held.[109] Hindus were a nation because they shared not merely geography or association but "common blood."[110] Savarkar's list of ways in which Hindus were participants in the same civilization included legal regulations, social customs, and so on.[111] Those that did not share such characteristics were excluded. Muslims and Christians may share India's territory with Hindus. But even if they regarded the place as their *fatherland,* they did not view it as their *holy land.*[112] Their loyalties were elsewhere, the elements that constituted their past were distinct, and their outlook toward India was that of a foreigner.

Savarkar's presidential addresses at the annual sessions of the Hindu Mahasabha affirmed many of these themes. He defined a Hindu as a person who held "this *Bharatbhoomi* from the Indus to the Seas as his Fatherland and Holyland."[113] Again, Muslims, Christians, and so on fell outside this category. Muslims' faces were "ever turned towards Mecca and Medina," and Muslims were "often found to cherish an extraterritorial allegiance."[114] The distinction between Hinduism and Hindutva was stressed, with Savarkar asserting that the Mahasabha was not simply a religious body interested in theological doctrine. Its larger ambition was the prosperity of a Hindu nation. In developing his ideology, Savarkar articulated a particular notion of freedom. To be free, Hindus would have to do more than merely acquire geographical control over the territory of British India—they would need to construct a state that could protect and nourish their particular identity. For Savarkar, Hindus and Muslims shared centuries of enmity, and their collective presence in British India marked the presence of two separate nations on one soil. The communal problem was real, and the only solution was homogeneity: "India must be a Hindu land, reserved for the Hindus."[115] For Savarkar, the Indian National Congress had committed a fundamental error in disregarding the religious, racial, and cultural unity that was essential to the forming of a nation.[116]

Savarkar's emphasis was on the *nation,* with noticeably little mention of the state or formal institutions.[117] Though he deployed the language of religion, his thought was relatively weak and immodest in its religious components. In theological terms this kind of Hindu nationalism was "thin, because it is entirely indifferent to sectarian practices of everyday worship; indeed, its primary purpose is to make them redundant."[118] Instead, Savarkar's interest—his defining analytic maneuver—was to frame the question of nationhood in terms of identity. He thereby forced the question of which identity, which group, would be recognized as belonging in the Indian context, denying attempts to construct a nation on other terms. Savarkar's very question has been rightly termed as "a trap," for the framework of identity naturally led to the inclusion of some and the exclusion of others.[119]

Savarkar did not necessarily call for the exclusion of non-Hindus, but he did call for their subordination. Even if their territories were not given up, non-Hindus were not to assert their rights as a minority. The animating theme in Savarkar's thought—the stress on differences between Hindus and non-Hindus and the emphasis on similarities among Hindus—was furthered by a second prominent figure in Hindu nationalist thought, M. S. Golwalkar. A member of the Rashtriya Swayamsevak Sangh, Golwalkar interrogated the idea of nationhood in his 1939 work, *We or Our Nationhood Defined*.[120] The text depicted a magnificent ancient land of Hindus, stable and secure for thousands of years and surpassing all other civilizations in spiritual and intellectual progress. Eventually, however, it fell to foreign invaders, first to Muslims and subsequently to the British. Nonetheless, the Hindu nation retained its underlying spirit, as evidenced by events like the 1857 anticolonial revolt. According to Golwalkar, the Hindus were a nation because they shared the same territory, the same race, the same religion, the same spiritual and intellectual culture, and the same Sanskrit language. For him, it naturally followed that those who resided in this territory without satisfying the abovementioned criteria could not be considered as part of the nation. Without possessing these characteristics, they could only exist as foreigners, lacking the rights and benefits of citizenship.

Elsewhere, Golwalkar argued that distinctions in matters like language, caste, and custom had been erroneously used to deny that there was a distinctive Hindu way of living. He regarded such distinctions as superficial, akin to the various parts of a tree. Beneath the apparent diversity of such aspects was a form of unity that was organic. It was, for him, "ingrained in our blood from our very birth, because we are all born as Hindus."[121] Merely because Hindus had joined forces with Muslims or others against the British or because Muslims or others had resided in India, it did not follow that such groups could together form a nation. He claimed that such a theory of nationhood placed mistaken emphasis on territoriality. It assumed that residence was sufficient to make an individual part of a nation. For Golwalkar, a study of the past showed that "here was already a full-fledged ancient nation of the Hindus and the various communities which were living in the country were here either as guests, the Jews and Parsis, or as invaders, the Muslims and Christians."[122] As in the case of Savarkar, Golwalkar searched for a way to place all Hindus under one umbrella and exclude all others. His solution to the minority problem was nonrecognition of the minority.

In contrast to these wide-ranging positions, the writings of two figures stand out. The first was Lala Lajpat Rai. An influential member of the Indian nationalist movement who acquired a reputation for his interest in Hinduism and its reform, Rai died in 1928 after being severely injured during anticolonial protests. Even though he did not survive to see the furious unfolding of communal politics from the 1930s onward, Rai had already grasped the seriousness of the challenge at hand. His views are a reminder that the early Hindu Mahasabha, in which he played a prominent role, was not communal simply because it had religious commitments. Its politics was secular, and, interestingly enough, its commitment to Hinduism enabled it to take the question of religious diversity seriously. In the early years of the twentieth century, Rai occupied the unique position of acknowledging Hindu–Muslim differences as well as rejecting communal mechanisms for their resolution. "Hindus," he remarked, "shall never cease to be Hindus and Mohammedans shall never cease to be Mohammedans."[123] But recognition of this reality did not preclude a shared political life. He found "no reason why [Hindus and Muslims] cannot make common cause in political work."[124] But to try to create such solidarity within a communal framework would be a mistake and, in fact, a denial of genuine difference: "Nothing could be more disastrous to the success of representative institutions, than their constitution on a denominational basis."[125]

In the aftermath of the noncooperation movement of the early 1920s, Rai considered the demands of nationalist politics and the possibility of Hindu–Muslim unity. He saw a joint enterprise between communities as "not the merger or the absorption of one into the other, but the integration of all into one whole, without in any way injuring or lessening each group individually."[126] A shared political project need not deny religious communities spaces of autonomy. What frustrated Rai, however, was the superficial and indifferent treatment that the matter of representation had hitherto been given. Indian nationalists, he alleged, "have shouted Hindu–Muslim unity from a thousand platforms and from house-tops, in and out of season, but we have devoted little thought as to the process or processes by which we propose to achieve it."[127] What had emerged as a result was a "laissez-faire" approach where different communities had been engaged in competitive behavior to increase their power within the government, rather than shared principles that could make government as a whole responsible.[128]

He documented the spread of communal representation from Muslims to other groups, from legislative councils to local bodies, and from law-making bodies to public services and education. The trend was clear, and he viewed the mechanism as "a crude and clumsy device . . . likely to land us in difficulties which no one is thinking of at present."[129] The British had "created, fostered and nourished" this way of thinking and Indians had done little to imagine an alternative way of conceptualizing society.[130] For Rai, the fundamental intellectual error of his generation had been to either embrace a "collection of mutually warring, struggling, competing religious communities with chances of victory or domination for whatso-ever turns out to be the strongest, the most efficient, and the most powerful" or to argue for "a complete obliteration of all religious differences."[131]

Rai did not explicate a full-fledged theory of noncommunal represen-tation, but he did recognize that a secular political community could not take a sacrosanct position on every religious practice. Although religious belief may be beyond question, modern citizenship required the sacrificing of some portion of freedom.[132] For Rai, there was "no such thing as an absolute right vested in any individual or in any community forming part of a nation."[133] Just as one person's exercise of rights would inevitably clash with another person's rights, it was essential for rights to be "ad-justed and correlated that they might be exercised without doing injury to each other."[134] The regulation of rights depended on many factors, but it would in part rest on a distinction between religious practices that were essential and those that were nonessential.[135] He regretted how several religious reform movements had perpetuated the idea of religious rights being absolute. The movements among Sikhs and Muslims, the Arya Samaj, and so on, had all emphasized religious practices. Even Mohandas Gandhi's approach to the Khilafat movement had betrayed this sensi-bility, for he had chosen to give the movement a religious rather than a political hue.[136]

In providing a history of communal relations, Rai, like others, acknowl-edged the contribution of Syed Ahmed Khan. For him, Khan's fears were not without foundation, but the manner in which they had been posed had profoundly influenced the political arrangements that subsequently emerged.[137] In December 1925 Rai delivered the presidential address at the Bombay Hindu Mahasabha Conference. He used the opportunity to explain the self-perpetuating character of communal representation. A concession to one community would, he claimed, inevitably result in a concession to others, and political mobilization on community lines would only increase; community-based polarization was internal to the logic of the arrangement.[138] In the years preceding his death, Rai remained apprehensive about the direction Indian politics was taking and, more than two decades before British India was partitioned, predicted that "once you accept communal representation with separate electorates, there is no chance of its being abolished without a civil war."[139]

A second unusual intervention on representation was made by B. R. Ambedkar. His tract *Pakistan or the Partition of India* stands out for its unrelenting questioning of communal politics.[140] Initially published as *Thoughts on Pakistan* only months after the 1940 Lahore Resolution, the text viewed the problem of Pakistan as real. He rejected the idea that "the demand for Pakistan is the result of mere political distemper, which will pass away with the efflux of time."[141] The text was not a defense of the Muslim League's call for Pakistan, but it did show that the call could not be reduced to either prejudice or political strategy. It rested on claims that could not be summarily dismissed.

In the text, Ambedkar probed the impression that Hindus and Muslims formed one nation. They both may share experiences, speak the same language, enjoy relatable customs, and so forth, but none of this meant that they constituted one nation. The existing similarities were, for Ambedkar, "the result of certain purely mechanical causes."[142] They existed partly because even though some Hindus had converted to Islam, many such conversions were incomplete, thereby revealing shared social norms with Hindus. A further reason for similarities was that Hindus and Muslims had been exposed to a "common environment."[143] He moreover acknowledged the "remnants of a period of religious amalgamation between the Hindus and the Muslims" under the Mughal emperor Akbar, and referred to such remnants as "the result of a dead past which has no present and no future."[144] For Ambedkar, similarities between Hindus and Muslims had been falsely interpreted and mistakenly used to propose a theory of unity. He saw the past as offering no relief for supporters of an undivided India. Hindus and Muslims, he remarked, "have been just two armed battalions warring against each other."[145] There "was no cycle of participation for a common achievement," and what existed was "a past of mutual destruction, a past of mutual animosities, both in political as well as in the religious fields."[146] The unity was neither geographical (for this was the result of "nature") nor to do with ways of life (as this arose from an "exposure to a common environment") nor administrative (as shown by the easy partition of Burma in 1937 after over a century of being tied to India).[147] As far as he was concerned, any real union "must be founded on a sense of kinship, in the feeling of being kindred."[148] It was this fundamental spirit that he found missing.

The question was not only one of historical accuracy or consistency. There were, to be sure, issues pertaining to the past and to matters of principle that merited a response. Ambedkar pointed out, for instance, that "if the Hindus did not object to the severance of Burma from India, it is difficult to understand how the Hindus can object to the severance of an area like Pakistan, which . . . is politically detachable from, socially hostile and spiritually alien to, the rest of India."[149] He also observed that the Congress party had accepted territorial divisions on linguistic lines, and it was "no use saying that the separation of Karnatak and Andhra is based on a linguistic difference and that the claim to separation of Pakistan is based on a cultural difference."[150] Difference rooted in language was "simply another name for cultural difference."[151] However, the principal basis for the call for the creation of Pakistan was neither the validity of Muslim allegations of unfair treatment nor the reasonableness of the fears of Hindu tyranny. It was instead the same reason that Indian nationalists had given the British in the case for self-government: the consent of the governed.[152] Ambedkar felt that "the demand by a nationality for a national state does not require to be supported by any list of grievances."[153] For it to be justifiable, all it needs is the "will of the people."[154]

Ambedkar's *Pakistan or the Partition of India* drew attention to the gravity of the communal problem. Ambedkar attacked the Communal Award of 1932, which granted separate electorates in provincial and state legislatures and guaranteed weightage for Muslims in Hindu-majority provinces. He regarded it as "iniquitous inasmuch as it accords unequal treatment to the Hindu and Muslim minorities."[155] While in the Hindu provinces, the Muslim minority had the exclusive authority to "choose the kind of electorates it wants . . . in the Muslim provinces, it is the Muslim majority which is allowed to choose the kind of electorates it prefers and the Hindu minority is not permitted to have any say in the matter."[156] He also attacked the idea of communal provinces, for it left each majority province with significant minority populations. This scheme had been occasionally defended as promoting harmony by offering each community a chance to mistreat minorities, in the event that minorities were mistreated by the other community. Ambedkar took this to be depraved defense, an argument for a "system of protection, in which blast was to be met by counter-blast, terror by terror, and tyranny by tyranny."[157] The logic at work here, the "a system of communal hostages," offered no hope for enduring peace.[158]

For Ambedkar, the problem of Hindus and Muslims did not turn on their individual vices. He did reject several Hindu arguments that denied the individuality of Muslim identity, and he lamented the attitude of Muslim political leaders, who did not want to "recognize secular categories of life as the basis of their politics because to them it means the weakening of the community in its fight against the Hindus."[159] But the real issue was structural. The problem was "inherent in a situation where a minority is pitted against a majority"[160] and "sure to last as long as the Hindus and Muslims are required to live as members of one country under the mantle of a single constitution."[161] Ambedkar believed that it would be difficult to avoid such a problem with "two communities facing each other, one a majority and the other a minority, welded in the steel-frame of a single government."[162] The creation of Pakistan might solve the communal problem, though this would turn on how the boundaries were drawn. If the nation's boundaries tracked the North-West Provinces and Bengal, for example, that would exacerbate tensions: "The rule of the Hindu minorities by the Muslim majorities and the rule of the Muslim minorities by the Hindu majorities were the crying evils" of the proposed division.[163] Ambedkar concluded that an exit from the model of mixed states would be a superior solution to the communal problem, and thereby proposed the transfer of minorities.[164]

Throughout *Pakistan or the Partition of India*, we see Ambedkar's interest in the widespread failure to address Hindu–Muslim relations. Efforts to create harmony had been futile because the reality of difference had been ignored. This difference was not a function of material reasons. Rather, it was "formed by causes which take their origin in historical, religious, cultural and social antipathy, of which political antipathy is only a reflection."[165] Hindu nationalists and the Indian National Congress had failed to address the Muslim question effectively. The former simply sought to eradicate Muslims—their philosophy was "not merely arrogant but . . . arrant nonsense."[166] The latter mistakenly appeased the Muslim community, and the appeasement of demands and "policy of concession" had only increased Muslim aggression.[167]

In the revised edition of *Pakistan or the Partition of India,* Ambedkar added a new chapter that confirms that the book should not be seen as supporting the territorial division of British India. In the revised text, he went so far as to gesture at possible forms of a common political life organized around shared social and economic concerns. Rather than accept or reject the call for the partition of British India, Ambedkar's aim was to show that the call was serious and that acknowledging it in clear terms meant recognizing the inevitable tension that would persist in a united India. He was unclear on how precisely the division of territory would solve tensions in the Indian nation that remained. Hindustan, he noted, was likely to remain a state with Hindus and Muslims, unlike Pakistan, which could be imagined as a homogeneous entity. The spread of the Muslim population across India made it impossible to homogenize the population through the drawing of boundaries. At one place in the tract, Ambedkar appeared to suggest that Hindustan would still suffer from "disharmony" as a consequence of being "a composite state."[168] But subsequently he seemed more optimistic, predicting that each new territory that would be born could "become a strong and well-knit state"[169] and that a division would be better than "trading in safeguards which have proved so unsafe."[170] Pakistan may have "the demerit of cutting away parts of India," but it also had "the merit of introducing harmony in place of conflict."[171] Moving beyond the current communal scheme would liberate both Hindus and Muslims and take away their fears of tyranny and intrusion.[172] The partitioning of British India would result in two territories with greater internal homogeneity, and this could perhaps benefit both nations.[173]

Pakistan or the Partition of India reveals the extent to which Ambedkar confronted the representation dilemma. His essay is a remarkable account of the tensions involved in every possible solution to a framework structured around identity. The terms of the conversation had prevented any sustainable response. In Rai's and Ambedkar's contributions we find a recognition of just how unanswerable the problem of representation had become during the late colonial period, and a sense that a shared life would be possible only if matters were understood in a different manner. The only way to find some kind of enduring answer to the problem of representation would be to ask the question differently.

Citizens as Participants

When we come to terms with the stubborn hold that communal representation had on India's political imagination, the Constituent Assembly's turn away from such a conception is noteworthy. The Assembly rejected separate electorates, weighted representation, and reservations on the basis of religion. Only days before Indian independence and the partition of British India, Sardar Patel, in his capacity as chairman of the Advisory Committee on Minorities and Fundamental Rights, wrote to the president of the Assembly to explain why separate electorates had been rejected. The electoral scheme, he stated, "has, in the past, sharpened communal differences to a dangerous extent and has proved one of the main stumbling blocks to the development of a healthy national life."[174] He registered the Committee's view that it was "specially necessary to avoid these dangers in the new political conditions that have developed in the country."[175] In prior months, Indian leaders like Patel had openly declared that communal electorates were bound to encourage communal sentiments.[176] Mohandas Gandhi went so far as to remark that one "cannot have a healthy political life in any country where the electorates which should exercise the sovereign controlling power are based upon religion, race, creed, or caste."[177] Now, with the birth of two separate nations, such fears had been realized.

In the Constituent Assembly, Patel turned to the further decision to drop reservations based on religion. Previously such reservations had been permitted because "conditions were different and even the effect of partition was not fully comprehended or appreciated."[178] The *new conditions*— namely, the territorial split of British India—had changed matters and demonstrated the failure of communal representation on its own terms. What conclusions we draw from the division of territory turns on how we read the years preceding the end of colonial rule. For some participants in the Assembly, the lesson was not "abolishing even the niggardly safeguards that were given to the Muslims and other minorities . . . [but] giving them better and real safeguards."[179] But for a great many other members, the event of partition exposed the inability of communal representation to provide for a sustainable political environment. In response to the Muslim League's call for differentiated citizenship, Patel countered that such a scheme had already been tried and had led to the division of territory.[180] Notes and memoranda by members of the Assembly expressed the same sentiment. K. T. Shah, for example, lamented that "every attempt [to solve the problem of representation] has so far ended in failure, making the tension and virulence worse than ever before."[181] A sense emerged that the framework of identity, the search for a standard metric by which a citizen would be recognized, was the basis of the problem.

Muslims had been granted separate electorates by the Morley–Minto reforms of 1909.[182] The four decades following the 1909 reforms were spent trapped in power-sharing schemes of Byzantine complexity, ranging from territorial autonomy to separate electorates to weightage to reserved quotas. The failure of the 1946 Cabinet Mission Plan—which proposed a federation with strong provinces divided according to their religious makeup and a single center with limited powers—was the last stage in these game-theoretic proposals. A representative model centered on individual agency arose from the ruins of these schemes, out of an *internal* critique of communal representation. Such representation had engendered a form of politics where representatives were fated to speak with sole reference to their community. The system was condemned to endless negotiations over the appropriate balance of one community with another, until its logic left available no further option other than the breakdown of politics. The colonial schematic had long raised fairness concerns; now it even raised problems of stability.

The partition of British India dealt a blow to the Indian imagination. Partition brought elements of real tragedy, losses of life and livelihood, and a recasting as naïve the idea of civilizational unity that Gandhi and Nehru had taken to be India's destiny. Political events had followed their own rationality. What appeared to be artificial differences, gasps of momentary fear and insecurity, plaints that defied common sense, maneuvers of the imperial ideology, had split the South Asian subcontinent. Just as one could not escape the reality of what had occurred, one could not avoid its philosophical implications. Partition exposed the insistence and shortcomings of a politics performed through communal eyes. And it showed the power of such politics—its internal rules and justifications, its potential for disruption, and its capacity to transform. The partition of the colonial state revealed the plasticity of human passions, and in turn opened the door to a second, more normatively grounded rationale for noncommunal representation: the relationship between such representation and democracy.[183] There was the need for a principle that could stand above India's diversity—a principle that could avoid Savarkar's trap—rather than the perpetuation of a schema that would categorize citizens and view their groupings as permanent.

The lesson of the partition of British India was that no internal formulation could resolve the problem of representation if majority and minority groups were taken as established and unchangeable. In such a scenario, groups with numerical strength would insist on majority rule, while those who lacked the security of numbers would fear oppression. "Partition," it has been correctly noted, "was a non-solution, but a non-solution to a problem that had proved insoluble."[184] But how could one pose the problem differently? The answer lay in moving away from a representative framework that sought to express identities that were regarded as stable and fixed, and in moving toward a model of citizenship centered on the political participation of individuals. Such a model would allow the categories of majority and minority to be constantly defined and redefined within the fluid domain of politics, and it would thereby offer the greatest form of security. Previously, communal schemes like separate electorates and weighted representation had been regarded as anti-democratic in the elementary sense that they did not neatly respect the preference of the majority.[185] Now, with the shift in focus engendered by the partition of territory, further reflection ensued on the meaning of political participation in a free society. A self-governing polity, India's founders contended, called for a conception of representation that was unlike that present in an autocratic state. The Congress party leader Govind Ballabh Pant underlined this difference in a famous speech on separate electorates:

> In the olden days, whatever be the name under which our Legislatures functioned, in reality they were no more than advisory bodies. The ultimate power was vested in the British and the British Parliament was the ultimate arbiter of our destiny. So long as the power was vested in the foreigners, I could understand the utility of separate electorates. Then perhaps the representatives of different communities could pose as the full-fledged advocates of their respective communities and as the decision did not rest with the people of the country they could satisfy themselves with that position. But it is not merely a question of advocacy now. It is a question of having an effective decisive voice in the affairs and in the deliberations of the Legislatures and the Parliament of this free country. Even if in an advisory capacity one were a very good advocate, he cannot be absolutely of any use whether to his clients or to himself if the Judge whom he has to address does not appreciate his arguments, sentiments or feelings, and there is no possibility of the Advocate ever becoming a Judge. I want the Advocate to have also before him the prospect of becoming a Judge. In the new status that

we have now secured, every citizen in this country should in my opinion be able to rise to the fullest stature and always have the opportunity of influencing the decisions effectively; so I believe separate electorates will be suicidal to the minorities and will do them tremendous harm.[186]

As far as Pant was concerned, the question was whether citizens were recipients or participants. The state in a democracy was a collaborative project, not a paternal entity. A representative model that attended to communities rather than individuals did not involve such voluntary collaboration. Instead, by balancing fixed interests, it created "rival loyalties" rather than one form of association "centered round the state."[187] But this sat oddly with the idea of self-rule, for to be a democratic citizen meant to participate in a joint venture. It meant to exercise agency in determining the outcomes that the enterprise produced. This conception was linked in significant ways to the idea of equality: people were equal in part because they were equal partners in a collective political project. To deny this was, in some elemental sense, to deny that every voter should have equal impact on the electoral system.[188]

The anthropology behind such reasoning is worth unpacking. One's preconceived identity mattered even if one could vote independently: when people conceive of someone in a certain way, the person is required to respond to that conception, and this very fact results in their identity being reordered.[189] For India's founders, one could not be a political agent unless one's political identity was self-created. Without this, there was little sense in which a person's actions could count as theirs. In the colonial era, much contestation had taken place over the accuracy of contrasting representative claims. The Indian National Congress and the Muslim League, for example, often challenged one another over which party spoke for India's Muslims. Such contests had some rationale in situations without universal suffrage. One had to *divine* the real representative of a certain section of the population, and communal representation was understood to be a way to reflect the interests of different communities. But such reasoning was unsuitable in democratic conditions because people could now choose their representatives for themselves. Their views did not need to be inferred.

Both communal representation under colonialism and noncommunal representation under democracy were, by certain yardsticks, forms of *representation*. But whereas the former involved the representation of one's predetermined identity, the latter related to the representation of one's vote. By forcing a democratic people into communally organized categories, one could not enable this latter form of representation.[190] A model of communal representation was centered on reflecting a predetermined composition of society. In such a framework, being a representative was not about having authority but instead about being accountable for the exercise of that authority. It was a means of offering information rather than acting, a way to stand in for another.[191] In other words, the colonial model focused on the type of person that one happened to be rather than the actions one performed. Here, as it has been observed in a study of descriptive representation, "what seems important is less what the legislature does than how it is composed."[192] One problem with this, as many Indians saw, was that the recognition of communal distinctions would mean the disavowal of many other distinctions.[193] The schema, in and of itself, did not provide guidance for negotiating between cleavages.

But the more serious problem with the colonial approach, as Indians later came to understand, was the denial of agency. Such representation necessarily proceeded on the assumption that individuals within certain groups would act collectively and in specific ways. They were denied the capacity to deliberate and act for themselves as individuals.[194] In the framing of citizenship prior to India's independence, the "majority" and "minority" groups were taken to be permanent ones. The imperial ideology predetermined the attributes that were salient for politics, and it thereby predetermined how individuals would act. When the Indian Franchise Committee rejected universal suffrage in 1932, its alternative proposal was to "give reasonable representation to the main categories of the population."[195] In this way it condemned voters to those categories. One can see why such a viewpoint would disturb a democratic sensibility. A core justification for voting is that it treats individuals as *agents*. This is why, for example, voting is preferable to mechanisms like a lottery, because individual preferences *contribute* to the common life that is created.[196] It is a form of participation by which one can bring about an outcome. India's founders would now and again describe communal arrangements in much the same way as they described the princely kingdoms: both were taken to be relics from an age long past. Setting aside the rhetorical apparatus at work here, there is a crucial sense in which communal arrangements were premodern. A hallmark of modernity was the idea that one's political universe could be constructed: it was neither inherited nor natural. To be a citizen in the modern world was to be a participant in an act of creation. To presuppose the set of individuals who constitute a majority is to disallow that set from being an outcome of individual agency. The entire promise of a majoritarian decision-making process—the central organizing feature of modern democracies—is, after all, that it provides persons with the capacity to construct the majority by offering them a neutral mechanism for making decisions where each participant is treated equally.[197] It is not that a "majority" and "minority" are empowered by the institution of democracy. More fundamentally, they are created by it, and it is this fact that provides salience to the familiar features of democratic politics ranging from public reasoning to bargaining to persuasion. Thus, the idea of *agency* is related to the idea of *authority*. In the colonial system of identification, a person's identity gave him or her the authority to speak on behalf of another person sharing the same identity, whereas in a democratic order, authority was acquired through the process of authorization.

Recent scholarship has paid careful attention to the relationship between political identities and the colonial state. It has been recognized, for example, that the colonial construction of identity was "not only a way of acknowledging difference but also . . . a way of shaping, and sometimes even creating, difference," and that the use of legal measures "to manage and reproduce difference" was vital to this enterprise.[198] The process of enumeration conducted by the colonial state had three crucial implications: it meant that a community now had a sense of its numerical strength, and this empowered it to act as a collective; it resulted in a community becoming an abstract entity with features and characteristics that each member of the community was seen to possess; and it signified that the community was the site of agency.[199] The belief that the British engineered Hindu–Muslim conflict had animated Indian political thought for much of the first half of the twentieth century. Now, with the partition of British India and the advent of democracy, this idea acquired a very particular form. Previously, the British role in communal politics had been emphasized to deny the reality of such politics. But the trajectory of communal politics had made such denial impossible. It had become clear that such politics had acquired a life of its own. The British role was now highlighted to show how identities could change. The colonial scheme of representation had *made* some differences politically salient. To put the point simply, the colonial vision of representation had shown that representation could create its own reality.[200] It had demonstrated that Hindu–Muslim conflict *could* be engineered. This hard lesson enabled a radical, even gratifying, take on democracy. The classification and enumeration performed by the colonial state had accorded permanence and tangibility to the social world. But the imagery sketched by democratic life, with its shifting conceptions of majorities and minorities, was radically distinct and rested on the fluidity of political identities. The world prior to colonial citizenship has been accurately described as "a world of minorities, because this world was not governed by a form of politics which would make a statistical majority a vital principle of advantage."[201] And it has been correctly stated that, for this reason, it is "deeply misleading . . . to suggest, even absent-mindedly, that there were majorities and minorities before the colonial enumeration process."[202]

Politics under democratic conditions was understood to be something other than the effective advocacy of preset interests. The adoption of communal categories in a democracy would only isolate predefined minorities.[203] The rationale for such categories under autocratic rule had vanished with the arrival of popular authorization. To have frozen interests was to be antipolitical, for it was to presume that certain interests were fixed and outside the realm of politics. In this fundamental way, communal representation was viewed as incompatible with the idea of modern democratic citizenship. The belief that the presence of varying religious commitments in a single society would necessarily result in a certain kind of behavior contradicted the view that individuals in that society would have the power to act as they wished. Such a belief would be at odds with the very basis of democratic authority—namely, that individuals were governed by laws because such laws had been freely created by them. The argument against a correspondence between real or imagined social realities and political action was an extension of the anticolonial argument that denied the difference between the British and Indians: it followed from the claim that an Indian could be *any* kind of person.[204]

The argument from agency had both an individual and a collective dimension. With regard to the former, it meant that a citizen would be self-governing because his or her relationship with the state would not be mediated by a predestined identity. In terms of the latter, it meant that citizens would relate differently to one another and consequently occupy a different shared identity. In Chapter 2 we saw how the turn from localism involved a new kind of intersubjectivity. The same is true for the rejection of communal representation. In both cases, the very constitution of one's identity as a citizen was itself a form of freedom. To be recognized by the state in abstract and impersonal terms was a form of equality:

each person was anonymized. This made possible the association between freedom and the state, because it required state power to be not only an outcome of collective decision-making but also a form of coercion that would be justifiable to all persons regardless of who they were. The absence of such a justification had been an important feature of the fragility and tension experienced in communal representation.

The rejection of communal representation was an act of some political imagination.[205] To give Indians the right to vote without giving them the right to determine their interests would be to imagine that they were only capable of associating on communal terms. This would be to hold that they lacked the capacity to form other kinds of arrangements and act on other considerations.[206] This turn from communal representation was made possible by the recognition that—as the colonial period had so powerfully shown—any kind of political identity would be not only a form of recognition but also an act of construction. Mohammad Ali Jinnah's achievement lay in posing the problem of representation at a time when few others were willing to address this issue. His failure lay in an intransigent commitment to an earlier form of politics. He tried to place an old model of representation onto a new system, which unsurprisingly territorialized the question at hand. For Jinnah, it was impossible to imagine that political life might be performed on different terms. Indeed, the limits of his thought are best captured by his demand for a separate state, for the underlying premise of such a demand was that minorities would have security only within an arrangement that converted them into a majority.[207] For India's founders, the practical failure of communal arrangements and the constitutive promise of democracy suggested a different hypothesis.

The Caste Question

We have thus far considered why representation centered on collective identities was rejected by India's founders. The context for our study has been the relationship between political representation and religious difference. But this was not the only association that posed a challenge for citizenship. The institution of caste—specifically, the condition of lower-caste groups—was an additional matter of concern. At India's founding, the Constitution permitted reserved quotas for such groups, a fact that seems at odds with the turn away from communal representation. Why was group-based representation rejected when it came to Muslims but granted when it came to the lower castes? Some scholars have viewed the stance toward lower-caste groups as indicative of the Constitution's ambivalence and paradoxical orientation.[208] Some have regarded it as an acknowledgment of the limitations of formal equality and the exceptional status of lower-caste groups.[209] For some, it has encouraged the telling of the story of Indian citizenship through a less conceptually unifying narrative. The effort has been to study each case by itself, distinguishing between the Muslim dilemma and lower-caste dilemma as shaped by the separate concerns of majoritarian rule and discrimination, respectively.[210]

There is some virtue in these approaches, but there is another way to understand the treatment of caste. I shall argue that reserved quotas for the lower castes were determined by concerns pertaining to democracy, and should be understood as falling under the same normative umbrella as the rejection of communal representation. This rejection was driven by a distinct conception of citizenship. A member of a democratic society was seen as a political participant. Communal representation was suitable for societies where one was a subject rather than an agent. The conceptual unity that I hope to capture is partly achieved by better understanding the precise commitment toward lower-caste groups, a matter that has received surprisingly little scrutiny. Though it may appear *ex facie* that preferential treatment was a way to recognize a group identity, the approach to caste was, as in the case of religion, driven by a desire to unchain imposed group identities and liberate the individual. A study of the problem of caste helps us understand why the same objective resulted in somewhat different constitutional arrangements.[211]

From the 1920s onward, largely due to the efforts of B. R. Ambedkar, *dalits* (outcastes, once called untouchables) emerged as a distinct political category. Their historical encounter with discrimination and exclusion was novel. Ambedkar's writings are worth investigating not least because he was among the first thinkers to theorize about the possibilities and limitations of group representation under democratic conditions. His writings betray various, sometimes incompatible, points of view, experimenting as he did with different negotiating positions to safeguard the interests of lower-caste groups. He nonetheless expressed a number of consistent beliefs. One of his most significant claims was that the caste system was artificial. The text of his 1936 speech "The Annihilation of Caste" charged the system with creating the "unnatural division of laborers into watertight compartments."[212] "In no other country," Ambedkar noted, "is the division of labor accompanied by this gradation of laborers."[213] Thus, caste was not merely a division of labor but was also a division of laborers. The *unnatural* character of the institution meant, in the first instance, that the division was "not spontaneous" and "not based on natural aptitudes."[214] Rather than allowing people to choose their careers, the caste system was "an attempt to appoint tasks to individuals in advance, selected not on the basis of trained original capacities, but on that of the social status of the parents."[215] By being "based on the dogma of predestination," it prevented people from being themselves.[216]

But the system was also unnatural in a related but somewhat different way: it was not founded on any racial distinction. As per Ambedkar's reading, the caste system "came into being long after the different races of India had commingled in blood and culture."[217] There was no racial affinity, for example, between a Brahmin of the Punjab and a Brahmin of Madras. Instead of depicting a difference between races, caste was a social division between members of the same race. To buttress this point, Ambedkar gave the example of subcastes: "If caste means race then differences of sub-castes cannot mean differences of race because sub-castes become *ex hypothesia* sub-divisions of one and the same race. Consequently the bar against intermarrying and inter-dining between sub-castes cannot be for the purpose of maintaining purity of race or of blood."[218] The link between caste and race had been a notable feature in Indian political thought. In distinguishing between the two, Ambedkar was departing from the previous generation of anti-caste thinkers like Jotirao Phule—a major figure who had confronted upper-caste authority and focused on the spread of education. In his 1873 text *Gulamgiri* (Slavery), Phule had compared caste with race in America, referring to the treatment toward both the lower castes and blacks as slavery. He argued that "the only difference between [the lower castes in India] and the slaves in America is that whereas the blacks were captured and sold as slaves, the *shudras* and *atishudras* were conquered and enslaved by the *bhats* and Brahmins."[219] Apart from this fact, however, there was no difference between the two groups. For Phule, a common feature of both caste-based discrimination and slavery was the psychological impact on the victim. Like slaves in America, India's *shudras* had come to internalize narratives of their own inferiority. They had been socialized into not only accepting their condition but resisting their liberation.[220] Phule felt that the "arguments of the Brahmins have been imprinted so firmly on the minds of the *shudras* that they, like the negro slaves in America, oppose the very people who are willing to fight for them, and free them from the chains of slavery."[221] Ambedkar's writings are filled with similar explorations of the psychological burdens of inequality, but his view that race presented a misplaced analogy was crucial to the claim that caste was unique—in its invention and in its domination.[222]

For Ambedkar, showing that caste was an unnatural institution was crucial to arguing that it *could* be eradicated. The next stage in his argument was an explication of the problem of caste. Here Ambedkar drew a relationship between democracy, fraternity, and inequality. The hallmark of the caste system was the status that it bestowed on different individuals. Those who belonged to particular caste groups were fated to choose occupations and perform lives differently from those that belonged to others. Certain tasks and rituals were kept for members of lower-caste groups, and the performance of these tasks and rituals enforced and entrenched their degraded status. The caste system consisted in not only the differentiation between but also the registering of particular groups—and the tasks they performed and lives they lived—as less worthy than others. This compulsory status was undoubtedly a form of inequality, but for Ambedkar it was also fundamentally undemocratic.

Hindus, he observed in "The Annihilation of Caste," did not constitute a society: "Men do not become a society by living in physical proximity any more than a man ceases to be a member of his society by living so many miles away from other men."[223] What prevented Hindus from constituting a society was the lack of communication. This fact disabled common activity and made it impossible to share in one another's feelings and emotions. Caste kept people in "isolated pockets," and individuals could not exit the caste system because of the caste group's right of excommunication.[224] In "The Annihilation of Caste" Ambedkar drew an analogy between *chaturvarnya,* a Hindu schema that divided society into four classes, and Plato's *Republic.* Both had wrongly concluded that individuals could be slotted into definite classes. In both cases, there was a rejection of the person and the absence of civic reciprocity. In claiming that fraternity was essential for democratic life, Ambedkar relied on materials that included John Dewey's work on the interactive spirit of self-rule and Thomas Carlyle's idea of "organic filaments" in *Sartor Resartus.*[225]

In prior years Ambedkar had similarly observed the segregation that caste practices like endogamy perpetuated.[226] He had noted that it was the "isolation of the groups that is the chief evil."[227] What political independence required was not only the absence of social divisions but, more significantly, a shared sense of community. Fraternity was communication, participation, and interaction between groups. In 1945, in an essay attacking the Congress party and Gandhi, Ambedkar stated that India lacked the "endosmosis between groups" that had in Europe created "a society which can be depended upon for community of thought, harmony of purposes and unity of action."[228] Different caste groups in India were not merely "non-social," but were actively "anti-social."[229] The institution of caste meant that individuals would not see one another as equal citizens, and modern democratic politics would thus be impossible to achieve.

The interdependence of democracy, fraternity, and inequality was crucial to Ambedkar's thought, but it did not by itself help determine how one should respond to the problem of caste. In the colonial era Ambedkar's primary concern was the restrictions on franchise that had led to the *de facto* exclusion of lower-caste groups. As a consequence, he poured his energy into seeing that lower-caste groups receive some kind of representation. At that time he flirted with numerous possible strategies to make this possible. In 1919 his submissions to the Southborough Committee on Franchise included the interesting argument that instead of lower-caste groups being offered separate electorates or reserved seats, they should instead benefit from "a low-pitched franchise."[230] By making the franchise for the non-Brahmin even lower than the franchise for the Brahmin, "the Marathas would improve their position on the voters' list and the altogether favored position of the Brahmin would be equalized."[231] The disproportionate influence that Brahmins exerted could be mitigated only by reducing their influence in politics. He believed that both communal representation and reservations for lower-caste groups could be avoided by the extension of franchise.[232] But he also suggested that communal electorates could enable "a new cycle of participation in which the representatives of various castes who were erstwhile isolated and therefore antisocial will be thrown into an associated life."[233]

Yet, speaking before the Simon Commission in 1928, he characterized the "depressed classes" as "a distinct and independent minority" and sought reserved seats if they were accompanied by the introduction of universal franchise.[234] In the absence of universal franchise, the demand was for separate electorates.[235] Communal electorates, he openly suggested, were "an evil" and "adult suffrage should be introduced not only because of its inherent good but because it can enable us to get rid of the evil of communal electorates."[236] Ambedkar denied that any community, such as Muslims, had special interests that were not shared by the general public.

But even if such interests existed, he contended, they would be better served through a system of joint electorates. A system of communal electorates would condemn a minority to its allotted share. Under the joint system, however, much greater fluidity was possible.[237] He adopted the same position at the Roundtable Conference in 1930, declaring, "If you give us adult universal suffrage, the Depressed Classes . . . will be prepared to accept joint electorates and reserved seats; but if you do not give us adult suffrage, then we must claim representation through separate electorates."[238] In 1943 he called for the untouchables to be represented as a separate category.[239] He suggested that separate electorates were "the only mechanism by which real representation can be guaranteed to the untouchables."[240] Whereas political majorities and minorities were "fluid bodies," the case of the Hindus and untouchables was different.[241]

As we can see, Ambedkar's stance on lower-caste representation under colonialism varied over time. Despite this variance, two themes recur: First, that the kind of protection lower-caste groups might require would at least in part turn on the franchise restrictions in operation. The calculation on behalf of such groups was made by factoring in the extent of the franchise and the limitations on the right to vote. Second, that a constitutional scheme cannot ignore the reality of caste. In one form or another, it would have to be confronted. Every constitutional system, he noted in 1945, had its own set of safeguards to consider. The checks and balances required in the Indian system were those that counteracted upper-caste oppression.[242] "Self-government and democracy become real," he argued, "not when a constitution based on adult suffrage comes into existence but when the governing class loses its power to capture the power to govern."[243] He had similarly stated, only a couple of years previously, that the principal failure of India's politicians was their presumption that democracy is simply a form of government. He proposed the alternative understanding that a "democratic form of government presupposes a democratic form of society."[244] What this required, among other things, was "a social organization free from rigid social barriers."[245]

How such barriers were to be broken was a question that came to be answered in the Constituent Assembly. With the introduction of universal suffrage, an opportunity arose for the caste question to be addressed in a comprehensive fashion. The question of representation was no longer framed under conditions of restricted suffrage. The first order of business was a careful reexamination of the exact problem at hand. Here, what was vital was the recognition that caste and religion tendered fundamentally distinct problems. In the case of religion, the challenge was to strike a balance between a common politics and distinct religious faiths—what can loosely be called accommodation. With regard to caste, however, the aim was not survival but extinction. India's founders envisioned a country where many religions could thrive, and where one's identity as a political agent was not tied to one's religious affiliation. But when it came to caste, the ambition was to put an end to the institution—to eliminate the markers it created and the practices it encompassed. Caste involved no group identity to protect, only an identity to dismantle.

The twin objectives of annihilating caste and securing the lower castes posed a puzzle for political representation.[246] The explicit recognition of caste threatened to make permanent an identity that Ambedkar and several other members in the Assembly had characterized as contingent. The schemes of descriptive representation under colonial rule had turned caste-based social practices into a concrete, firm legal identity.[247] Such an approach risked confirming instead of annihilating this constructed identity, so it is clear why the special recognition of caste might have been the subject of concern. But it is worth asking why such recognition was thought to be valuable in the first place. What exactly was inadequate about a policy of constitutional silence?

To answer this, we must recall the constraints that forced identities imposed on individualism. Unlike in the case of religion, the identities created by the caste system were both compulsory and hierarchical. The various caste groups were not merely different; they were *categorically different*. The concern with constitutional silence—that is, with indifference to caste in the political domain—was that Indian society would remain untransformed and the power of the upper castes would stay intact. Given the force of caste-based practices, the worry was that extrapolitical forms of power could dominate the sphere of the political. This is similar to the contemporary fear of concentrated economic or social power translating into political power.[248] In the case of caste, the concern was that upper-caste groups' power over lower-caste groups could infiltrate democratic politics, making it impossible to insulate public institutions from social forces. For individual liberty to be realized, the stubborn practices of superior groups needed to end. Because the democratic individual could emerge only when the energy exerted by powerful blocs was reduced, it was deemed necessary that the Constitution diminish the power of dominant groups in order to achieve the individualization of identity.

Domination could occur where powerful, obstinate hierarchies existed. Seeing the problem through this lens—where domination was the problem—led to an effort at abstraction. A category of "backwardness" was developed, which could in principle be filled by any group but was at the time neatly applicable to the lower castes.[249] The groups that one might regard as backward would depend on a range of socioeconomic factors extant at the time. A mutable category like backwardness allowed for any group to be the subject of special treatment. The concept of backwardness, K. M. Munshi noted, "signifies that a *class of people*—does not matter whether you call them untouchables or touchables, belonging to this community or that—a class of people who are so backward that special protection is required in the services."[250] The focus on backwardness shows that there was no particular group identity that the Constitution sought to protect. It did not aim to enable freedom *through* a group association. The fact that it was lower-caste groups that needed protection at the time was a contingent outcome. That there was no caste identity to protect, no balancing between caste groups to be performed, is evidenced not least by the fact that the preferential treatment toward caste groups in particular was seen as temporary.

For Ambedkar, the concept of "backwardness" could reconcile the equality of opportunity with the inclusion of specific communities in public life. The former principle held that "every individual who is qualified for a particular post should be free to apply for that post, to sit for examinations and to have his qualifications tested so as to determine whether he is fit for the post or not."[251] Ambedkar recognized that one could hold that a strict reading of this principle disabled any form of preferential treatment. But he also acknowledged the contrasting perspective that "although theoretically it is good to have the principle that there shall be equality of opportunity, there must at the same time be a provision made for the entry of certain communities which have so far been outside the administration."[252] This is where backwardness entered the picture. The concept of backwardness ensured that any scheme of reservations would have to be sensitive to the principle of equality of opportunity. For example, reservations would have to be "confined to a minority of seats," and if, say, they were made for 70 percent of public jobs and only 30 percent were left unreserved, such a proposal would be invalid.[253] This illustration captured the relative character of the proposal: a group could be considered backward only when it was placed in the context of other groups that were less backward. The confining of reservations to a minority of seats made the concept of backwardness intelligible because the halfway mark signified the statistical mean that would make such relative judgments possible.

A further attribute of backwardness was its capacity to serve a "qualifying" role.[254] To receive preferential treatment, it was not enough to simply belong to a minority. The Sikh community, for instance, was a numerical minority but it was denied special treatment because it was not backward relative to other communities.[255] The Constituent Assembly's subcommittee noted that the Sikh community did not suffer from any handicap and was therefore ineligible for any distinct treatment.[256] As one member in the Assembly stated, "The fundamental question is whether the Sikhs are a backward community either socially, educationally, or economically or even in any other sphere . . . they are not."[257] The issue was the counteracting of dominant forces outside the domain of politics, not the blanket recognition of a community on the basis of its size.

The turn to backwardness also captured the distinction between the problems of discrimination and representation. In 1930, at the First Roundtable Conference in London, Ambedkar had remarked that the "Depressed Classes are not entitled, under present circumstances, to certain civic rights which the other minorities by law enjoy."[258] Here he pointed to discriminatory practices in employment, the use of public spaces and public transport, the use of public utilities, and so on. With such practices in mind, Ambedkar demanded the outlawing of untouchability and an antidiscrimination regime.[259] The Constitution gave effect to this demand. It contained not only a general equal protection clause but also a wide set of antidiscrimination provisions and explicitly outlawed practices such as untouchability.[260] The problem of discrimination was addressed through the framework of rights. It may not be wrong to see this as capturing the relative substitutability between rights and representation: both can be viewed as mechanisms for the protection of weak groups.[261] But though a certain functional similarity between rights and representation may exist, it should be noted that the phenomena of backwardness and discrimination were analytically distinct. A member of a backward group might be more at risk of being subject to discriminatory state action, but discriminatory state action that was without legitimate basis was a problem regardless of the person who was targeted. Conversely, a group might be backward—say, as a result of economic inequality—without that backwardness translating into serious discrimination. Yet such economic inequality would need tackling not least because of the influence of wealth over the political process (even if the laws that were generated satisfied antidiscrimination norms). Special representation for backward groups was not, in other words, an aid to antidiscrimination. Insofar as discrimination was a problem, it was met by the rights regime that was put in place. And the limitations of such a regime would have to be addressed by the creation of a more effective rights regime. Here, as previously, abstraction could articulate the problem at hand. Caste-based discrimination raised concerns about unequal state action. A regime of rights could respond to such action regardless of whether the inequality, in any given instance, rested on caste prejudice.

One final point may be made about this constitutional settlement. The ideological differences between Mohandas Gandhi and B. R. Ambedkar on the subject of caste are familiar.[262] Both leaders were responsible for making caste a concern of national importance, and both strove hard for the abolition of untouchability. But whereas Ambedkar sought the explicit recognition of lower-caste groups, Gandhi viewed special treatment as a form of segregation. Gandhi also resisted Ambedkar's reading of Hinduism, as exemplified by the exchanges that followed Ambedkar's "The Annihilation of Caste." The contrast was between Gandhi's internal approach to change, both in the sense of the individual and in terms of Hinduism, and Ambedkar's call for structural reform. Like Ambedkar, Gandhi sought to delegitimize the caste system, but he identified society rather than the state as the site of alteration. Gandhi had feared that preferential legal measures would engender rigidity, that converting lower-caste groups into a distinct statutory category would only further their exclusion.[263] The difference between Muslims and untouchables was that recognition in the latter case would result in the perpetuation of a fixed identity: "The Mussalmans will never cease to be Mussalmans by having separate electors. Do you want the untouchables to remain untouchables forever? Well, the separate electorates would perpetuate the stigma."[264] For Gandhi, the distinction between a *de facto* outcome and a *de jure* one was crucial. Future legislatures would do well to be entirely composed of the lower castes, but the entry of such members should occur through the channels of politics.[265]

Much of the contrast between Gandhi and Ambedkar is well known, but for our purpose it is interesting to see the Constitution's eventual framework in light of this contest. The Constitution's final arrangement on caste reflects Ambedkar's views, not Gandhi's, but its details capture a shared feature of their thought—the discomfort with caste recognition in and of itself. It is sometimes suggested that the Constitution "mandated" caste-based reservations for lower-caste groups.[266] This way of framing matters is misleading, though, because the Constitution permitted such measures and the description confuses a permissive legal rule with a mandatory one, and because it does not accurately represent the nature of beneficiary identification. The possibility of special treatment was driven by the social and educational circumstances of a group—circumstances that applied at India's founding to members of particular castes—and not by the sense that there was something essential about the group's condition. By requiring the state to justify the preferential treatment on principle, the treatment could be legitimized and made acceptable to those that did not receive it. The turn to an abstract constitutional principle thus achieved elements of both what Gandhi desired and what Ambedkar desired, because it meant that the special treatment toward the lower castes was the *consequence* rather than the *object* of the constitutional arrangement.

Conclusion

In previous chapters we saw that the codification of rules and the centralization of state authority were means to address prevailing ways of thinking and existing webs of association, and to engineer deliberation in a manner applicable to a self-governing regime. In this chapter, we have considered a third element in the creation of a democratic citizen: the framework of representation. Here India's founders drew a different image of the nation than the one they had inherited from colonialism and reimagined the possibility of representation in a divided society under conditions of universal suffrage. That is to say, they reevaluated the political implications of India's social makeup.

In the context of religion, the breakdown of Hindu-Muslim relations and the disunion of British India had underscored the limits of communal representation. This collapse came in conjunction with a fresh understanding of representation in a setting involving popular authorization. The failure of communal representation was partly caused by a transition away from its previous nonterritorial, functional character. Once controversies over communal representation traversed into questions of territory, its internal logic had no resolution to offer. But the territorializing of communal representation was itself a consequence of its conceptual structure.

It was the next stage in the contestation between communities. In addition to its political and practical failure, communal representation came to be seen as limited for normative reasons: it would condemn citizens to predetermined, compulsory identities. A modern democratic state was conceptualized as one where people could create their own political identities and could authorize and effectuate change by exercising preferences in their capacity as agents.

The prevalence of caste gave rise to a slightly different problem than that advanced by religion, though in both cases the Constitution sought to immobilize forces that limited individualism. The caste question invited attention to the power exercised by groups over individuals. Caste-based domination was so entrenched that the problem could not be entirely solved by suffrage. In the face of strong and invidious group identities, the path to the individualization of identity lay in permitting special treatment toward members of groups that had remained constrained. The Constitution posited an overarching principle for beneficiary identification, one that considered the relative positioning of peoples, the potential for historical and social change, and the burden of justification for authority to be legitimized. Whether in the case of religion or caste, the hope that was the Constitution would liberate individuals and allow them to participate in politics as free and equal persons.

Conclusion

Constitutional Democracy Today

The majority of the world's constitutions were written in the past three decades.[1] The crafting of canonical legal texts has become as ubiquitous a political reality as the existence of nation-states.[2] But constitution-making in the age after the mid-twentieth-century postcolonial moment has been more than merely widespread: it has been an attempt to negotiate unfamiliar and uncertain waters. Unlike the revolutions of the late eighteenth century, whose public image still informs so many cries for freedom, contemporary revolutions have occurred in regions characterized by low levels of education and economic growth, intense ethnic and social divisions, and immediate rather than gradual democratization. For the writers of constitutions in such conditions, much of recent world history is not reassuring. But what it can offer is some historical precedent. The Indian founding is the critical reference point for such constitutional moments.

Though constitutions have become omnipresent, concern has grown over their capacity to produce radical change. Whether constitutions are perceived as complicit in the grand ills of our time, modest tools for social management, or silent bystanders to other realities, they have spread just as their influence is increasingly being questioned. It is thus not all that surprising that the key themes in this book—the significance of shared rules, the consequence of common authority, and the logic behind the construction of identities—resonate so deeply with our present controversies. In studies on the character of the state, the role of representative bodies, the place of supranational and subnational institutions, and the political recognition of difference, we are left wondering whether the ex-pectations that were once associated with self-rule in the modern world can ever be realized.[3]

Our present-day concerns over the spread and survival of constitu-tional democracy share similarities with the perspectives that once ratio-nalized colonial rule. For the imperial ideology of the nineteenth century, democracy could not travel wherever it pleased. Its existence and dura-bility were linked to specific historical and sociological conditions, which countries like India lacked. To recall the conceptual foundations of modern India is to recall how such concerns were met. Indians challenged the very logic of colonialism, claiming that imperial rule had given India a partic-ular historical and sociological construction, and that India's reality could be changed by an alternative political ordering. To create a democratic citizen, the new arrangement would have to provide Indians with new kinds of knowledge and power. This was the central aim of the constitu-tional proposal studied in this book. The manner in which rules were cod-ified, the state was conceived, and representation was formulated could disable the established forms of understanding, displace prevailing notions of authority, and move beyond accepted methods of identification. Each aspect of the scheme shared a relationship to the idea of self-government, for each liberated Indians from associations and constraints that mini-mized the individual. The consequence of the constitutional arrangement was that Indians would view themselves and one another differently, and a democratic citizen would thereby emerge from the practices of demo-cratic politics.

In recognizing this, one must acknowledge that India's founders held a certain conception of a democratic citizen. Like the imperialists that they fought, the makers of modern India too sought an enlightened politics. They did not attack the idea of modernity or the attributes of constitu-tional democracy.[4] Indeed, Indian nationalists fought for these alien ideals with hope and fury. Why should Indians, they frequently asked, be gov-erned by a different concept of freedom? The birth of the postcolonial state was a conversation between Western and non-Western possibilities and burdens, but it was above all an affirmation of a certain kind of uni-versalism. In asking what it might mean to be Indian, the nation's founders were asking what it might mean to be free individuals, persons who ruled themselves. This necessitated both an inquiry into the transformation of Indian society in its journey through colonialism, as well as a dialogue with Western political concepts. The rejection of imperial ideology was a universalist rejection, and it serves as a reminder that the postcolonial world is not, in fact, postcolonial but instead a space that once was colonized.[5]

The universalism of India's founding moment is borne out by the striking fact that the anticolonial struggle, despite its fervent attack on foreign rule, did not turn away from India's problems. Many of the major figures that have been studied in this book, such as Jawaharlal Nehru and B. R. Ambedkar, believed that Indian society was perforated with forms of life where power was personalized, and the sense of a collective was far from present. Their unflinching critiques of Indian society made such figures revolutionary. Where they departed from the imperial ideology was in their understanding of the causes and consequences of this situation, in seeing its assumptions and conclusions as entailed by a particular political project. The path to an enlightened politics did not lie in an enlightened despotism. Rather, it lay in the practices of politics itself. This claim was radical in the sense that it would alter Indian life in its most elemental aspects. It was a claim driven by the thought that Indians, like men and women elsewhere, were the products of circumstances to which they were not doomed. The imperial project had granted itself more knowledge of the social world than it was entitled to have. As Mohandas Gandhi had observed in *Hind Swaraj:* "The English . . . have a habit of writing history; they pretend to study the manners and customs of all peoples. God has given us a limited mental capacity, but they usurp the function of the Godhead and indulge in novel experiments. They write about their own researches in most laudatory terms and hypnotize us into believing them. We, in our ignorance, then fall at their feet."[6] To belong to the modern world was to resist such presumption. To progress beyond divine laws and divine rights was to see human life as contingent. To think deterministically that Indians were of certain stripes, that they only acted on certain considerations, that their motivations were set, was to deny them the agency to act freely. If their behavior was already an established matter, then there was no meaningful way in which they could be self-governing.

The constructivist project at the heart of India's founding is situated at some distance from the general preoccupations of contemporary constitutional theory. Within existing bodies of scholarship, the most common subject of inquiry has been the relationship between constitutions and state power, a matter that is often studied through the language of checks, balances, and justifications. Here the substance of rights, the restrictions on the use of public power, the working of independent institutions, and the mechanisms for constitutional change have been familiar topics of engagement. A second theme in contemporary research has been the role of constitutions in the creation of political forms that represent the citizenry. In studies on wealth and democracy, regulatory bodies and their participatory features, electoral rules and restrictions, and so forth, constitutionalism is seen as a means to generate a site of representation. A third way to understand constitutions has been to see them as elite bargains that contend with competing interests. Such work sheds light on the strategic accommodations that make constitutional transitions and political stability possible. In the American context, for example, this way of seeing things frequently considers the balance struck between slavery and freedom at the nation's birth.[7]

There is something to be said for each of these approaches. What is revealing, however, is the extent to which they take for granted a set of circumstances and realities that do not quite obtain in much of the world. The global challenge for constitutionalism since the mid-twentieth century has been to construct democracy in settings where its imagined ingredients are seen as absent—under conditions where the people as free citizens must be created rather than assumed. In such situations, a constitution must be regarded, not as a kind of *rulebook,* but instead as a type of *textbook*—a pedagogical apparatus that can bring into being a certain kind of citizen. That process must necessarily involve the use of authority. In the Indian case, the shaping of intersubjectivity, the structuring of deliberation, and the framework of participation—in sum, the new universe of knowledge and power—presented a conception of individual agency that could legitimize such authority.

These features of the constitutional framework did not, however, exhaust its democratic character and carry the full weight of legitimation. Our study has explored how India's Constitution created and structured the postcolonial state so as to transform subjects into citizens. The democratic character of the state was partly enabled by universal suffrage, exercised in a specific institutional manner. By way of voting, Indians would choose their representatives and participate in an act of authorization. But a further dimension crucial to a system of self-government is the process by which a constitution can be changed. Elections maintain the interconnection between democracy and government, and the amendment procedure preserves the relation between *democracy* and *constitutionalism,* and each process occurs within particular structural forms. This final piece of the framework allows us to see India's founding text as instituting not only democracy but also constitutionalism.

The Constitution specified three paths to change. For the most part, the Constitution could be amended by a two-thirds majority of Parliament, present and voting. In select instances that implicated the nation's federal scheme, ratification was required by at least half of the state legislatures. Finally, some provisions could be changed by way of a simple parliamentary majority, in the same manner that Parliament might enact a statute.[8] The path that would be normally used—two-thirds parliamentary approval—was seen as a middle ground between two extreme possibilities: the British route, which did not distinguish between constitutional and ordinary legal change and gave a basic majority complete authority, and the American alternative that specified a rigid amendment procedure.

The amendment procedure in India's Constitution was thus striking for its ease. After surveying numerous choices, the Constituent Assembly had settled on a path where constitutional change would face little resistance.[9] B. R. Ambedkar observed that the ordinary process of amendment, which could amend "a very large part of the Constitution" and did not require the sanction of India's regional units, prevented the text from falling prey to "the faults of rigidity or legalism."[10] "It is difficult," he felt, "to conceive of a simpler method of amending the Constitution."[11] Ambedkar did concede that the process could have been even easier. Barring certain exceptional cases, the Constitution could not, after all, be amended by a simple majority. But he noted that no major single constitutional text could be amended merely by a simple majority. When placed alongside other texts, the constraints imposed by the Indian Constitution were limited. To reject even the bare requirement of two-thirds parliamentary approval would, in effect, be a rejection of constitutionalism altogether. As Ambedkar put it, "the purpose of a constitution is not merely to create the organs of the state but to limit their authority, because if no limitation was imposed upon the authority of the organs, there will be complete tyranny and complete oppression."[12] Through the act of voting, the sovereign people would choose their government; and the chosen government would be bound by the rules stipulated by the sovereign—namely, the constitutional text. When a parliamentary body elected on the basis of universal franchise would speak in a supermajority and amend the Constitution, it would be seen as effectively speaking for the sovereign people.

The representative character of the Assembly, both because of the means by which it was composed and because of a two-thirds consensus within the body, was taken to capture the sovereign will. In this way the schema could be constructed and reconstructed by the people, and its popular legitimacy could be sustained.

India's Constituent Assembly did not base its legitimacy on democratic grounds, even though it enjoyed clear and widespread support. The Assembly was not elected by universal suffrage, nor was the final constitutional text ratified by the people. But once the Constitution came into being, the people had real power to amend it by way of a supermajority consensus among their representatives.[13] The three features that have been covered in this book—codification, centralization, and representation—would constitute Indians in distinct ways. Indians would not only be democratic citizens during and between elections, they would also be constitutional citizens who could amend the foundational rules on which the overall system rested. Seen in this way, it is hardly surprising that India's Constitution was not a straightforward product of the people. At the birth of the Indian Republic, the people were yet to transition from subjecthood to citizenship. The important point is that this transition was to occur through a democratic constitution.

One can notice the contrast between this scenario and what transpired in the United States. The American Constitution had origins that we can recognize as more democratic. The text was ratified by conventions that had been specially convened. It is true that the Federalists had numerous advantages on their side during the ratification process.[14] Nonetheless, the fact of ratification, even if not the same as direct popular participation, signified an appeal to the people. Moreover, the conventions were composed more inclusively than we might expect: "Eight states elected convention delegates under special rules that were more populist and less property-focused than normal, and two others followed standing rules that let virtually all taxpaying adult male citizens vote."[15] Yet a striking fact of American constitutionalism is the disjuncture between this democratic past and the limits on popular expression in the present. The requirements of Article 5 of the American Constitution, which provides the procedure for amendment, are such that a formal change in the text is today viewed as practically impossible.

Thus, the world's oldest democracy and the world's largest democracy differ in an interesting way. The undemocratic origins of India's creation led to a schema that can be amended with comparative ease, whereas the relatively democratic ratification of the American founding has resulted in a system that is more immune to alteration. And yet neither nation has resolved the difficulties that burden modern democratic constitutionalism. In India, a key concern has been to prevent representative institutions from usurping sovereign power, a worry that has revealingly played out in controversies over substantive limitations on the power to amend the Constitution.[16] In the United States, on the other hand, a core dilemma has been to locate a way for the people to speak in the absence of the possibility of formal constitutional change. This has opened up the problem of present consent and the rule of the dead over the living, an anxiety that has contributed to intense conflicts over constitutional interpretation and the role and power of unelected judges.[17] In both cases, a tension persists between authority and authorization, between what representation produces and what legitimacy requires.

Such challenges are hard to avoid for any constitutional democracy. But they can find resolution, if at all, only within the crucible of politics. At a time when the terms of individual and collective freedom have acquired fresh attention in even the world's established democracies, the predicaments faced by India's founders are in many ways those of the contemporary world and they call on us to scrutinize the conclusions that are ever so often drawn about particular societies and the political forms that are associated with them. For India's founders, the point was not that the imperial facts about the social world were empirically false. It was instead that the conception of the social world that emerged from such facts was a product of the colonizers' broader political project. After all, the imperialists had constructed the colonialized peoples, an act which served to validate their case against self-rule.[18] The remarkable irony of the present crisis of constitutional democracy is its uncanny resemblance to the imperial ideology. In much the same way as the absence of faith in Indian self-rule made Britain conceive of the colony in particular historical and sociological terms, present studies of the challenges faced by self-government around the world may well reflect our own lack of faith in democracy. Over time, the relationship between political ideology and political developments is likely to emerge as a mutually constitutive one, for—as we have observed at the outset—politics has the potential to produce its own brand of essentialism.

Modern political life, in its normative aspiration to self-rule, will of course remain an arena of rational and irrational contests, a sphere that is home to frustrated hopes, dangerous fantasies, and surprising victories.

But even to concede the space for politics is to acknowledge the potential for transformation. For India's founders, the plasticity of one's political condition was a mark of possibility, just as it was a reminder of the fragility of any state of being.[19] The endurance of the Indian project would, the founders felt, ultimately rest on whether reasons were present for individuals to remain committed to that project. Any kind of institutional change could not rely only on the idea of force. There would have to be some underlying sense of why people would accept the institutional project. And motives for allegiance would depend as much on political action—on the use of authority—as on political belief. Indeed, much of the tragedy of contemporary politics, in India or elsewhere, is the shift in expectations. The global unraveling of constitutional democracy risks feeding nicely into the political ontology of the age of colonialism, where individual actors are defined in specific ways and they are somewhat condemned to the terms of their shared existence. Such a narrative would be not only tragic but also perilous. For freedom, whether at the end of the British empire or now, has been endangered not only by extremism but perhaps even more so by cynicism.

Notes

Acknowledgments

Index

NOTES

Introduction

1. Speech by Jawaharlal Nehru, Constituent Assembly of India, December 13, 1946, in *Constituent Assembly Debates,* 12 vols. (New Delhi: Lok Sabha Secretariat, 2009 [1950]) (hereafter cited as *CAD*), 64.

2. See Alexis de Tocqueville, *Democracy in America,* trans. Arthur Goldhammer, 2 vols. (New York: Library of America, 2004 [1835–1840]); John Stuart Mill, *On Liberty and Other Writings,* ed. Stefan Collini (New York: Cambridge University Press, 1989 [1859]); Mill, *Considerations on Representative Government* (New York: Cambridge University Press, 2010 [1861]).

3. See Walter Bagehot, *The English Constitution,* ed. Miles Taylor (New York: Oxford University Press, 2001 [1867]); A. V. Dicey, *Lectures Introductory to the Study of the Law of the Constitution* (London: Macmillan and Co., 1885).

4. James Mill, *The History of British India,* 3 vols. (New York: Cambridge University Press, 2010 [1817]).

5. See Karuna Mantena, *Alibis of Empire: Henry Maine and the Ends of Liberal Imperialism* (Princeton: Princeton University Press, 2010).

6. See David Singh Grewal, *The Invention of the Economy: A History of Economic Thought* (Cambridge, MA: Harvard University Press, forthcoming) (draft on file with author).

7. Thomas Hobbes, *Leviathan,* ed. Richard Tuck (New York: Cambridge University Press, 1996 [1651]).

8. See Emmanuel Joseph Sieyès, "What Is the Third Estate?," in *Political Writings,* trans. Michael Sonenscher (Indianapolis: Hackett, 2003 [1789]).

9. Alexander Hamilton, James Madison, and John Jay, *The Federalist* (Cambridge, MA: Harvard University Press, 2009 [1787–1788]).

10. See Robert Dahl, *How Democratic Is the American Constitution?,* 2nd ed. (New Haven: Yale University Press, 2003); Sanford Levinson, *Our Democratic*

Constitution: Where the Constitution Goes Wrong (and How We the People Can Correct It) (New York: Oxford University Press, 2008); Lawrence Lessig, *Republic, Lost: How Money Corrupts Congress—and a Plan to Stop It* (New York: Twelve, 2012); Jedediah Purdy, "Wealth and Democracy," in *Wealth,* ed. Jack Knight and Melissa Schwartzberg (New York: NYU Press, 2017), 235–260.

11. See Uday Singh Mehta, *Liberalism and Empire: A Study in Nineteenth-Century British Liberal Thought* (Chicago: University of Chicago Press, 1999); Jennifer Pitts, *A Turn to Empire: The Rise of Imperial Liberalism in Britain and France* (Princeton: Princeton University Press, 2006); Sankar Muthu, *Enlightenment against Empire* (Princeton: Princeton University Press, 2003); Mantena, *Alibis of Empire;* Duncan Bell, *Reordering the World: Essays on Liberalism and Empire* (Princeton: Princeton University Press, 2016).

12. For a recent contribution in this regard that considers anticolonial efforts in the international realm and the relationship between state sovereignty and the global order, see Adom Getachew, *Worldmaking after Empire: The Rise and Fall of Self-Determination* (Princeton: Princeton University Press, 2019).

13. In the Indian context, the definitive treatment of the psychological burdens of colonialism remains Ashis Nandy, *The Intimate Enemy: Loss and Recovery of Self under Colonialism* (New Delhi: Oxford University Press, 1983).

14. On historicism and postcolonial thought, see Dipesh Chakrabarty, *Provincializing Europe: Postcolonial Thought and Historical Difference* (Princeton: Princeton University Press, 2007).

15. G. W. F. Hegel, *The Philosophy of History,* trans J. Sibree (New York: Dover, 1956 [1824]), 139. On Western visions of India, see Ronald Inden, *Imagining India* (Oxford: Basil Blackwell, 1990).

16. Hegel, *The Philosophy of History,* 144.

17. Ibid., 162.

18. This was visible across the Indian political spectrum. See, for example, Lala Lajpat Rai, "The Political Future of India," 1919, in *The Collected Works of Lala Lajpat Rai,* ed. B. R. Nanda, vol. 8 (New Delhi: Manohar, 2006), 299–308; Subhas Chandra Bose, Presidential Address at the Maharashtra Provincial Conference, May 3, 1928, in *The Essential Writings of Netaji Subhas Chandra Bose,* ed. Sisir K. Bose and Sugata Bose (New Delhi: Oxford University Press, 1997), 83. The point here was that there was no essential difference between the East and the West, as Nehru would assert on several occasions. See, for instance, Jawaharlal Nehru, "Evolution of British Policy in India," 1928, in *Selected Works of Jawaharlal Nehru,* ed. S. Gopal, 1st ser., vols. 1–15 (New Delhi: Orient Longman, 1972–1982) (hereafter cited as *Selected Works*), 2:332–334.

19. Jawaharlal Nehru, *The Discovery of India* (New Delhi, Penguin 2004 [1946]).

20. Jawaharlal Nehru, "The Psychology of Indian Nationalism," 1927, in *Selected Works,* 2:266.

21. Nehru, *The Discovery of India,* 52.

22. The literature here is too vast to cite, but definitive contributions include Bernard Bailyn, *The Ideological Origins of the American Revolution* (Cambridge, MA: Belknap Press of Harvard University Press, 1992); Gordon S. Wood, *The*

Creation of the American Republic, 1776–1787 (Chapel Hill: University of North Carolina Press, 1998). See also Bruce Ackerman, *We the People: Foundations* (Cambridge, MA: Harvard University Press, 1991); Akhil Reed Amar, *America's Constitution: A Biography* (New York: Random House, 2005). For recent provocations, see Eric Nelson, *The Royalist Revolution: Monarchy and the American Founding* (Cambridge, MA: Harvard University Press, 2014); Michael J. Klarman, *The Framers' Coup: The Making of the United States Constitution* (New York: Oxford University Press, 2016).

23. James Bryce, *Modern Democracies*, 2 vols. (New York: Macmillan, 1921), 1:42.

24. David Runciman, *The Confidence Trap: A History of Democracy in Crisis from World War I to the Present* (Princeton: Princeton University Press, 2013), 77.

25. See, for example, an afterword jointly authored by Jawaharlal Nehru, Narendra Dev, and K. T. Shah to a work by Shah on the Government of India Act of 1935. K. T. Shah, *Federal Structure* (Bombay: Vora and Co., 1937), 510–511.

26. This is captured by Ira Katznelson's revealing study, which regards the New Deal as "the most important twentieth-century testing ground for representative democracy in an age of mass politics." Ira Katznelson, *Fear Itself: The New Deal and the Origins of Our Time* (New York: Liveright, 2013), 9.

27. See Mark Mazower, *Dark Continent: Europe's Twentieth Century* (New York: Vintage Books, 1998).

28. Jawaharlal Nehru, Letter to Vallabhbhai Patel, March 26, 1949 (containing a reproduction of a letter from C. R. Attlee to Nehru, March 20, 1949), in *Sardar Patel's Correspondence, 1945–50*, ed. Durga Das, 10 vols. (Ahmedabad: Navajivan, 1971–1974), 8:7.

29. Philip Spratt, *India and Constitution Making* (Calcutta: Renaissance, 1948), 82.

30. M. C. Setalvad, *The Common Law in India* (London: Stevens and Sons, 1960), 204. There were, one should note—and expect, given the historical circumstances involved—international dimensions to India's anticolonial struggle and its founding. See Erez Manela, *The Wilsonian Moment: Self-Determination and the International Origins of Anticolonial Nationalism* (New York: Oxford University Press, 2007).

31. This is not to suggest that these other constitutional moments do not raise important questions. The case of Japan, for example, has invited reflection on the idea of imposed constitutionalism. See Noah Feldman, "Imposed Constitutionalism," *Connecticut Law Review* 37 (2005): 857–889; Ray A. Moore, *The Birth of Japan's Postwar Constitution*, trans. Koseki Shoichi (Boulder, CO: Westview Press, 1997); Shigenori Matsui, *The Constitution of Japan: A Contextual Analysis* (Oxford: Hart, 2011), 13–16; David S. Law, "The Myth of the Imposed Constitution," in *The Social and Political Foundations of Constitutions*, ed. Denis J. Galligan and Mila Versteeg (New York: Cambridge University Press, 2013), 239–268.

32. For helpful overviews of the extant literature, see Tom Ginsburg, Zachary Elkins, and Justin Blount, "Does the Process of Constitution-Making Matter?,"

Annual Review of Law and Social Science 5 (2009): 201–223; Mark Tushnet, "Constitution-Making: An Introduction," *Texas Law Review* 91 (2013): 1983–2013.

33. Ackerman's ongoing multivolume project on the global spread of constitutionalism is an important exception to this trend, and it acknowledges the distinct revolutionary character of the Indian founding. See Bruce Ackerman, *Revolutionary Constitutions: Charismatic Leadership and the Rule of Law* (Cambridge, MA: Harvard University Press, 2019), 59–63.

34. On Jennings's contribution and legacy, see H. Kumarasingham, ed., *Constitution-Making in Asia: Decolonization and State-Building in the Aftermath of the British Empire* (Oxon: Routledge, 2016).

35. Ivor Jennings, *The Approach to Self-Government* (Cambridge: Cambridge University Press, 1958), 1.

36. Ibid., 28–32.

37. Ibid., 82.

38. Ibid., 63.

39. Ibid., 65. For the lessons that Jennings drew from the Asian wave of decolonization, see also Ivor Jennings, *Problems of the New Commonwealth* (Durham, NC: Duke University Press, 1958).

40. Edwin S. Montagu and Lord Chelmsford, *Report on Indian Constitutional Reforms* (Calcutta: Superintendent Government Printing, 1918), 85.

41. Ibid., 98.

42. Indian Statutory Commission, *Report of the Indian Statutory Commission* (London: His Majesty's Stationary Office, 1930), 2:91.

43. Indian Franchise Committee, *Report of the Indian Franchise Committee* (Calcutta: Government of India Central Publication Branch, 1932), 1:20.

44. Clause I.3, The Congress–League Scheme, 1916, in *The Framing of India's Constitution: Select Documents,* ed. B. Shiva Rao et al., 5 vols. (New Delhi: Universal Law Publishing, 1966), 1:26.

45. Report of the Committee of the All Parties Conference, 1928, in *Selected Works of Motilal Nehru,* ed. Ravinder Kumar and Hari Dev Sharma, 6 vols. (New Delhi: Vikas, 1995), 6:76.

46. Supplementary Report of the Committee of the All Parties Conference, 1928, in *Selected Works of Motilal Nehru,* 6:141.

47. *Constitutional Proposals of the Sapru Committee* (Bombay: Padma, 1945), 167–168 (emphasis mine).

48. Ibid., 168. India's first minister of education estimated that adult literacy levels were at 10 percent at the time of India's independence. See Maulana Abul Kalam Azad, Speech at a UNESCO Seminar, November 2, 1949, in *The Selected Works of Maulana Abul Kalam Azad,* ed. Ravindra Kumar, vol. 4 (New Delhi: Atlantic, 1992), 138–139.

49. See, for example, Motilal Nehru, Speech on the Government of India Act, April 18, 1924, in *Selected Works of Motilal Nehru,* ed. Ravinder Kumar and Hari Dev Sharma (New Delhi: Vikas, 1986), 4:212.

50. Mohandas K. Gandhi, "The Only Way," *Harijan,* November 25, 1939, 352–353. See also Mohandas K. Gandhi, "Illiterates v. Literates," October 3, 1937, in

The Collected Works of Mahatma Gandhi, 100 vols. (Government of India: Publications Division, 1956–1994) (hereafter cited as *Collected Works*), 66:197.

51. On new liberalism, see Stefan Collini, *Liberalism and Sociology: L. T. Hobhouse and Political Argument in England, 1880–1914* (Cambridge: Cambridge University Press, 1979).

52. L. T. Hobhouse, "Liberalism," in *Liberalism and Other Writings,* ed. James Meadowcroft (New York: Cambridge University Press, 1994), 112, cited in B. R. Ambedkar, Evidence before the Southborough Committee on Franchise, 1919, in *Dr. B. R. Ambedkar: Writings and Speeches,* ed. Vasant Moon, 17 vols. (New Delhi: Dr. Ambedkar Foundation, 2014), 1:261.

53. B. R. Ambedkar, Report on the Constitution of the Government of Bombay Presidency, 1929, in *Dr. B. R. Ambedkar,* 2:337. It seems that Ambedkar did not embrace his view of suffrage with as much consistency as one might have liked. He observed, "With regard to the criminal tribes, it might not be a good thing to give them adult suffrage, because by occupation they are a people who have more the interest of their own particular community in mind, and they are not very particular as regards the means whereby they earn their living; but I do not think that there is any harm in giving aborigines the right to vote." B. R. Ambedkar, Evidence before the Indian Statutory Commission, October 23, 1928, in *Dr. B. R. Ambedkar,* 2:471.

54. Ambedkar, Report, Bombay Presidency, 338–340.

55. Ibid., 341.

56. Ibid., 343.

57. B. R. Ambedkar, First Roundtable Conference, December 22, 1930, in *Dr. B. R. Ambedkar,* 2:558.

58. John Dewey, *Democracy and Education: An Introduction to the Philosophy of Education* (New York: Free Press, 1997 [1916]), 87. Ambedkar does not explicitly reference *Democracy and Education,* but this appears to be the work he draws upon. On Dewey's conception of democracy, see also John Dewey, *The Public and Its Problems: An Essay in Political Inquiry* (University Park: Pennsylvania State University Press, 2012 [1946]).

59. Ambedkar, First Roundtable Conference, December 22, 1930, 559.

60. See Dadabhai Naoroji, *Poverty and Un-British Rule in India* (Delhi: Government of India Press, 1962 [1901]); R. C. Dutt, *The Economic History of India,* 2 vols. (New York: Ben Franklin, 1970 [1906]).

61. Jawaharlal Nehru, "Exploitation of India," October 2, 1933, in *Selected Works,* 6:40.

62. Mohandas K. Gandhi, Resolution, March 1, 1940, in *Collected Works,* 71:441.

63. Congress Working Committee's Resolution, May 24, 1946, in Mohandas K. Gandhi, *Collected Works,* 84:483.

64. See Granville Austin, *The Indian Constitution: Cornerstone of a Nation* (New Delhi: Oxford University Press, 1966), 12–13n38 (estimating that 28 percent of the populace could vote in the provincial assembly elections). Shani has recently observed that the "estimates for the proportion of the adult population that could

vote under the 1935 Act ranged between 20% and 25% at most." Ornit Shani, *How India Became Democratic: Citizenship and the Making of the Universal Franchise* (Cambridge: Cambridge University Press, 2018), 3n9. Some estimates are far lower. See, for example, Sumit Sarkar, "Indian Democracy: The Historical Inheritance," in *The Success of India's Democracy,* ed. Atul Kohli (Cambridge: Cambridge University Press, 2001), 35 (stating that elections to the provincial legislatures had taken place on a franchise of "around 10 per cent").

65. Austin refers to Nehru, Azad, Patel, and Prasad as forming an "oligarchy within the Assembly." Austin, *The Indian Constitution,* 21.

66. See Gandhi, "The Only Way." See also Mohandas K. Gandhi, "Question Box (Pakistan and Constituent Assembly)," June 29, 1940, in *Collected Works,* 72:200; Gandhi, "Independence," July 28, 1946, in *Collected Works,* 85:34. For Gandhi's prior faith in a constituent assembly, see Gandhi, statement to the *News Chronicle,* December 4, 1939, in *Collected Works,* 71:6; Gandhi, "Independence," December 17, 1939, in *Collected Works,* 71:44; Gandhi, "Question Box (Constituent Assembly)," January 29, 1940, in *Collected Works,* 71:154; Gandhi, "My Answer to Quaid-E-Azam," March 26, 1940, in *Collected Works,* 71:372.

67. Speech by Rajendra Prasad, Constituent Assembly of India, October 7, 1949, in *CAD,* 10:21. See also speech by Rajendra Prasad, Constituent Assembly of India, November 26, 1949, in *CAD,* 11:986–987.

68. See, for example, speech by Alladi Krishnaswami Ayyar, Constituent Assembly of India, November 8, 1948, in *CAD,* 7:336; speech by R. K. Sidhwa, Constituent Assembly of India, November 17, 1949, in *CAD,* 11:624; speech by Shibban Lal Saksena, Constituent Assembly of India, November 19, 1949, in *CAD,* 11:705; speech by Nandkishore Das, Constituent Assembly of India, November 23, 1949 in *CAD,* 11:850–851.

69. Speech by B. Das, November 17, 1949, Constituent Assembly of India, in *CAD,* 11:637.

70. Speech by Thirumala Rao, Constituent Assembly of India, November 22, 1949, in *CAD,* 11:818.

71. Speech by Mahavir Tyagi, Constituent Assembly of India, November 25, 1949, in *CAD,* 11:963.

72. Speech by Frank Anthony, Constituent Assembly of India, November 25, 1949, in *CAD,* 11:939.

73. Speech by K. T. Shah, Constituent Assembly of India, June 2, 1949, in *CAD,* 8:552.

74. Speech by Alladi Krishnaswami Ayyar, Constituent Assembly of India, November 23, 1949, in *CAD,* 11:835.

75. See, for example, Alan Gledhill, *The Republic of India: The Development of Its Laws and Constitution* (London: Steven and Sons, 1951), 11–12. India's postcolonial setup was taken to be a mark of British success in transferring the liberal tradition to India. See, for instance, R. J. Moore, *Liberalism and Indian Politics: 1872–1922* (London: Edward Arnold, 1966), 127.

76. See, for example, Perry Anderson's recent diatribe against Indian nationalism, where he credits the Baldwin cabinet with the core of the Indian Constitution. Perry Anderson, *The Indian Ideology* (New York: Verso, 2013), 106–107. Anderson's

study has invited many responses. See, especially, Sudipta Kaviraj, "The Curious Persistence of Colonial Ideology," *Constellations* 21 (2014): 186–198. The ubiquity of Anderson's views should not be underestimated. Traces of it are visible even in broad-ranging studies of decolonization. See, for example, Dietmar Rothermund, *The Routledge Companion to Decolonization* (New York: Routledge, 2006), 245.

77. See Ayesha Jalal, *Democracy and Authoritarianism in South Asia: A Comparative and Historical Perspective* (Cambridge: Cambridge University Press, 1995), 36.

78. V. S. Srinivasa Sastri, Kamala Lectures, 1926, in *Speeches and Writings of the Right Honourable V. S. Srinivasa Sastri*, 2 vols. (Madras: Jupiter Press, 1969), 1:120.

79. See Sections 80A and 81A, Government of India Act, 1919.

80. James Fitzjames Stephen, "Foundations of the Government of India," *Nineteenth Century* 14 (1883): 544.

81. Earl of Minto, cited in Sir Penderel Moon, *The British Conquest and Dominion of India,* vol. 2 (New Delhi: India Research Press, 1999 [1989]), 955.

82. I borrow the distinction between representative and responsible government from Reginald Coupland, who nicely blamed the continuance of British rule and extant tensions on local factors. Sir Reginald Coupland, *The Indian Problem, 1833–1935* (Oxford: Clarendon Press, 1942), 45. See, also, Reginald Coupland, *Constitutional Problem in India* (New York: Oxford University Press, 1944). On constitutional law and politics prior to Indian independence, see Rohit De, "Constitutional Antecedents," in *The Oxford Handbook of the Indian Constitution*, ed. Sujit Choudhry, Madhav Khosla, and Pratap Bhanu Mehta (Oxford: Oxford University Press, 2016), 17–37.

83. See H. M. Seervai, *The Position of the Judiciary under the Constitution of India* (Bombay: University of Bombay, 1970), 54–55.

84. See Anil Seal, *The Emergence of Indian Nationalism: Competition and Collaboration in the Later Nineteenth Century* (New York: Cambridge University Press, 1968); John Gallagher, Gordon Johnson, and Anil Seal, eds., *Locality, Province and Nation: Essays on Indian Politics* (Cambridge: Cambridge University Press, 1977); Christopher Baker, Gordon Johnson, and Anil Seal, eds., *Power, Profit and Politics: Essays on Imperialism, Nationalism and Change in Twentieth Century India* (Cambridge: Cambridge University Press, 1981).

85. John Strachey's leading work was *India: Its Administration and Progress,* 3rd ed. (London: Macmillan and Co., 1903).

86. Tapan Raychaudhuri, "Indian Nationalism as Animal Politics," *Historical Journal* 22 (1979): 747–763.

87. See C. A. Bayly, *Recovering Liberties: Indian Thought in the Age of Liberalism and Empire* (New York: Cambridge University Press, 2012).

88. Sudipta Kaviraj, *The Enchantment of Democracy and India* (Ranikhet: Permanent Black, 2011), 15–17; Sunil Khilnani, "The Indian Constitution and Democracy," in *India's Living Constitution: Ideas, Practices, Controversies,* ed. Zoya Hasan, E. Sridharan, R. Sudarshan, et. al. (Delhi: Permanent Black, 2002), 65–70.

89. See Louis Hartz, *The Liberal Tradition in America* (New York: Harcourt, Brace and World, 1955).

90. Kaviraj rightly observes that, given the vibrant criticisms of individualism that had emerged in Indian thought, "the legal structure of the Constitution was a

surprising one, since a large part of its fundamental principles and technical legal apparatus presuppose a liberal-individualist understanding of democratic politics." Kaviraj, *Enchantment of Democracy,* 292.

91. A notable example is Ramachandra Guha, *India after Gandhi: The History of the World's Largest Democracy* (New York: HarperCollins, 2007), 1–15.

92. See Arend Lijphart, "The Puzzle of Indian Democracy: A Consociational Interpretation," *American Political Science Review* 90 (1996): 258–268; Ashutosh Varshney, "Why Democracy Survives," *Journal of Democracy* 9 (1998): 36–50; Devesh Kapur, "Explaining Democratic Durability and Economic Performance," in *Public Institutions in India,* ed. Devesh Kapur and Pratap Bhanu Mehta (New Delhi: Oxford University Press, 2005), 28–76; Ashutosh Varshney, *Battles Half Won: India's Improbable Democracy* (New Delhi: Penguin, 2013), 11–15.

93. See Jalal, *Democracy and Authoritarianism;* Philip Oldenburg, *India, Pakistan, and Democracy: Solving the Puzzle of Divergent Paths* (New York: Routledge, 2010); Maya Tudor, *The Promise of Power: The Origins of Democracy in India and Autocracy in Pakistan* (New York: Cambridge University Press, 2013).

94. For a classic treatment, see Samuel P. Huntington, *Political Order in Changing Societies* (New Haven: Yale University Press, 1968).

95. See, generally, Seymour Martin Lipset, "Some Social Requisites of Democracy: Economic Development and Political Legitimacy," *American Political Science Review* 53 (1959): 69–105; Barrington Moore, *The Social Origins of Dictatorship and Democracy: Lord and Peasant in the Making of the Modern World* (Boston: Beacon Press, 1966); Carles Boix, *Democracy and Redistribution* (Cambridge: Cambridge University Press, 2003); Daron Acemoglu and James A. Robinson, *Economic Origins of Dictatorship and Democracy* (New York: Cambridge University Press, 2006); Daniel Ziblatt, *Conservative Parties and the Birth of Democracy* (New York: Cambridge University Press, 2017).

96. John Dunn, *Breaking Democracy's Spell* (New Haven: Yale University Press, 2014), 103.

97. Shani's recent book is noteworthy in this regard for studying how democratic citizenship was created in India. Her contribution lies in a careful analysis of the administrative mechanics that the task involved. Her book "focuses on the practical—rather than ideological—steps through which the nation and its democracy were built." Shani, *How India Became Democratic,* 5. *India's Founding Moment* is different in two key respects. First, I might well be seen as focusing on the ideological rather than the practical. Second, my discussions link democratization to other features of the overall constitutional order and are not focused exclusively on suffrage.

98. Sunil Khilnani, *The Idea of India* (New Delhi: Penguin, 1997), 34. Khilnani is, of course, alive to the significance of the Constituent Assembly debates, seeing them as "perhaps India's most remarkable moment of deliberation and discussion." Sunil Khilnani, "Democracy and Its Indian Pasts," in *Arguments for a Better World: Essays in Honor of Amartya Sen,* 2 vols., ed. Kaushik Basu and Ravi Kanbur (New York: Oxford University Press, 2009), 2:497. For a recent, exceptional essay that does attend to the anxieties about popular rule at India's founding, see

Udit Bhatia, "Precautions in a Democratic Experiment: The Nexus between Political Power and Competence," in *Constituent Assemblies,* ed. Jon Elster et. al. (New York: Cambridge University Press, 2018), 109–137.

99. Speech by Alladi Krishnaswami Ayyar, Constituent Assembly of India, November 23, 1949, in *CAD,* 11:835.

100. Speech by G. L. Mehta, Constituent Assembly of India, August 21, 1947, in *CAD,* 5:77.

101. B. R. Ambedkar, "On Participation in the War," October 26, 1939, in *Dr. B. R. Ambedkar,* 2:245.

102. The challenge might be seen as similar to one that Appiah once observed in the case of "ideological decolonization"—namely, that it is "bound to fail if it neglects either endogenous 'tradition' or exogenous 'Western' ideas." See Kwame Anthony Appiah, *In My Father's House: Africa in the Philosophy of Culture* (New York: Oxford University Press, 1992), x.

103. As is well established, it is a feature of effective authority that it claims legitimacy. See Joseph Raz, *The Authority of Law: Essays on Law and Morality,* 2nd ed. (New York: Oxford University Press), 28–29.

104. Jean-Jacques Rousseau, *The Social Contract and Other Later Political Writings,* ed. and trans. Victor Gourevitch (Cambridge: Cambridge University Press, 1997). On Rousseau's conception of this idea, see Frederick Neuhouser, "Freedom, Dependence, and the General Will," *Philosophical Review* 102 (1993): 363–395.

105. For a recent inquiry of this nature, see Pierre Rosanvallon, *Good Government: Democracy beyond Elections,* trans. Malcolm DeBevoise (Cambridge, MA: Harvard University Press 2018).

106. See Austin, *The Indian Constitution;* Uday Singh Mehta, "Constitutionalism," in *The Oxford Companion to Politics in India,* ed. Niraja Gopal Jayal and Pratap Bhanu Mehta (New Delhi: Oxford University Press, 2010), 15–27; Uday Singh Mehta, "Indian Constitutionalism: Crisis, Unity, and History," in *The Oxford Handbook of the Indian Constitution,* ed. Sujit Choudhry, Madhav Khosla, and Pratap Bhanu Mehta (Oxford: Oxford University Press, 2016), 38–54; Jalal, *Democracy and Authoritarianism.* For a recent meditation on the question of colonial continuity that is attentive to some of the peculiarities of the Indian founding, see Sandipto Dasgupta, "'A Language Which Is Foreign to Us': Continuities and Anxieties in the Making of the Indian Constitution," *Comparative Studies of South Asia, Africa, and the Middle East* 34 (2014): 228–242. The themes of continuity and displacement have also featured in works on the legal system in India. See D. A. Washbrook, "Law, State and Agrarian Society in Colonial India," *Modern Asian Studies* 15 (1981): 649–721; Marc Galanter, *Law and Society in Modern India,* ed. Rajeev Dhavan (Delhi: Oxford University Press, 1989).

107. For a classic contribution in this genre, see Ranajit Guha, *Elementary Aspects of Peasant Insurgency in Colonial India* (Delhi: Oxford University Press, 1983).

108. On liberalism, the right to vote, and the "discourse of capacity," see Alan S. Kahan, *Liberalism in Nineteenth-Century Europe: The Political Culture of Limited Suffrage* (New York: Palgrave Macmillan, 2003).

1. The Grammar of Constitutionalism

1. See, for example, Gyan Prakash, "Anxious Constitution-Making," in *The Post-colonial Moment in South and Southeast Asia*, ed. Gyan Prakash, Michael Laffan, and Nikhil Menon (London: Bloomsbury, 2018), 146. The size of the original Constitution of 1950 is different from the current text. Provisions have been added and removed. But the size of both documents is nonetheless awesome.

2. Carl Schmitt, *Legality and Legitimacy,* ed. and trans. Jeffrey Seitzer (Durham, NC: Duke University Press, 2004 [1958]), 98.

3. Ibid., 99–100. In contrast, Ernest Barker began his notable work *Principles of Social and Political Theory* by referring to the Indian Constitution, seeing it as an extension of, rather than a departure from, Western political theory: "I ought to explain, as I end, why the preamble to the Constitution of India is printed after the table of contents. It seemed to me, when I read it, to state in a brief and pithy form the argument of much of the book; and it may accordingly serve as a key-note. I am the more moved to quote it because I am proud that the people of India should begin their independent life by subscribing to a political tradition which we in the West call Western, but which is now something more than Western." Ernest Barker, *Principles of Social and Political Theory* (Oxford: Clarendon Press, 1951), vi.

4. The relationship between codification and common knowledge goes back all the way to Athens in the classical period. See Josiah Ober, *Democracy and Knowledge: Innovation and Learning in Classical Athens* (Princeton: Princeton University Press), 211–263.

5. See Charles Taylor, "Interpretation and the Sciences of Man," *Review of Metaphysics* 25 (1971): 3–51.

6. See H. L. A. Hart, *The Concept of Law,* ed. Penelope A. Bulloch and Joseph Raz, 2nd ed. (New York: Oxford University Press, 1994), 91–99.

7. See Frederick Schauer, *Playing by the Rules: A Philosophical Examination of Rule-Based Decision-Making in Law and in Life* (Oxford: Clarendon Press, 1991), 135–166.

8. Ibid., 151–152.

9. Ibid., 138–139.

10. See K. C. Wheare, *Modern Constitutions,* 2nd ed. (London: Oxford University Press, 1966), 1–2.

11. See John Gardner, *Law as a Leap of Faith: Essays on Law in General* (Oxford: Oxford University Press, 2012), 97–103. On constitutions, see also Kent Greenawalt, *Interpreting the Constitution* (New York: Oxford University Press, 2015), 3–19.

12. See, generally, Peter Winch, *The Idea of a Social Science and Its Relation to Philosophy* (London: Routledge, 1958), 42–48.

13. See Bijay Kisor Acharyya, *Codification in British India* (Calcutta: S. K. Banerji and Sons, 1914).

14. See K. Lipstein, "The Reception of Western Law in India," *International Social Science Journal* 9 (1957): 85–95.

15. See Bernard S. Cohn, *Colonialism and Its Forms of Knowledge: The British in India* (Princeton: Princeton University Press, 1996), 57–75. See also J. Duncan M. Derrett, *Religion, Law and the State in India* (New York: Free Press, 1968), 237–250.

16. Speech by Thomas Babington Macaulay, July 10, 1833, in *Parliamentary Debates (Hansard),* vol. 1 (London: House of Commons, 1833), 531–532.

17. See W. H. Rattigan, "Possibilities of Codification in India," *Law Quarterly Review* 14 (1898): 367–378.

18. Karuna Mantena, *Alibis of Empire: Henry Maine and the Ends of Liberal Imperialism* (Princeton: Princeton University Press, 2010), 91.

19. Eric Stokes, *The English Utilitarians and India* (Oxford: Clarendon Press, 1959), 225.

20. James Fitzjames Stephen, "Codification in India and England," *Fortnightly Review* 12 (1872): 654. For a provocative comparison between English and Indian law, see David Skuy, "Macaulay and the Indian Penal Code of 1862: The Myth of the Inherent Superiority and Modernity of the English Legal System Compared to India's Legal System in the Nineteenth Century," *Modern Asian Studies* 32 (1998): 513–557. For a historical and contemporary perspective on Macaulay's legacy, see Wing-Cheong Chan, Barry Wright, and Stanley Yeo, eds., *Codification, Macaulay and the Indian Penal Code: The Legacies and Modern Challenges of Criminal Law Reform* (Oxon: Routledge, 2016).

21. See Whitley Stokes, *The Anglo-Indian Codes* (Oxford: Clarendon Press, 1887), xxii–xxiii. The specific strategies undertaken in each statute would, of course, relate to the area of law involved. In the case of property, for example, see Shyamkrishna Balganesh, "Codifying the Common Law of Property in India: Crystallization and Standardization as Strategies of Constraint," *American Journal of Comparative Law* 63 (2015): 33–76.

22. I do not mean this as a technical claim about the legal status of such statutes. This clarification is required after the decision of the High Court of England and Wales in Thoburn v. Sunderland City Council, [2003] QB 151. See, generally, Mark Elliott, "Embracing 'Constitutional' Legislation: Towards Fundamental Law?," *Northern Ireland Legal Quarterly* 54 (2003): 25–42. In recent years, the idea of some statutes possessing a superior status has also gained interest in the United States. See William N. Eskridge Jr., and John Ferejohn, *A Republic of Statutes: The New American Constitution* (New Haven: Yale University Press, 2013).

23. See Anil Chandra Banerjee, *The Constitutional History of India*, vol. 1, *1600–1858* (Delhi: Macmillan, 1977), 66–122.

24. Rohit De, "Constitutional Antecedents," in *The Oxford Handbook of the Indian Constitution,* ed. Sujit Choudhry, Madhav Khosla, and Pratap Bhanu Mehta (Oxford: Oxford University Press, 2016), 25.

25. See Ronald Dworkin, *Freedom's Law: The Moral Reading of the American Constitution* (Cambridge, MA: Harvard University Press, 1996), 1–38.

26. See Jeremy Waldron, *Political Theory: Essays on Institutions* (Cambridge, MA: Harvard University Press, 2016), 23–44.

27. See N. W. Barber, *The Principles of Constitutionalism* (Oxford: Oxford University Press, 2018), 1–19.

28. See Jeremy Waldron, *Law and Disagreement* (New York: Oxford University Press, 1999).

29. The scholarship here is too large to reference in any meaningful way, but for a recent iteration of this debate, see Jeremy Waldron, "The Core of the Case against Judicial Review," *Yale Law Journal* 115 (2006): 1346–1406; Richard Fallon, "The Core of an Uneasy Case for Judicial Review," *Harvard Law Review* 121 (2008): 1693–1736; Mark Tushnet, "How Different Are Waldron's and Fallon's Core Cases for and against Judicial Review?," *Oxford Journal of Legal Studies* 30 (2016): 49–70.

30. The contrast between legal and political constitutionalism is often framed as the contrast between American and British constitutionalism, respectively. This is not without reason, but one should note that Britain has shared a more complex historical relationship with written constitutionalism than is often supposed. See Linda Colley, "Empires of Writing: Britain, America and Constitutions, 1776–1848," *Law and History Review* 32 (2014): 237–266. The intellectual relationship is equally complex. When constitutional rights were, for instance, beginning to gain attention in the first half of the twentieth century, Ernest Barker—to give one prominent example—noted that although the "English temper is apt to mistrust enunciations of legal and political principle . . . there is something to be said, nonetheless, in favour of declarations of rights." Ernest Barker, *Reflections on Government* (Oxford: Oxford University Press, 1942), 32–33.

31. Speech by B. R. Ambedkar, Constituent Assembly of India, July 29, 1947, in *Constituent Assembly Debates,* 12 vols. (New Delhi: Lok Sabha Secretariat, 2009 [1950]) (hereafter cited as *CAD*), 4:918.

32. Speech by B. R. Ambedkar, Constituent Assembly of India, July 30, 1949, in *CAD,* 9:12.

33. Speech by B. R. Ambedkar, Constituent Assembly of India, December 9, 1948, in *CAD,* 7:953.

34. Ibid.

35. Speech by Brajeshwar Prasad, Constituent Assembly of India, October 10, 1949, in *CAD,* 10:45.

36. Ibid. See also letter from Vallabhbhai Patel to All Provincial Premiers, November 3, 1949, in *Sardar Patel's Correspondence, 1945–50,* ed. Durga Das, 10 vols. (Ahmedabad: Navajivan Publishing House, 1971–1974), 8:393.

37. See Uday Singh Mehta, "Constitutionalism," in *The Oxford Companion to Politics in India,* ed. Niraja Gopal Jayal and Pratap Bhanu Mehta (New Delhi: Oxford University Press, 2010), 15–27; Uday Singh Mehta, "Indian Constitutionalism: Crisis, Unity, and History," in Choudhry et al., *The Oxford Handbook of the Indian Constitution,* 38–54. Scholars have sometimes focused on specific themes to make similar arguments. With regard to free speech, for example, see Gautam Bhatia, "The Conservative Constitution: Freedom of Speech and the Constituent Assembly Debates," in *The Indian Constituent Assembly: Deliberations on Democracy,* ed. Udit Bhatia (Oxford: Routledge, 2008), 103–129.

38. Speech by Somnath Lahiri, Constituent Assembly of India, April 29, 1947, in *CAD,* 3:405.

39. Jawaharlal Nehru, *An Autobiography* (New Delhi: Penguin 2004 [1936]), 416. See also Nehru, *The Discovery of India* (New Delhi: Penguin, 2004 [1946]),

548. On the police and the maintenance of order during the colonial era, see Rajnarayan Chandavarkar, *Imperial Power and Popular Politics: Class, Resistance and the State in India, 1850–1950* (Cambridge: Cambridge University Press, 1998), 180–233; T. K. Vinod Kumar and Arvind Verma, "Hegemony, Discipline and Control in the Administration of Police in Colonial India," *Asian Journal of Criminology* 4 (2009): 61–78.

40. On the rule of law in colonial India, see Radhika Singha, *A Despotism of Law: Crime and Justice in Early Colonial India* (New Delhi: Oxford University Press, 1998); Nasser Hussain, *The Jurisprudence of Emergency: Colonialism and the Rule of Law* (Ann Arbor: University of Michigan Press, 2003); Elizabeth Kolsky, *Colonial Justice in British India: White Violence and the Rule of Law* (Cambridge: Cambridge University Press, 2010).

41. This typology is only one among many, though it dominates studies of constitutionalism. For an examination of constitutional typologies, see Dieter Grimm, "Types of Constitutions," in *The Oxford Handbook of Comparative Constitutional Law,* ed. Michel Rosenfeld and Andras Sajo (New York: Oxford University Press, 2013), 98–132.

42. See Resolutions adopted by the Second Session of the Indian National Congress, December 27–30, 1886, in *INC: The Glorious Tradition,* ed. A. M. Zaidi, vols. 1–4 (New Delhi: Indian Institute of Applied Political Research, 1987–1988), 1:27–28.

43. *Constitutional Proposals of the Sapru Committee* (Bombay: Padma, 1945), 190–197.

44. Speech by Jawaharlal Nehru, Constituent Assembly of India, November 25, 1948, in *CAD,* 7:588–589.

45. James Bryce, *Studies in History and Jurisprudence,* 2 vols. (New York: Oxford University Press, 1901), 1:129.

46. Ibid., 143.

47. See Ivor Jennings, *Some Characteristics of the Indian Constitution* (Madras: Oxford University Press, 1953), 9–29.

48. M'Culloch v. State, 17 U. S. 316 (1819).

49. Ibid., 407.

50. Ibid.

51. Jawaharlal Nehru, "Whiter India?," October 1933, in *Selected Works of Jawaharlal Nehru,* ed. S. Gopal, 1st ser., vols. 1–15 (New Delhi: Orient Longman, 1972–1982) (hereafter cited as *Selected Works*), 6:13.

52. Ibid.

53. Jawaharlal Nehru, "Evolution of British Policy in India," 1928, in *Selected Works,* 2:347.

54. On the stability of rules, see Schauer, *Playing by the Rules,* 156–157.

55. Speech by H. V. Pataskar, Constituent Assembly of India, November 18, 1949, in *CAD,* 11:673.

56. Speech by Gopal Narain, Constituent Assembly of India, November 22, 1949, in *CAD,* 11:803–804.

57. Speech by Rajendra Prasad, Constituent Assembly of India, April 29, 1947, in *CAD,* 3:418.

58. Ibid.

59. George Grote, *A History of Greece,* 12 vols. (New York: Cambridge University Press, 2009 [1847]), 4:204–216.

60. Speech by B. R. Ambedkar, Constituent Assembly of India, November 4, 1948, in *CAD,* 7:38. See Pratap Bhanu Mehta, "What Is Constitutional Morality?," *Seminar* 615 (2010): 17–22.

61. B. R. Ambedkar, "Communal Deadlock and a Way to Solve It," May 1945, in *Dr. B. R. Ambedkar: Writings and Speeches,* ed. Vasant Moon, 17 vols. (New Delhi: Dr. Ambedkar Foundation, 2014) (hereafter cited as *Dr. B. R. Ambedkar*), 1:360.

62. Ibid.

63. Ibid.

64. Speech by B. R. Ambedkar, Constituent Assembly of India, November 4, 1948, in *CAD,* 7:38.

65. Article 37, Constitution of India, 1950.

66. For a recent effort to theorize the idea of directive principles in constitutional law, see Lael K. Weis, "Constitutional Directive Principles," *Oxford Journal of Legal Studies* 37 (2017): 916–945.

67. Nehru, *An Autobiography,* 400.

68. Jawaharlal Nehru, "Swaraj and Socialism," August 11, 1928, in *Selected Works,* 3:371.

69. Nehru, *An Autobiography,* 452, 603.

70. Jawaharlal Nehru, "The Unity of India," October 8, 1937, in *Selected Works,* 8:621.

71. Ibid.

72. Jawaharlal Nehru, "Before India Is Reborn," June 1936, in *Selected Works,* 7:636.

73. See Dadabhai Naoroji, *Poverty and Un-British Rule in India* (Delhi: Government of India Press, 1962 [1901]); R. C. Dutt, *The Economic History of India,* 2 vols. (New York: Ben Franklin, 1970 [1906]).

74. See Nehru, *An Autobiography,* 175.

75. Ibid., 295.

76. Jawaharlal Nehru, Interview on the 1935 Act, January 27, 1936, in *Selected Works,* 7:80.

77. Jawaharlal Nehru, "India's Problems," February 21, 1936, in *Selected Works,* 7:115.

78. See Jawaharlal Nehru, "The Congress and World Crisis," November 5, 1937, in *Selected Works,* 7:536; Nehru, "The Unity of India," 620.

79. Jawaharlal Nehru, "The Need for Understanding India," June 27, 1938, in *Selected Works,* 9:28.

80. Jawaharlal Nehru, "Roads to Freedom," sometime after April 1919 (incomplete review), in *Selected Works,* 1:142.

81. Jawaharlal Nehru, "On Fascism and Democracy," October 28, 1933, and Speech at the Inauguration of the Civil Liberties Union at Madras, October 8, 1936, both in *Selected Works,* 6:115, 7:437.

82. Ibid.

83. Jawaharlal Nehru, Presidential Address at the Lucknow Congress, April 12, 1936, and Nehru, "Fascism and Communism," December 18, 1933, both in *Selected Works*, 7:173, 6:134.

84. Nehru, *An Autobiography*, 175.

85. Jawaharlal Nehru, Letter to Beltie Shah Gilani, December 3, 1933, in *Selected Works*, 6:126.

86. Jawaharlal Nehru, "The Congress and Socialism," January 13, 1937, in *Selected Works*, 7:61. See also Nehru, "Violence and Non-violence," January 16, 1942, in *Selected Works*, 12:77.

87. Nehru, *An Autobiography*, 565–566.

88. Jawaharlal Nehru, "On Federal Government," 1937, in *Selected Works*, 8:598. The editor of the selected writings, S. Gopal, credits Nehru with the authorship of this note, but it is worth mentioning that its publication in print was jointly credited to Jawaharlal Nehru, Narendra Dev, and K. T. Shah and the note appeared as the afterword to Shah's book on the Government of India Act of 1935. See K. T. Shah, *Federal Structure* (Bombay: Vora and Co., 1937), 510–511.

89. Nehru, "On Federal Government," 603.

90. Ibid., 610.

91. Ibid.

92. Report of the Committee of the All Parties Conference, 75.

93. Ibid., 76.

94. Resolutions adopted by the Forty-Fifth Session of the Indian National Congress, March 29–31, 1931, in *INC: The Glorious Tradition*, 3:185.

95. See Resolutions, Forty-Fifth Session, Indian National Congress, 186.

96. Nehru, *An Autobiography*, 279–280.

97. Mohandas K. Gandhi, Speech on Fundamental Rights, Karachi Congress, March 31, 1931, in *The Collected Works of Mahatma Gandhi*, 100 vols. (Government of India: Publications Division, 1956–1994) (hereafter cited as *Collected Works*), 45:372. See also Gandhi, "What We Can Do Today," July 30, 1931, in *Collected Works*, 47:235.

98. Alladi Krishnaswami Ayyar, Note on Fundamental Rights, March 14, 1947, in *The Framing of India's Constitution: Select Documents*, ed. B. Shiva Rao et al., 5 vols. (New Delhi: Universal Law Publishing, 1966), 2:67.

99. Minutes of the Meetings of the Sub-Committee on Fundamental Rights, February 27, 1947, in Rao et al., *Framing of India's Constitution*, 2:115.

100. Minutes of the Meetings of the Sub-Committee on Fundamental Rights, March 27, 1947, in Rao et al., *Framing of India's Constitution*, 2:125.

101. K. M. Munshi, Note and Draft Articles on Fundamental Rights, March 17, 1947, in Rao et al., *Framing of India's Constitution*, 2:69.

102. Ibid.

103. Ibid., 2:70.

104. Ibid., 2:73.

105. K. T. Shah, Note of Dissent, Sub-Committee on Fundamental Rights, April 16, 1947, and see also Shah, Comments on the Draft Report, Sub-Committee on Fundamental Rights, April 10, 1947, both in Rao et al., *Framing of India's Constitution*, 2:153, 192.

106. Shah, Dissent, Sub-Committee on Fundamental Rights, 2:192.

107. Ibid.

108. Niraja Gopal Jayal, *Citizenship and Its Discontents: An Indian History* (Cambridge, MA: Harvard University Press, 2013), 148.

109. B. R. Ambedkar, Memorandum and Draft Articles on the Rights of States and Minorities, March 24, 1947, in Rao et al., *Framing of India's Constitution,* 2:97–98.

110. Ibid., 2:89–90.

111. Ibid., 2:99.

112. Ibid.

113. Ibid., 2:100.

114. Ibid., 2:101.

115. Speech by B. R. Ambedkar, Constituent Assembly of India, November 4, 1948, in *CAD,* 7:41.

116. Jayal, *Citizenship and Its Discontents,* 152–153.

117. Ibid., 151.

118. Ambedkar's position is hardly surprising, considering that global trends at the time offered few precedents for strong rights-based review by courts. See, for example, Michaela Hailbronner, *Traditions and Transformations: The Rise of German Constitutionalism* (Oxford: Oxford University Press, 2015), 48–53.

119. This focus is no doubt partly shaped by contemporary debates on socio-economic rights. The recognition of such rights by constitutional documents, like the South African Constitution of 1996, and by constitutional courts, ranging from Colombia to India, has inspired an outpouring of literature on the possibility of justiciable socioeconomic rights. Important contributions include Cécile Fabre, *Social Rights under the Constitution: Government and the Decent Life* (New York: Oxford University Press, 2000); Martha C. Nussbaum, "Foreword—Constitutions and Capabilities: 'Perception' against Lofty Formalism," *Harvard Law Review* 121 (2007): 4–97; Mark Tushnet, *Weak Courts, Strong Rights: Judicial Review and Social Welfare Rights in Comparative Constitutional Law* (Princeton: Princeton University Press, 2007); Sandra Fredman, *Human Rights Transformed: Positive Rights and Positive Duties* (New York: Oxford University Press, 2008); Amartya Sen, *The Idea of Justice* (Cambridge: Harvard University Press, 2009), 379–385; Jeff King, *Judging Social Rights* (New York: Cambridge University Press, 2012). On the Indian experience, see Madhav Khosla, "Making Social Rights Conditional: Lessons from India," *International Journal of Constitutional Law* 8 (2010): 739–765.

120. Jayal, *Citizenship and Its Discontents,* 154–158.

121. Ibid., 152.

122. Resolutions adopted by the All India Congress Committee, November 15–17, 1947, in *INC: The Glorious Tradition,* 4:303.

123. Harel has offered one answer to this question. He has argued that the inclusion of the directive principles rests on a republican conception of freedom (i.e., freedom as nondomination). The incorporation of the directive principles, he suggests, confirmed that India's Parliament was not sovereign and was limited in the exercise of its powers. See Alon Harel, *Why Law Matters* (Oxford: Oxford University Press, 2014), 158–168. Harel is clearly on to something, but his suggestion does

not seem entirely satisfactory, if only because the political goal to which it appeals had already been achieved by the very fact of a written constitutional text that recognized the judicial review of legislation and separated power both vertically and horizontally. The account, moreover, does not fully capture the relationship between the directive principles and democratization. A different suggestion has been made by Khaitan, who has argued that the directive principles enabled the Indian constitution-making process to accommodate dissenters, and the technique thereby allowed the process to succeed by giving rebels a reason to buy into the enterprise. See Tarunabh Khaitan, "Directive Principles and the Expressive Accommodation of Ideological Dissenters," *International Journal of Constitutional Law* 16 (2018): 389–420. Among other things, this argument struggles to succeed on its own terms. If the directive principles had no meaning and were simply a device to accommodate rebels, then why would rebels consent to them? And if they had meaning, then their independent ideological, substantive weight cannot be reduced to the strategic, expressive accommodation of rebels.

124. For a recognition of this point in another context, see Noah Feldman, "Imposed Constitutionalism," *Connecticut Law Review* 37 (2005): 872.

125. The commitment to welfare would have to negotiate rights more generally, of course. This was to become one of the most contentious issues in independent India's constitutional politics. See Upendra Baxi, "Directive Principles and the Sociology of Indian Law," *Journal of the Indian Law Institute* 11 (1969): 245–272; P. K. Tripathi, *Spotlights on Constitutional Interpretation* (Bombay: N. M. Tripathi, 1972), 291–322; Gautam Bhatia, "Directive Principles of State Policy," in Choudhry et al., *The Oxford Handbook of the Indian Constitution,* 644–661.

126. Speech by B. R. Ambedkar, Constituent Assembly of India, November 25, 1949, in *CAD,* 11:975.

127. Sub-Committee on Fundamental Rights, Letter to the Chairman, Advisory Committee on Minorities, Fundamental Rights, etc., April 3, 1947, in Rao et al., *Framing of India's Constitution,* 2:137.

128. Speech by B. R. Ambedkar, Constituent Assembly of India, December 9, 1948, in *CAD,* 7:953.

129. B. N. Rau, Notes on Fundamental Rights, September 2, 1946, in Rao et al., *Framing of India's Constitution,* 2:33.

130. See Articles 40–45, Constitution of Ireland, 1945; H. Lauterpacht, *An International Bill of the Rights of Man* (New York: Oxford University Press, 2013 [1945]). On aspects of the twentieth-century approach to socioeconomic guarantees, see Samuel Moyn, *Not Enough: Human Rights in an Unequal World* (Cambridge, MA: Harvard University Press, 2018).

131. Lauterpacht, *International Bill,* 90.

132. Ibid., 134.

133. Ibid.

134. Speech by B. R. Ambedkar, Constituent Assembly of India, November 4, 1948, in *CAD,* 7:41.

135. Ibid.

136. Ibid.

137. Ibid.

138. B. R. Ambedkar, Report on the Constitution of the Government of Bombay Presidency, 1929, in *Dr. B. R. Ambedkar,* 2:323, 337.

139. See Jayal, *Citizenship and Its Discontents,* 155–156.

140. B. R. Ambedkar, "Ranade, Gandhi, and Jinnah," January 18, 1943, in *Dr. B. R. Ambedkar,* 1:222.

141. B. R. Ambedkar, "Labour and Parliamentary Democracy," September 17, 1943, in *Dr. B. R. Ambedkar,* 10:108.

142. Ambedkar, "Ranade, Gandhi, and Jinnah," 222.

143. Rau, Notes on Fundamental Rights, 34.

144. This is vividly portrayed by the focus of the Sapru Committee. See *Constitutional Proposals of the Sapru Committee.*

145. Resolutions adopted by the Special Session of the Indian National Congress, August 29–September 1, 1918, in *INC: The Glorious Tradition,* 1:408.

146. Jawaharlal Nehru, Report on the Brussels Congress, February 19, 1927, in *Selected Works,* 2:290.

147. Resolutions adopted by the Thirty-Fourth Session of the Indian National Congress, December 27–29, 1919, in *INC: The Glorious Tradition,* 1:436–437.

148. Resolutions adopted by the Fiftieth Session of the Indian National Congress, December 27–28, 1936, in *INC: The Glorious Tradition,* 3:339.

149. Nehru, "On Federal Government," 601.

150. *Constitutional Proposals of the Sapru Committee,* 257.

151. V. S. Srinivasa Sastri, Kamala Lectures, 1926, in *Speeches and Writings of the Right Honourable V. S. Srinivasa Sastri,* 2 vols. (Madras: Jupiter Press, 1969), 1:89.

152. Ibid.

153. Ibid., 1:95.

154. See, for example, clause 4(iv), Report of the Committee of the All Parties Conference, 1928, 75: "The right of free expression of opinion, as well as the right to assemble peaceably and without arms, and to form associations or unions, is hereby guaranteed for purposes not opposed to public order or morality."

155. Speech by Somnath Lahiri, Constituent Assembly of India, April 29, 1947, in *CAD,* 3:404.

156. Ibid.

157. Ibid., 3:405.

158. Speech by K. T. Shah, Constituent Assembly of India, November 17, 1949, in *CAD,* 11:619.

159. Ibid., 11:620.

160. Ibid.

161. Speech by Hukum Singh, Constituent Assembly of India, December 1, 1948, in *CAD,* 7:732.

162. Ibid., 7:733.

163. Speech by Hriday Nath Kunzru, Constituent Assembly of India, April 29, 1947, in *CAD,* 3:401.

164. Speech by Kazi Syed Karimuddin, Constituent Assembly of India, December 2, 1948, in *CAD,* 7:756.

165. Ibid.

166. Speech by B. R. Ambedkar, Constituent Assembly of India, November 4, 1948, in *CAD*, 7:40.

167. Gitlow v. New York, 268 U. S. 652 (1925), 666, cited in Speech by B. R. Ambedkar, Constituent Assembly of India, November 4, 1948, in *CAD*, 7:40.

168. Speech by B. R. Ambedkar, Constituent Assembly of India, November 4, 1948, in *CAD*, 7:41.

169. Ibid.

170. Speech by Alladi Krishnaswami Ayyar, Constituent Assembly of India, November 8, 1948, in *CAD*, 7:336.

171. Speech by Alladi Krishnaswami Ayyar, Constituent Assembly of India, November 23, 1949, in *CAD*, 11:837.

172. Ibid.

173. Rau, Notes on Fundamental Rights, 21–36.

174. Connolly v. Union Sewer Pipe Company, 184 U. S. 540 (1902).

175. Tigner v. Texas, 310 U. S. 141 (1940).

176. Rau, Notes on Fundamental Rights, 24.

177. Section 9, Illinois Trust Act, 1893.

178. Connolly v. Union Sewer Pipe Company, 563–564.

179. Tigner v. Texas, 146.

180. Ibid., 147.

181. Fox v. Standard Oil Co. of New Jersey, 294 U. S. 87 (1935).

182. Stewart Dry Goods v. Lewis, 294 U. S. 550 (1935).

183. Madden v. Kentucky, 309 U. S. 83 (1940).

184. Stewart Dry Goods v. Lewis, 560.

185. Ibid., 565–566.

186. Ibid., 566.

187. B. N. Rau, *India's Constitution in the Making*, ed. B. Shiva Rao (New Delhi: Orient Longmans, 1960), 364. The fear over uncertainty was also noticeable in topics that I have been unable to cover. A noteworthy example is executive power and federalism. See, for instance, Speech by T. T. Krishnamachari, Constituent Assembly of India, December 30, 1948, in *CAD*, 7:1133: "It is conceivable that if we say nothing about the exercise of the executive powers in the concurrent list, the courts may interpret it one way or the other and the Constitution may become more federal or less federal as circumstances arise and the views of the judges in this regard and the decisions that they arrive at."

188. This argument has been made with great force in Grégoire Webber, *The Negotiable Constitution: On the Limitation of Rights* (New York: Cambridge University Press, 2009).

189. Speech by K. M. Munshi, Constituent Assembly of India, December 6, 1948, in *CAD*, 7:851.

190. Ibid.

191. Speech by Thakur Das Bhargava, Constituent Assembly of India, September 15, 1949, *CAD*, 9:1503.

192. Speech by Mahboob Ali Baig Sahib Bahadur, December 6, 1948, in *CAD*, 7:845.

193. Speech by Z. H. Lari, December 6, 1948, in *CAD,* 7:855.

194. On the history and meaning of due process in the United States, see Nathan S. Chapman and Michael W. McConnell, "Due Process as Separation of Powers," *Yale Law Journal* 121 (2012): 1584–2031.

195. Rau, Notes on Fundamental Rights, 29.

196. Ibid.

197. B. N. Rau, Report by the Constitutional Adviser on his visit to USA, Canada, Ireland, and England, October–December 1947, in Rao et al., *Framing of India's Constitution,* 2:67.

198. Rau, Notes on Fundamental Rights, 31.

199. Ibid.

200. Louisville Joint Stock Land Bank v. Radford, 295 U. S. 555 (1935).

201. B. N. Rau, Notes on the Draft Report, April 8, 1947, in Rao et al., *Framing of India's Constitution,* 2:151.

202. Lochner v. New York, 198 U. S. 45 (1905); Bunting v. Oregon, 243 U. S. 426 (1917).

203. Adkins v. Children's Hospital of the District of Columbia, 261 U. S. 525 (1923); West Coast v. Parrish, 300 U. S. 379 (1937).

204. Ferguson v. Skrupa, 372 U. S. 726 (1963), 731.

205. Austin, *The Indian Constitution,* 110n12.

206. Speech by Alladi Krishnaswami Ayyar, Constituent Assembly of India, December 6, 1948, in *CAD,* 7:853.

207. Ibid.

208. Speech by Alladi Krishnaswami Ayyar, Constituent Assembly of India, September 15, 1949, in *CAD,* 9:1537.

209. Alladi Krishnaswami Ayyar, Speech in Advisory Committee proceedings, April 21–22, 1947, in Rao et al., *Framing of India's Constitution,* 2:242.

210. Ayyar, Note on Fundamental Rights, 67.

211. Speech by Kazi Syed Karimuddin, Constituent Assembly of India, December 6, 1948, in *CAD,* 7:843.

212. Speech by Alladi Krishnaswami Ayyar, Constituent Assembly of India, September 1, 1949, in *CAD,* 9:852.

213. Speech by B. R. Ambedkar, Constituent Assembly of India, December 13, 1948, in *CAD,* 7:999–1001.

214. Speech by B. R. Ambedkar, Constituent Assembly of India, September 16, 1949, in *CAD,* 9:1588.

215. See Article 22, Constitution of India, 1950.

216. Speech by B. R. Ambedkar, Constituent Assembly of India, September 15, 1949, in *CAD,* 9:1500.

217. See Gardner, *Law as a Leap of Faith,* 116–124.

218. It is only rarely that scholars recognize that the role of a constitutional text might be far greater in certain circumstances and societies than in others. For a noteworthy example, see David A. Strauss, "Common Law Constitutional Interpretation," *University of Chicago Law Review* 63 (1996): 923–924.

219. For a leading statement of this position, see Cass R. Sunstein, *Legal Reasoning and Political Conflict,* 2nd ed. (New York: Oxford University Press, 2018).

On silence as a key characteristic of constitutions, see Martin Loughlin, "The Silences of Constitutions," *International Journal of Constitutional Law* 16 (2018): 922–935.

220. See Rosalind Dixon and Tom Ginsburg, "Deciding Not to Decide: Deferral in Constitutional Design," *International Journal of Constitutional Law* 9 (2011): 636–672; Mark Tushnet, "Constitution-Making: An Introduction," *Texas Law Review* 91 (2013): 2007–2012. In a recent study, Lerner has applied the idea of deferral to the Indian founding. See Hanna Lerner, *Making Constitutions in Deeply Divided Societies* (New York: Cambridge University Press, 2011). She suggests that India's founders hoped to mitigate social conflict through a strategic adoption of "ambiguous constitutional formulations in the area of personal law and national language" (148). Like the statist reading of India's founding, this account of constitutional incrementalism casts the moment in an antirevolutionary light. The strategy, it is claimed, involved "transferring the most controversial choices regarding the foundational aspect of their constitution from the constitutional arena to the political one" (10). Though provocative, such an argument is hard to sustain. It rests entirely on decisions pertaining to two matters—language and personal laws—without any effort to explain the vast number of other choices. Moreover, the two examples themselves merit further interrogation. On the issue of language, for example, the constitutional text is not vague. In an innovative and precise manner, the language-related provisions disaggregated the choice of official language into different institutional settings. Rather than bracket the choice of a sovereign language, the text developed a mechanism by which one language need not trump all others. See Sujit Choudhry, "Managing Linguistic Nationalism through Constitutional Design: Lessons from South Asia," *International Journal of Constitutional Law* 7 (2009): 577–618.

221. See Charles Taylor, "Interpretation and the Sciences of Man," 27–29.

222. The classic study of law and its normative construction remains Robert M. Cover, "Foreword: *Nomos* and Narrative," *Harvard Law Review* 97 (1983): 4–68.

223. Speech by B. R. Ambedkar, Constituent Assembly of India, November 25, 1949, in *CAD*, 11:978.

224. On constitutions as precommitment devices, see Stephen Holmes, *Passions and Constraint: On the Theory of Liberal Democracy* (Chicago: University of Chicago Press, 1995), 134–177.

225. See John Gardner, "How to Be a Good Judge," *London Review of Books*, July 8, 2010, 15.

2. The Location of Power

1. See Duncan Bell, *The Idea of Greater Britain: Empire and the Future of World Order, 1860–1900* (Princeton: Princeton University Press, 2007); Mark Hewitson and Matthew D'Auria, eds., *Europe in Crisis: Intellectuals and the European Idea, 1917–1957* (New York: Berhahn Books, 2012); Frederick Cooper, *Citizenship between Empire and Nation: Remaking France and French Africa, 1945–1960* (Princeton: Princeton University Press, 2014); Gary Wilder, *Freedom Time: Negritude, Decolonization, and the Future of the World* (Durham, NC: Duke University

Press, 2015); Gil Rubin, "From Federalism to Binationalism: Hannah Arendt's Shifting Zionism," *Contemporary European History* 24 (2015): 393–414; William Selinger, "The Politics of Arendtian Historiography: European Federation and the Origins of Totalitarianism," *Modern Intellectual History* 13 (2016): 417–446; Or Rosenboim, *The Emergence of Globalism: Visions of World Order in Britain and the United States, 1939–1950* (Princeton: Princeton University Press, 2017); Quinn Slobodian, *Globalists: The End of Empire and the Birth of Neoliberalism* (Cambridge, MA: Harvard University Press, 2018); Adom Getachew, *Worldmaking after Empire: The Rise and Fall of Self-Determination* (Princeton: Princeton University Press, 2019).

2. Speech by B. R. Ambedkar, Constituent Assembly of India, November 25, 1949, in *Constituent Assembly Debates,* 12 vols. (New Delhi: Lok Sabha Secretariat, 2009 [1950]) (hereafter cited as *CAD*), 11:976–977.

3. See Article 3, Constitution of India, 1950.

4. K. C. Wheare, *Federal Government,* 4th ed. (London: Oxford University Press, 1963), 28. See also Benjamin N. Schoenfeld, *Federalism in India* (Washington, DC: Public Affairs, 1960), 14–15.

5. C. H. Alexandrowicz, "Is India a Federation?," *International and Comparative Law Quarterly* 393 (1954). On Alexandrowicz's work and legacy, see David Armitage and Jennifer Pitts, "'This Modern Grotius': An Introduction to the Life and Thought of C. H. Alexandrowicz," in C. H. Alexandrowicz, *The Law of Nations in Global History,* ed. David Armitage and Jennifer Pitts (Oxford: Oxford University Press, 2017), 1–31.

6. Some scholars have thus referred to India as a form of "holding together" rather than "coming together" federalism. See Alfred Stephan, *Arguing Comparative Politics* (New York: Oxford University Press, 2001), 320–323.

7. Alexandrowicz, "Is India a Federation?," 403. The atypical character of Indian federalism was noticed a great many times during the proceedings of the Constituent Assembly. See, for example, the speech by G. L. Mehta, Constituent Assembly of India, August 21, 1947, in *CAD,* 5:76–79.

8. Uday Singh Mehta's recent work has rightly underlined the founding commitment to a strong state. See Uday Singh Mehta, "Constitutionalism," in *The Oxford Companion to Politics in India,* ed. Niraja Gopal Jayal and Pratap Bhanu Mehta (New Delhi: Oxford University Press, 2010), 15–27; Uday Singh Mehta, "Indian Constitutionalism: Crisis, Unity, and History," in *The Oxford Handbook of the Indian Constitution,* ed. Sujit Choudhry, Madhav Khosla, and Pratap Bhanu Mehta (Oxford: Oxford University Press, 2016), 38–54. My account is different in key ways, not least of all because I take the choice to have occurred alongside crucial constraints on state power. Importantly, Mehta's work says very little about the motivations behind the centrality of the state. For studies that interrogate the motivations behind the statist commitment at India's birth, see Partha Chatterjee, *Nationalist Thought and the Colonial World: A Derivative Discourse* (London: Zed Books, 1986); Sudipta Kaviraj, *The Enchantment of Democracy and India* (Ranikhet: Permanent Black, 2011).

9. This standard way of understanding centralization would see it as similar to the choice of parliamentary over presidential government, which was sometimes

defended on the basis that it would enable harmonious legislative–executive relations and prevent institutional conflict in a new democracy. For this defense of parliamentarianism, see the Speech by Alladi Krishnaswami Ayyar, Constituent Assembly of India, December 10, 1948, in *CAD*, 7:985–986.

10. See Karuna Mantena, "Popular Sovereignty and Anti-Colonialism," in *Popular Sovereignty in Historical Perspective*, ed. Richard Bourke and Quentin Skinner (Cambridge: Cambridge University Press, 2016), 297–301. On other colonial visions of the future, see Manu Goswami, "Imaginary Futures and Colonial Internationalisms," *American Historical Review* 117 (2012): 1461–1485.

11. It should not be assumed that such an inward-looking investigation is a necessary part of the colonial experience. See Aung San Suu Kyi, "Intellectual Life in Burma and India under Colonialism," in *Freedom from Fear and Other Writings*, ed. Michael Aris (London: Penguin, 2010), 83–100.

12. On this shift, see Sudipta Kaviraj, *The Imaginary Institution of India: Politics and Ideas* (New York: Columbia University Press, 2010), 172–173.

13. Mohandas K. Gandhi, *Hind Swaraj and Other Writings*, ed. Anthony J. Parel (Cambridge: Cambridge University Press, 1997 [1909]), 26.

14. Ibid., 28.

15. Ibid.

16. Ibid., 29.

17. Ibid.

18. Ibid.

19. Ibid.

20. Ibid., 31.

21. Ibid., 32.

22. Ibid., 35.

23. Ibid., 36.

24. Ibid., 37.

25. Ibid., 42.

26. Ibid., 37.

27. Ibid., 39.

28. Ibid., 7.

29. Ibid., 33.

30. Ibid., 38.

31. For a careful analysis of the conceptual relationship between anticolonialism and anti-statism, see Karuna Mantena, "On Gandhi's Critique of the State: Sources, Contexts, Conjectures," *Modern Intellectual History* 9 (2012): 535–563.

32. Gandhi, *Hind Swaraj*, 6.

33. Ibid., 10–11.

34. Ibid., 31.

35. Ibid., 34.

36. Edward Carpenter, *Civilization: Its Cause and Cure, and Other Essays* (London: Swan Sonnenschein, 1891), 1.

37. Ibid., 3.

38. Ibid.

39. Ibid., 31.

40. Gandhi, *Hind Swaraj,* 57.

41. Ibid., 59.

42. Ibid., 63.

43. Ibid.

44. Ibid., 49.

45. Ibid., 107.

46. See the petition to the Natal Legislative Assembly, June 28, 1894, in *The Collected Works of Mahatma Gandhi,* 100 vols. (Government of India: Publications Division, 1956–1994) (hereafter cited as *Collected Works*), 1:128. On Gandhi's early efforts in South Africa, see Ramachandra Guha, *Gandhi before India* (New Delhi: Allen Lane, 2013), 55–81. For Maine's analysis of the Indian village, see Henry Sumner Maine, *Village-Communities in the East and West* (London: John Murray, 1871).

47. Mohandas K. Gandhi, "The Indian Franchise," December 16, 1895, in *Collected Works,* 1:269–270.

48. Ibid.

49. Mohandas K. Gandhi, "Baroda: A Model Indian State," June 3, 1905, in *Collected Works,* 4:457.

50. Ibid.

51. Mohandas K. Gandhi, Preface to Leo Tolstoy's "Letter to a Hindoo," November 19, 1909, in *Collected Works,* 10:4.

52. Ibid.

53. See, for example, Mohandas K. Gandhi, "Village Industries," November 15, 1934, in *Collected Works,* 59:255; Gandhi, Speech at Gandhi Seva Sangh, November 30, 1934, in *Collected Works,* 59:408; Gandhi, Letter to Jhaverbhai Patel, August 23, 1944, in *Collected Works,* 78:45; Gandhi, "How to Improve Village Industries," May 21, 1945, in *Collected Works,* 80:152; Gandhi, Speech at Industries Ministers Conference, July 31, 1946, in *Collected Works,* 85:95; Gandhi, "Decentralisation," October 15, 1946, in *Collected Works,* 85:459.

54. Mohandas K. Gandhi, "What of the West?," September 3, 1925, in *Collected Works,* 28:147.

55. Mohandas K. Gandhi, Letter to Jawaharlal Nehru, October 5, 1945, in *Collected Works,* 81:319.

56. Mohandas K. Gandhi, "Independence," July 21, 1946, in *Collected Works,* 85:33.

57. Mohandas K. Gandhi, "Panchayats," May 28, 1931, in *Collected Works,* 46:240.

58. Mohandas K. Gandhi, "Democracy and Non-Violence," May 13, 1940, in *Collected Works,* 72:60. On the relationship between democratic politics and violence in Gandhi's thought, see Uday Singh Mehta, "Gandhi on Democracy, Politics, and the Ethics of Everyday Life," *Modern Intellectual History* 7 (2010): 355–371.

59. See Mantena, "On Gandhi's Critique."

60. Radhakamal Mukerjee, *The Foundations of Indian Economics* (London: Longmans, Green and Co., 1916), 3–4.

61. Radhakamal Mukerjee, *Democracies of the East: A Study in Comparative Politics* (London: P. S. King and Son, 1923).

62. Ibid., viii.

63. Ibid., x.

64. Ibid., xxvi.

65. Ibid., xvi.

66. Ibid., xxv. On Mukerjee's idea of human community, see also Radhakamal Mukerjee, *The Community of Communities* (Bombay: Manaktala, 1966).

67. Mukerjee, *Democracies of the East,* 12.

68. Ibid., 15–16.

69. Ibid., 24.

70. Ibid., 76–77.

71. Ibid., 102.

72. Ibid., 89.

73. Ibid., 166.

74. Ibid., 115–116.

75. Radhakumud Mookerji, *Local Government in Ancient India* (Oxford: Clarendon Press, 1919).

76. Ibid., 10.

77. Ibid., 19.

78. Ibid., 20.

79. See Mukerjee, *Democracies of the East,* 150–160.

80. Ibid., 22.

81. Ibid., 122–131.

82. *The Fifth Report from the Select Committee of the House of Commons on the Affairs of the East India Company,* July 28, 1812, ed. Walter Kelly Firminger, vol. 1 (Calcutta: R. Cambray and Co., 1917), 158.

83. Ibid.

84. Minutes of Charles T. Metcalfe, November 7, 1830, *Minutes of Evidence Taken before the Select Committee on the Affairs of the East India Company,* pt. 3 (London: J. L. Cox and Son, 1833), 331.

85. See Mantena, "On Gandhi's Critique," 540–545. For Maine's account of the village community, see Maine, *Village-Communities;* Henry Sumner Maine, *Ancient Law: Its Connection with the Early History of Society, and Its Relation to Modern Ideas* (London: John Murray, 1861).

86. Mukerjee, *Democracies of the East,* 297.

87. Ibid., 34.

88. Mantena, "On Gandhi's Critique." The literature on political pluralism is vast, but notable contributions include David Runciman, *Pluralism and the Personality of the State* (Cambridge: Cambridge University Press, 1997); Marc Stears, *Progressives, Pluralists, and the Problems of the State: Ideologies of Reform in the United States and Britain, 1906–1926* (Oxford: Oxford University Press, 2002).

89. Mukerjee, *Democracies of the East,* 339, citing George H. Sabine, "The Concept of the State as Power," *Philosophical Review* 29 (1920): 301–318.

90. Harold J. Laski, "A Note on M. Duguit," *Harvard Law Review* 31 (1917): 186.

91. Harold J. Laski, *Studies in the Problem of Sovereignty* (New Haven: Yale University Press, 1917), 12.

92. Mukerjee, *Democracies of the East*, 352.

93. Ibid., 357.

94. Ibid., 364.

95. Ibid., 156.

96. Mantena, "On Gandhi's Critique," 553–558.

97. Mukerjee, *Democracies of the East*, 146.

98. Ibid., 326.

99. Ibid., 166.

100. Ibid., 325.

101. Ibid., 360.

102. Ibid., 361.

103. Ibid., 363.

104. Ibid., 149.

105. Shriman Narayan Agarwal, *Gandhian Constitution for Free India* (Allahabad: Kitabistan, 1946). The text featured a foreword by Gandhi.

106. Shriman Narayan Agarwal, *The Gandhian Plan of Economic Development for India* (Bombay: Padma, 1944). This text, too, contained a foreword by Gandhi. An important figure within Gandhian economic thought was J. C. Kumarappa. See Benjamin Zachariah, *Developing India: An Intellectual and Social History* (New Delhi: Oxford University Press, 2005), 156–210; Venu Madhav Govindu and Deepak Malghan, *The Web of Freedom: J. C. Kumarappa and Gandhi's Struggle for Economic Justice* (New Delhi: Oxford University Press, 2016); Taylor C. Sherman, "A Gandhian Answer to the Threat of Communism? Sarvodaya and Postcolonial Nationalism in India," *Indian Economic and Social History Review* 53 (2016): 249–270.

107. Ibid., 5.

108. Mohandas K. Gandhi, Interview to P. Ramachandra Rao, June 19, 1945, in *Collected Works*, 80:353.

109. Agarwal, *Gandhian Constitution for Free India*, 11.

110. Ibid.

111. Ibid., 51.

112. Ibid., 68.

113. Ibid., 97.

114. Ibid., 98.

115. Ibid., 135.

116. Although my focus is on Indian political thought, colonial efforts at planning are to be acknowledged. See Raghabendra Chattopadhyay, "An Early British Government Initiative in the Genesis of Indian Planning," *Economic and Political Weekly* 22 (1987): 19–29.

117. M. Visvesvaraya, *Reconstructing India* (London: P. S. King and Son, 1920).

118. Ibid., 17–35.

119. Ibid., 1–16.

120. See Shiv Visvanathan, *Organizing for Science: The Making of an Industrial Research Laboratory* (Delhi: Oxford University Press, 1985).

121. See ibid., 97–132.

122. See Sugata Bose, *His Majesty's Opponent: Subhas Chandra Bose and India's Struggle against Empire* (Cambridge, MA: Harvard University Press, 2011), 137–146.

123. Among major Indian thinkers who underlined the importance of the state and industrial development, one figure worth mentioning is Mahadev Govind Ranade. See Mahadev Govind Ranade, *Essays on Indian Economics: A Collection of Essays and Speeches* (Madras: G. A. Natesan and Co., 1898). For a brief description, see Joseph J. Spengler, *Indian Economic Thought: A Preface to Its History* (Durham, NC: Duke University Press, 1971), 148–150.

124. Jawaharlal Nehru, Presidential Address at the Lucknow Congress, April 12, 1936, in *Selected Works of Jawaharlal Nehru,* ed. S. Gopal, 1st ser., vols. 1–15 (New Delhi: Orient Longman, 1972–1982) (hereafter cited as *Selected Works*), 7:181.

125. Ibid., 7:182.

126. See Jawaharlal Nehru, *Soviet Russia,* 1928, in *Selected Works,* 2:377.

127. See Sarvepalli Gopal, *Jawaharlal Nehru: A Biography,* vol. 1 (New Delhi: Oxford University Press, 1975), 245–248.

128. Jawaharlal Nehru, Note to the National Planning Committee, June 4, 1939, in *Selected Works,* 9:378.

129. Ibid.

130. Ibid., 9:377–378.

131. See Jawaharlal Nehru, Note on the Guidelines for Planning, June 19, 1939, in *Selected Works,* 9:386.

132. See Jawaharlal Nehru, "China Rebuilds for Democracy," July 2, 1942, in *Selected Works,* 12:569–571.

133. Jawaharlal Nehru, Letter to Mohandas K. Gandhi, October 4, 1945, in *Selected Works,* 14:554.

134. Ibid.

135. Ibid., 14:555.

136. Jawaharlal Nehru, "The Purpose of Planning," October 4, 1940, in *Selected Works,* 11:315.

137. Ibid.

138. Nehru, Letter to Mohandas K. Gandhi, October 4, 1945, 555.

139. Ibid., 556.

140. Jawaharlal Nehru, *An Autobiography* (New Delhi: Penguin, 2004 [1936]), 435.

141. Jawaharlal Nehru, Letter to Krishna Kripalani, September 29, 1939, in *Selected Works,* 10:540.

142. Jawaharlal Nehru, "Roads to Freedom," sometime after April 1919 (incomplete review), in *Selected Works,* 1:142.

143. Ibid.

144. Nehru, *An Autobiography,* 452.

145. Jawaharlal Nehru, "The Feudal Demand for Pakistan," December 17, 1945, in *Selected Works,* 14:269–270. See also Jawaharlal Nehru, *The Discovery of India* (New Delhi: Penguin, 2004 [1946]), 552.

146. Jawaharlal Nehru, Interview, July 8, 1945, in *Selected Works,* 14:36. Nehru had previously expressed similar faith in the responsiveness of democratic politics. See Nehru, *An Autobiography,* 465.

147. See Jawaharlal Nehru, Interview, May 22, 1942, in *Selected Works,* 12:327.

148. M. Visvesvaraya, *Prosperity through Industry: Move towards Rapid Industrialisation* (Bombay: All-India Manufacturers' Organisation, 1943).

149. Ibid., 1–2.

150. Ibid., 51.

151. Sir Purshotamdas Thakurdas et al., *A Plan of Economic Development for India* (London: Penguin, 1945).

152. P. S. Lokanathan, "The Bombay Plan," *Foreign Affairs* 23 (1945): 685. On the Bombay Plan and its historical context, see Srinath Raghavan, *India's War: The Making of Modern South Asia, 1939–1945* (London: Allen Lane, 2016), 435–438.

153. See Resolutions passed by the Congress Working Committee, January 17–20, 1950, in *INC: The Glorious Tradition,* 4:464–468.

154. Nehru, *An Autobiography,* 153.

155. Jawaharlal Nehru, Report to the All India Congress Committee at Haripura, February 17, 1938, in *Selected Works,* 8:756.

156. Nehru, *An Autobiography,* 122.

157. B. R. Ambedkar, "Labour and Parliamentary Democracy," September 17, 1943, in *Dr. B. R. Ambedkar: Writings and Speeches,* ed. Vasant Moon, 17 vols. (New Delhi: Dr. Ambedkar Foundation, 2014) (hereafter cited as *Dr. B. R. Ambedkar*), 10:107.

158. Ibid., 10:108–109.

159. B. R. Ambedkar, *What Congress and Gandhi Have Done to the Untouchables,* 1945, in *Dr. B. R. Ambedkar,* 9:282–283.

160. Ibid., 9:283.

161. Ibid., 9:284.

162. Gandhi, "How to Improve Village Industries," 152.

163. Ambedkar, *What Congress and Gandhi Have Done to the Untouchables,* 290–291.

164. B. R. Ambedkar, "On Village Panchayats Bill: 1," October 6, 1932, in *Dr. B. R. Ambedkar,* 2:106.

165. See, for example, K. T. Shah, *Federal Structure* (Bombay: Vora and Co., 1937), 101. See also B. R. Ambedkar, "Federation versus Freedom," January 29, 1939, in *Dr. B. R. Ambedkar,* 1:279.

166. Jawaharlal Nehru, "Where Are We?," March 1939, in *Selected Works,* 9:501–502.

167. Clause 3, Aims and Objects Resolution, Constituent Assembly of India, in *CAD,* 1:59.

168. Speech by Sachchidananda Sinha, Constituent Assembly of India, December 9, 1946, in *CAD,* 1:5, citing James Bryce, *The American Commonwealth,* vol. 1 (Indianapolis: Liberty Fund, 1995 [1914]), 14.

169. Speech by Jawaharlal Nehru, Constituent Assembly of India, December 13, 1946, in *CAD,* 1:58.

170. Ibid.

171. See the speeches by N. Gopalaswami Ayyangar, Constituent Assembly of India, December 18, 1946, in *CAD*, 2:127–130; S. Radhakrishnan, Constituent Assembly of India, January 20, 1947, in *CAD*, 2:271–272.

172. Ibid.; Shrikrishna Sinha, Constituent Assembly of India, December 16, 1946, in *CAD*, 1:89.

173. Speech by Purushottam Das Tandon, Constituent Assembly of India, December 13, 1946, in *CAD*, 1:67.

174. Speech by B. R. Ambedkar, Constituent Assembly of India, December 17, 1946, in *CAD*, 1:102. Even when Ambedkar argued for provincial autonomy during colonial rule, he was against any substantial weakening in central power. He regarded federations as fragile entities because their power rested on the power of the units. A federation was only as strong as its constituent parts. By contrast, Ambedkar wanted a central government "so independent that not only should it survive even when all provincial governments have vanished or changed into wholly different bodies, but it should have the power to carry on provincial administration when a provincial government by rebellion or otherwise has ceased to function." Ambedkar, Report on the Constitution of the Government of Bombay Presidency, 1929, in *Dr. B. R. Ambedkar*, 385.

175. Speech by R. K. Sidhwa, Constituent Assembly of India, December 18, 1946, in *CAD*, 1:117. In earlier decades, too, there were calls for local autonomy, but these were attempts toward greater Indian participation and increased self-government. See Resolutions adopted by the Thirtieth Session of the Indian National Congress, December 27–29, 1915, in *INC: The Glorious Tradition*, 1:376.

176. Speech by K. M. Munshi, Constituent Assembly of India, July 14, 1947, in *CAD*, 4:546.

177. Ibid.

178. Speech by N. Gopalaswami Ayyangar, Constituent Assembly of India, August 20, 1947, in *CAD*, 5:38.

179. Letter from Jawaharlal Nehru, Chairman of the Union Powers Committee, to President, Constituent Assembly of India, July 5, 1947, in *CAD*, 5:58–59.

180. Speech by Brajeshwar Prasad, Constituent Assembly of India, November 9, 1948, in *CAD*, 7:371.

181. Speech by P. R. Thakur, Constituent Assembly of India, January 25, 1947, in *CAD*, 2:357.

182. See Speech by Hriday Nath Kunzru, Constituent Assembly of India, August 25, 1947, in *CAD*, 5:146; Speech by Shibban Lal Saksena, Constituent Assembly of India, August 2, 1949, in *CAD*, 9:109.

183. Speech by Brajeshwar Prasad, Constituent Assembly of India, November 9, 1948, in *CAD*, 7:372.

184. Speech by S. H. Prater, Constituent Assembly of India, January 21, 1947, in *CAD*, 2:307.

185. Speech by K. M. Munshi, Constituent Assembly of India, June 16, 1949, in *CAD*, 8:927–928.

186. Speech by Brajeshwar Prasad, Constituent Assembly of India, November 15, 1949, in *CAD*, 11:515.

187. Article 356, Constitution of India, 1950.

188. Speech by Shibban Lal Saksena, Constituent Assembly of India, August 2, 1949, in *CAD*, 9:109.

189. Speech by Alladi Krishnaswami Ayyar, Constituent Assembly of India, July 25, 1947, in *CAD*, 4:847.

190. See, for example, K. T. Shah, *Provincial Autonomy* (Bombay: Vora and Co., 1937), 246–248.

191. Speech by Alladi Krishnaswami Ayyar, Constituent Assembly of India, August 3, 1949, in *CAD*, 9:151.

192. See Andrew Muldoon, *Empire, Politics, and the Creation of the 1935 India Act* (Surrey: Ashgate, 2009).

193. See Ian Copland, *The Princes of India in the Endgame of Empire, 1917–1947* (Cambridge: Cambridge University Press, 1997).

194. Speech by Vallabhbhai Patel, Constituent Assembly of India, October 12, 1949, in *CAD*, 10:167–168.

195. Speech by R. K. Sidhwa, Constituent Assembly of India, October 13, 1949, in *CAD*, 10:179–182.

196. Speech by Mahomed Sheriff, Constituent Assembly of India, August 21, 1947, in *CAD*, 5:69–70. See also Speech by Kamlapati Tiwari, November 23, 1949, in *CAD*, 11:863–864.

197. Speech by Mahboob Ali Baig Sahib Bahadur, Constituent Assembly of India, November 8, 1948, in *CAD*, 7:296. See also Speech by K. Hanumanthaiya, Constituent Assembly of India, November 8, 1948, in *CAD*, 7:339; Speech by Maulana Hasrat Mohani, October 17, 1949, in *CAD*, 10:432–434; Speech by Bhopinder Singh Man, Constituent Assembly of India, November 21, 1949, in *CAD*, 11:721.

198. Speech by K. V. Kamath, Constituent Assembly of India, August 2, 1949, in *CAD*, 9:105.

199. Speech by Lokanath Misra, Constituent Assembly of India, November 5, 1948, in *CAD*, 7:241.

200. Speech by Rohini Kumar Chaudhari, Constituent Assembly of India, November 17, 1948, in *CAD*, 7:446–447.

201. Speech by Naziruddin Ahmad, Constituent Assembly of India, August 3, 1949, in *CAD*, 9:161.

202. Speech by P. T. Chacko, Constituent Assembly of India, November 21, 1949, in *CAD*, 11:746.

203. See Speech by K. T. Shah, Constituent Assembly of India, November 17, 1948, in *CAD*, 7:438; Speech by Hriday Nath Kunzru, October 16, 1949, in *CAD*, 10:370–371; Speech by T. Prakasam, Constituent Assembly of India, November 19, 1949, in *CAD*, 11:702.

204. Speech by Hriday Nath Kunzru, Constituent Assembly of India, November 22, 1949, in *CAD*, 11:784.

205. Speech by Sarangadhar Das, Constituent Assembly of India, October 13, 1949, in *CAD*, 10:186.

206. See Speech by Lokanath Misra, Constituent Assembly of India, November 22, 1949, in *CAD*, 11:798.

207. Speech by H. V. Pataskar, Constituent Assembly of India, November 18, 1949, in *CAD*, 10:671; see also Speech by Lakshminarayan Sahu, Constituent Assembly of India, November 17, 1949, in *CAD*, 11:614.

208. Speech by K. Hanumanthaiya, Constituent Assembly of India, November 17, 1949, in *CAD*, 11:616.

209. See Speech by Syamanadan Sahaya, Constituent Assembly of India, November 22, 1949, in *CAD*, 11:789.

210. See Speech by T. Prakasam, Constituent Assembly of India, November 22, 1948, in *CAD*, 7:521–522; Speech by Govind Das, Constituent Assembly of India, November 23, 1948, in *CAD*, 7:521–522; Speech by B. P. Jhunjhunwala, Constituent Assembly of India, November 23, 1949, in *CAD*, 11:831–834.

211. Speech by T. T. Krishnamachari, Constituent Assembly of India, August 2, 1949, in *CAD*, 9:122.

212. Letter from Jawaharlal Nehru to Lord Wavell, October 15, 1946, in *Sardar Patel's Correspondence, 1945–50*, ed. Durga Das, 10 vols. (Ahmedabad: Navajivan, 1971–1974), 3:183–184.

213. Speech by B. R. Ambedkar, Constituent Assembly of India, November 25, 1949, in *CAD*, 11:977.

214. Speech by B. R. Ambedkar. Constituent Assembly of India, November 4, 1948, in *CAD*, 7:36.

215. Ibid., 7:39.

216. Ibid.

217. Ibid.

218. Speech by B. Pocker Sahib Bahadur, Constituent Assembly of India, December 30, 1948, in *CAD*, 7:1129–1131.

219. T. T. Krishnamachari, Constituent Assembly of India, December 30, 1948, in *CAD*, 7:1132.

220. Ibid., 7:1133.

221. Ibid., 7:1133–1134.

222. Ibid., 7:1135.

223. Ibid., 7:1136.

224. Speech by B. R. Ambedkar, Constituent Assembly of India, December 30, 1948, in *CAD*, 7:1137.

225. Section 126, Government of India Act, 1935.

226. Section 126A, Government of India Act, 1935.

227. Speech by B. R. Ambedkar, Constituent Assembly of India, December 30, 1948, in *CAD*, 7:1138.

228. See Speech by B. R. Ambedkar, Constituent Assembly of India, November 4, 1948, in *CAD*, 7:34–35.

229. Speech by B. R. Ambedkar, Constituent Assembly of India, December 30, 1948, in *CAD*, 7:1140.

230. Speech by Balkrishna Sharma, Constituent Assembly of India, August 21, 1947, in *CAD*, 5:77. In a description of the Soviet Union Constitution in 1928, Nehru had noted the sovereign character of the republics forming the Union but recognized that "the Communist Party, although it has apparently no official status

in the constitution, is really a pillar of the Soviet regime." Jawaharlal Nehru, "The Constitution of U.S.S.R.," May 24, 1928, in *Selected Works*, 2:397.

231. Speech by Alladi Krishnaswami Ayyar, Constituent Assembly of India, November 8, 1948, in *CAD*, 7:335.

232. See Speech by K. M. Munshi, Constituent Assembly of India, June 16, 1949, in *CAD*, 8:927–928.

233. See Speech by Alladi Krishnaswami Ayyar, Constituent Assembly of India, November 23, 1949, in *CAD*, 11:838–839.

234. Vallabhbhai Patel, Letter to All Provincial Premiers, November 3, 1949, in *Sardar Patel's Correspondence*, 8:394.

235. Although in this chapter I have not studied the place of India's tribal regions within the constitutional framework, the dynamic between regional state authority and pluralism is crucial to understanding the approach taken toward the governance of these regions. It is this dynamic, rather than a straightforward fear about democratization, that explains the constitutional schema. For an account that notes the schema but focuses simply on democratization rather than this dynamic, see Udit Bhatia, "Precautions in a Democratic Experiment: The Nexus between Political Power and Competence," in *Constituent Assemblies*, ed. Jon Elster et al. (New York: Cambridge University Press, 2018), 109–137.

236. This point is acknowledged in some form in the study of comparative politics. See, for example, Daniel Ziblatt, *Structuring the State: The Formation of Italy and Germany and the Puzzle of Federalism* (Princeton: Princeton University Press, 2006).

237. For an attempt to see federalism in practical terms, see Edward L. Rubin, "Federalism as a Mode of Governance: Autonomy, Identity, Power, and Rights" in *The Federal Idea: Public Law between Governance and Political Life*, ed. Amnon Lev (Oxford: Hart, 2017), 125–144.

238. One should note that the power and influence of Indian *society* has been an important theme in comparative historical studies. See, for example, Francis Fukuyama, *The Origins of Political Order: From Prehuman Times to the French Revolution* (London: Profile Books, 2011), 151–188.

239. On these features of political pluralism, see Runciman, *Pluralism*, 180–193.

240. On the failure of Gandhian thought, see Chatterjee, *Nationalist Thought*, 117–125.

241. See Runciman, *Pluralism*.

242. It is hardly surprising, therefore, that critics of pluralism in Europe noted that "pluralism seemed possible only against the background of an overarching moral consensus about the limits of politics, as well as a great deal of mutual tolerance." Jan-Werner Müller, *Contesting Democracy: Political Ideas in Twentieth-Century Europe* (New Haven: Yale University Press, 2013), 53–54.

243. Manabendra Nath Roy is a figure who merits mentioning in this context. A prominent actor in the 1920s, Roy would later join the Congress party but have hardly any impact on its ideology, create his own party but achieve little political success, and eventually—with the birth of the new republic—initiate a new humanist movement. In his early writings, such as his 1922 work *India in Transition*, he underlined the class composition of society and argued that feudalism no longer characterized Indian power relations. Political opposition to British rule arose from both

capitalists, who sought to control resources and labor, and the poor, who desired material improvements in their standards of living. Even though both groups joined forces to end foreign rule, Roy cautioned against seeing them as one. It would be a mistake to confuse elite capitalist anxiety with mass struggle; and to commit such a mistake would blind one to the exploitative character of capitalism. The emphasis on class was part of the broader claim that capitalism had arrived in India, and that ongoing and future transformations in India were part of the story of capitalist exploitation. This broader claim was a challenge to both imperial and nationalist versions of Indian history. By offering a new account for the factors that contributed to change and the emergence of the Indian nation, Roy was both affirming collective agency but denying that such agency was always present. This analysis offered a fresh explanation for colonial rule: such rule was a consciously ruthless marriage between the British and local trading classes. See Manabendra Nath Roy, *India in Transition,* 1922, in *Selected Works of M. N. Roy,* ed. Sibnarayan Ray, vol. 1 (New Delhi: Oxford University Press, 1987), 183.

Roy's views changed considerably by the 1940s. His eventual proposal was for radical participation, with people's committees at multiple tiers, and the prevention of forms of representation, which in typical communist terms he regarded as forms of domination. It is not entirely clear, however, whether he quite gave up his search for a direct path to modernization. On the later Roy, see Manabendra Nath Roy, *Constitution of Free India* (Delhi: Radical Democratic Party, 1944). See also Roy, "Constituent Assembly," February 1928, in *Selected Works of M. N. Roy,* ed. Sibnarayan Ray, vol. 3 (New Delhi: Oxford University Press, 1990), 147–148; Spratt, *India and Constitution Making,* 73–74. For a thoughtful study of Roy's limitations, see Sudipta Kaviraj, "The Heteronomous Radicalism of M. N. Roy," in *Political Thought in Modern India,* ed. Thomas Pantham and Kenneth L. Deutsch (New Delhi: Sage, 1986), 201–227.

Two additional figures who should be taken note of are Subhas Chandra Bose, whose notion of centralized state power focused on nationalism and socialist reconstruction, and Rammanohar Lohia, who argued against a large state and made the case for a balance between urban and rural life. See, as merely indicative of their thought, Subhas Chandra Bose, Presidential Address at the Fifty-First Session of the Indian National Congress, February 1938, in *Netaji: Collected Works,* ed. Sisir Kumar Bose and Sugata Bose, vol. 9 (Delhi: Permanent Black, 2004), 16; Rammanohar Lohia, *Marx, Gandhi and Socialism* (Hyderabad: Navahind, 1963).

3. Identity and Representation

1. John Stuart Mill, *Considerations on Representative Government* (New York: Cambridge University Press, 2010 [1861]), 294–304.

2. James Mill, *The History of British India,* 3 vols. (New York: Cambridge University Press, 2010 [1817]); Mountstuart Elphinstone, *The History of India,* 2 vols. (New York: Cambridge University Press, 2013 [1841]); H. H. Risley, *The People of India,* 2nd ed. (London: W. Thacker, 1915). An egregious illustration of this outlook was the idea of criminal communities. See Criminal Tribes Act, 1871; Sanjay

Nigam, "Disciplining and Policing the 'Criminals by Birth,' Part 1: The Making of a Colonial Stereotype—The Criminal Tribes and Castes of North India," and Nigam, "Disciplining and Policing the 'Criminals by Birth,' Part 2: The Development of a Disciplinary System, 1871–1900," both in *Indian Economic and Social History Review* 27 (1990): 131–164, 257–287. For a classic treatment of the colonial creation of identity, see Bernard S. Cohn, *An Anthropologist among the Historians and Other Essays* (New Delhi: Oxford University Press, 1987), 224–254.

3. Other identities also posed challenges for the conceptualization of citizenship. For the resolution in the case of language, see Granville Austin, *The Indian Constitution: Cornerstone of a Nation* (New Delhi: Oxford University Press, 1966), 265–307. For a study of the case of the tribal population, see Niraja Gopal Jayal, *Citizenship and Its Discontents: An Indian History* (Cambridge, MA: Harvard University Press, 2013), 234–245. A third identity—one that has received the least attention of all—was gender.

4. See Ayesha Jalal, *The Sole Spokesman: Jinnah, the Muslim League, and the Demand for Pakistan* (Cambridge: Cambridge University Press, 1985).

5. Ibid., 57.

6. Ibid.

7. Ibid., 60.

8. Ibid., 58.

9. See Farzana Shaikh, *Community and Consensus in Islam: Muslim Representation in Colonial India, 1860–1947* (Cambridge: Cambridge University Press, 1989).

10. Ibid., 6.

11. Ibid., 195.

12. Venkat Dhulipala, *Creating a New Medina: State Power, Islam, and the Quest for Pakistan in Late Colonial North India* (Delhi: Cambridge University Press 2015), 4.

13. Jalal, *Sole Spokesman,* 59.

14. Mohammad Ali Jinnah, Presidential Address at the Twenty-Fifth Session of the All-India Muslim League, March 22, 1940, in *Quaid-i-Azam Mohammad Ali Jinnah Papers,* ed. Z. H. Zaidi, 3rd ser., vol. 15 (Islamabad: Government of Pakistan, 2007), 222.

15. Ibid., 223.

16. Ibid.

17. Mohammad Ali Jinnah, Letter to Mohandas K. Gandhi, January 21, 1940, in *Quaid-i-Azam Mohammad Ali Jinnah Papers,* 3rd ser., 15:76.

18. Ibid.

19. Mohammad Ali Jinnah, Letter to Mohandas K. Gandhi, September 17, 1944, in *Quaid-i-Azam Mohammad Ali Jinnah Papers,* ed. Z. H. Zaidi, 2nd ser., vol. 11 (Islamabad: Government of Pakistan, 2005), 164.

20. Ibid.

21. Ibid., 172.

22. Ibid.

23. See Peter Hardy, *The Muslims of British India* (Cambridge: Cambridge University Press, 1972), 94–104.

24. Syed Ahmed Khan, *The Causes of the Indian Revolt* (Karachi: Oxford University Press, 2000 [1873]).

25. Ibid., 13.

26. Ibid., 18.

27. Ibid., 12.

28. Ibid.

29. Ibid., 23.

30. Ibid.

31. Ibid., 34–35.

32. Ibid., 35.

33. Ibid.

34. Ibid.

35. Ibid., 44.

36. Syed Ahmed Khan, Speech on the Central Province Local Self-Government Bill of 1883, January 12, 1883, in *Writings and Speeches of Sir Syed Ahmed Khan,* ed. Shan Mohammad (Bombay: Nachiketa, 1972), 156.

37. See Speech by Viqar-ul-Mulk, and Speech by Nawab Salim-ul-lah, Inaugural Session of the All-India Muslim League, December 30, 1906, both in *Foundations of Pakistan,* ed. Syed Sharifuddin Pirzada (New Delhi: Metropolitan Book Co., 1982), 1:3–4, 7–10.

38. Speech by Viqar-ul-Mulk, Inaugural Session of the All-India Muslim League, 4.

39. Peter Hardy, *Partners in Freedom and True Muslims: The Political Thought of Some Muslim Scholars in British India, 1912–1947* (Sweden: Studentlitteratur, 1971), 21–23.

40. Ayesha Jalal, "Striking a Just Balance: Maulana Azad as a Theorist of Trans-National *Jihad," Modern Intellectual History* 4 (2007): 96.

41. Ibid., 106.

42. Hardy, *Partners in Freedom,* 22.

43. Ibid., 22–23. See also Jalal, "Striking a Just Balance," 105–107.

44. Hardy, *Partners in Freedom,* 28–29, 39–42.

45. Ibid., 30–31.

46. Maulana Abul Kalam Azad, Presidential Address at the Fifty-Third Session of the Indian National Congress, March 19, 1940, in *The Selected Works of Maulana Abul Kalam Azad,* vol. 1 (New Delhi: Atlantic Publishers, 1991), 113.

47. Ibid., 1:112–113.

48. Ibid., 1:113.

49. Ibid., 1:107.

50. Ibid., 1:109.

51. See Maulana Abul Kalam Azad, *India Wins Freedom* (New Delhi: Orient Longman, 1988), 147.

52. Maulana Abul Kalam Azad, Statement on Partition, April 15, 1946, in *The Selected Works of Maulana Abul Kalam Azad,* vol. 11 (New Delhi: Atlantic Publishers, 1992), 132.

53. Ayesha Jalal, "Azad, Jinnah and the Partition," *Economic and Political Weekly* 24 (1989): 1159–1160.

54. See Faisal Devji, *Muslim Zion: Pakistan as a Political Idea* (Cambridge, MA: Harvard University Press, 2013).

55. Resolutions adopted by the Twenty-Fourth Session of the Indian National Congress, December 27–29, 1909, in *INC: The Glorious Tradition,* 1:298.

56. It is telling that even the Sapru Committee linked communal tensions to economic realities. See *Constitutional Proposals of the Sapru Committee* (Bombay: Padma, 1945), 184. Often communal tensions were taken to be merely a practical obstacle to get out of the way so that focus could shift to the questions that really mattered. This was true even in the decades before Gandhi and Nehru acquired prominence. See, for example, Motilal Nehru, Views on the United Provinces Municipalities Bill of 1915, July 19, 1915, in *Selected Works of Motilal Nehru,* vol. 1 (New Delhi: Vikas Publishing House, 1982), 304.

57. See Jayal, *Citizenship and Its Discontents,* 208–215. Jayal proceeds to also regard Hindu nationalism as a form of universalism. Here, as the ensuing discussion reveals, I agree.

58. See Jawaharlal Nehru, "On Hindu–Muslim Unity," June 9, 1931, in *Selected Works of Jawaharlal Nehru,* ed. S. Gopal, 1st ser., vols. 1–15 (New Delhi: Orient Longman, 1972–1982) (hereafter cited as *Selected Works*), 5:282.

59. Jawaharlal Nehru, Presidential Address at the Punjab Provincial Conference, April 11, 1928, in *Selected Works,* 3:226.

60. Jawaharlal Nehru, "On Minorities and Nationalism," June 13, 1931, and Nehru, "On Hindu–Muslim Unity," June 9, 1931, both in *Selected Works,* 5:283, 282.

61. Jawaharlal Nehru, "Reality and Myth," January 5, 1934, in *Selected Works,* 6:182.

62. Ibid., 6:184; Jawaharlal Nehru, "The Need for Pachayati Rule," June 27, 1936, in *Selected Works,* 7:295.

63. Nehru, *An Autobiography* (New Delhi: Penguin, 2004 [1936]), 255.

64. Ibid., 307.

65. Ibid., 482.

66. Ibid., 146.

67. Jawaharlal Nehru, Presidential Address at the Lucknow Congress, April 12, 1936, in *Selected Works,* 7:189. See also Nehru, "On the Indian Situation," November 12, 1935, in *Selected Works,* 7:37.

68. Jawaharlal Nehru, "The Unity of India," *Foreign Affairs* 16 (1938): 238–239.

69. Jawaharlal Nehru, "The Worldwide Struggle against Imperialism," May 28, 1936, in *Selected Works,* 7:267.

70. Jawaharlal Nehru, Presidential Address at the All India Convention of Congress Legislators, March 19, 1937, in *Selected Works,* 8:62. See also Nehru, "The Parting of the Ways," August 10, 1940, in *Selected Works,* 11:112–113.

71. Jawaharlal Nehru, "The Congress and the Muslims," January 10, 1937, in *Selected Works,* 8:120.

72. Jawaharlal Nehru, "The Communal Approach of Jinnah," June 30, 1937, in *Selected Works,* 8:137.

73. See Jawaharlal Nehru, "On Communalism," August 11, 1937, and "On the Rights of Minorities," February 20, 1938, both in *Selected Works*, 8:174, 766.

74. See Jawaharlal Nehru, "India's Demand and England's Answer," January 6, 1940, in *Selected Works*, 10:280.

75. Jawaharlal Nehru, "On the Rights of Minorities," February 20, 1938, in *Selected Works*, 8:766.

76. Nehru, Presidential Address at the All India Convention of Congress Legislators, 62.

77. Jawaharlal Nehru, Letter to Stafford Cripps, January 17, 1940, in *Selected Works*, 10:301.

78. Jawaharlal Nehru, "Rally Round the Congress," April 28, 1940, in *Selected Works*, 11:215.

79. Jawaharlal Nehru, "India and Britain," July 6, 1938, in *Selected Works*, 9:49.

80. Ibid.

81. Ibid.

82. Ibid.

83. Jawaharlal Nehru, "Five Years Later," October 17, 1940, in *Selected Works*, 11:171–172. See also Nehru, letter to Syed Mahmud, February 2, 1942, in *Selected Works*, 12:511.

84. Jawaharlal Nehru, Note on the Indian Background, May 11, 1942, in *Selected Works*, 12:309.

85. Jawaharlal Nehru, "Can Indians Get Together?," July 19, 1942, in *Selected Works*, 12:521.

86. Jawaharlal Nehru, "The War and the People," January 31, 1942, in *Selected Works*, 12:16.

87. Jawaharlal Nehru, "A Clash of Outlooks," July 14, 1945, in *Selected Works*, 14:41.

88. Ibid., 14:42.

89. Jawaharlal Nehru, "The Absurdity of Partition," July 17, 1945, in *Selected Works*, 14:49.

90. Ibid., 14:49–50. For a similar view, see Rajendra Prasad, *India Divided* (New Delhi: Penguin, 2010 [1946]), 19–20.

91. Nehru, "The Absurdity of Partition," 51.

92. Jawaharlal Nehru, *The Discovery of India* (New Delhi: Penguin, 2004 [1946]), 588–590.

93. Nehru's relationship to religion should not be taken to be a rejection of faith, properly understood. For the importance that Nehru placed on *reason* as a source of authority, see Sunil Khilnani, "Nehru's Faith," *Economic and Political Weekly* 37 (2002): 4793–4799.

94. Mohandas K. Gandhi, Speech at Gathering of Schoolboys, October 23, 1931, in *The Collected Works of Mahatma Gandhi*, 100 vols. (Government of India: Publications Division, 1956–1994) (hereafter cited as *Collected Works*), 48:221.

95. Ibid.

96. Mohandas K. Gandhi, interview with the *New York Times*, March 23, 1939, in *Collected Works*, 69:77.

97. See Mohandas K. Gandhi, "Hindu–Mohammedan Unity," February 25, 1920, in *Collected Works*, 69:44.

98. Mohandas K. Gandhi, "Hindu–Muslim Riots," January 9, 1909, in *Collected Works*, 9:134.

99. Mohandas K. Gandhi, "To Hindus," August 29, 1920, in *Collected Works*, 18:203.

100. See Mohandas K. Gandhi, "Turkey," September 7, 1919, in *Collected Works*, 16:104–106.

101. Mohandas K. Gandhi, Speech at Public Meeting, April 7, 1921, in *Collected Works*, 19:538.

102. Ibid.

103. Gandhi, *Hind Swaraj*, 53.

104. Gandhi's non-institutional orientation meant that he did not call for a separation of religion from politics in a straightforward way. See Mohandas K. Gandhi, *My Experiments with Truth*, trans. Mahadev Desai (New Delhi: Penguin, 2012 [1940]), 435.

105. On the role of exemplary action in Gandhi's political thought, see Akeel Bilgrami, "Gandhi's Integrity," *Raritan* 21 (2001): 48–67.

106. Christophe Jaffrelot, *The Hindu Nationalist Movement in India* (New York: Columbia University Press, 1996), 25. On Hindu nationalism as an *ideology*, see John Zavos, *The Emergence of Hindu Nationalism in India* (New Delhi: Oxford University Press, 2000).

107. V. D. Savarkar, *Hindutva: Who Is a Hindu?*, 5th ed. (Bombay: Veer Savarkar Prakashan, 1969). My reading of Savarkar's text is a familiar one, though I employ it to make the less familiar argument about the crisis of liberal representation. For a somewhat different, provocative reading of Savarkar's text that highlights its rhetorical moves and its emphasis on territoriality, see Janaki Bakhle, "Country First? Vinayak Damodar Savarkar (1883–1966) and the Writing of *Essentials of Hindutva*," *Public Culture* 22 (2010): 149–186.

108. Savarkar, *Hindutva*, 39.

109. Ibid., 105.

110. Ibid., 84.

111. Ibid., 91–102.

112. Ibid., 113.

113. V. D. Savarkar, Presidential Address, Akhil Bharatiya Hindu Mahasabha, 1937, in *Hindu Rashtra Darshan*, 2nd ed. (Bombay: Veer Savarkar Prakashan, 1984), 8.

114. Ibid., 15.

115. V. D. Savarkar, Presidential Address, Akhil Bharatiya Hindu Mahasabha, 1938, in *Hindu Rashtra Darshan*, 57.

116. Ibid., 45.

117. See Sudipta Kaviraj, "Contradictions of Conservatism," *Studies in Indian Politics* 6 (2018): 8–10.

118. Sudipta Kaviraj, "On Thick and Thin Religion: Some Critical Reflections on Secularization Theory," in *Religion and the Political Imagination*, ed. Ira

Katznelson and Gareth Stedman Jones (New York: Cambridge University Press, 2010), 348.

119. Pratap Bhanu Mehta, "Hinduism and Self-Rule," *Journal of Democracy* 15 (2004): 118.

120. M. S. Golwalkar, *We or Our Nationhood Defined* (Nagpur: Bharat, 1939).

121. M. S. Golwalkar, *Bunch of Thoughts* (Bangalore: Vikrama Prakashan, 1966), 118.

122. Ibid., 142.

123. Lala Lajpat Rai, "Need for Vigorous Political Activity in Punjab," September 30, 1906, in *The Collected Works of Lala Lajpat Rai,* ed. B. R. Nanda, vol. 2 (New Delhi: Manohar, 2003), 61.

124. Ibid.

125. Lala Lajpat Rai, "The Mahomedan Demand," March 4, 1909, in *The Collected Works of Lala Lajpat Rai,* ed. B. R. Nanda, vol. 3 (New Delhi: Manohar, 2004), 199.

126. Lala Lajpat Rai, "The Program of Non-cooperation," 1924, in *The Collected Works of Lala Lajpat Rai,* ed. B. R. Nanda, vol. 10 (New Delhi: Manohar, 2008), 207.

127. Ibid., 10:208.

128. Ibid.

129. Ibid., 10:209.

130. Lala Lajpat Rai, "The Indian Problem: A Few Stray Thoughts," 1924, in *Collected Works of Lala Lajpat Rai,* 10:346–347.

131. Ibid., 10:348.

132. Lala Lajpat Rai, *Hindu–Muslim Unity: The Problem and Its Solution,* 1925, in *The Collected Works of Lala Lajpat Rai,* ed. B. R. Nanda, vol. 11 (New Delhi: Manohar, 2008), 145.

133. Ibid., 11:140.

134. Ibid., 11:142.

135. Ibid., 11:144.

136. Ibid., 11:143–146.

137. Ibid., 11:166–167.

138. Lala Lajpat Rai, Presidential Address at the Bombay Hindu Mahasabha Conference, December 5, 1925, in *The Collected Works of Lala Lajpat Rai,* 11: 271–273.

139. Rai, *Hindu-Muslim Unity,* 172.

140. B. R. Ambedkar, *Pakistan or the Partition of India,* 1946, in *Dr. B. R. Ambedkar: Writings and Speeches,* ed. Vasant Moon, 17 vols. (New Delhi: Dr. Ambedkar Foundation, 2014) (hereafter cited as *Dr. B. R. Ambedkar*), 8:1. For responses to this text, see Dhulipala, *Creating a New Medina,* 150–170.

141. Ambedkar, *Pakistan or the Partition of India,* 8:7.

142. Ibid., 8:33.

143. Ibid.

144. Ibid., 8:33–34.

145. Ibid., 8:35.

146. Ibid.

147. Ibid., 8:65–66.

148. Ibid.

149. Ibid.

150. Ibid., 8:28.

151. Ibid.

152. Ibid., 8:42.

153. Ibid., 8:35.

154. Ibid.

155. Ibid., 8:107–108.

156. Ibid.

157. Ibid., 8:110.

158. Ibid.

159. Ibid., 8:236.

160. Ibid., 8:111.

161. Ibid., 8:247–248.

162. Ibid., 8:11.

163. Ibid., 8:112.

164. Ibid., 8:116.

165. Ibid., 8:329.

166. Ibid., 8:269–270.

167. Ibid.

168. Ibid., 8:117.

169. Ibid., 8:220.

170. Ibid., 8:116.

171. Ibid., 8:220.

172. Ibid., 8:247–248.

173. Ibid., 8:220.

174. Letter from Vallabhbhai Patel to the President, Constituent Assembly of India, August 8, 1947, in *Constituent Assembly Debates,* 12 vols. (New Delhi: Lok Sabha Secretariat, 2009 [1950]) (hereafter cited as *CAD*), 5:243.

175. Ibid.

176. Letter from Vallabhbhai Patel to Amrit Lal Malhotra, January 30, 1946, in *Sardar Patel's Correspondence, 1945–50,* ed. Durga Das, 10 vols. (Ahmedabad: Navajivan Publishing House, 1971–1974), 2:301.

177. Mohandas K. Gandhi, Talk with Sir Stafford Cripps, April 10, 1946, in *Collected Works,* 94:262.

178. Speech by Vallabhbhai Patel, Constituent Assembly of India, May 25, 1949, in *CAD*, 8:269.

179. Speech by Mohamed Ismail Sahib, Constituent Assembly of India, May 25, 1949, in *CAD*, 8:277.

180. Speech by Vallabhbhai Patel, Constituent Assembly of India, August 28, 1947, in *CAD*, 5:270–272.

181. K. T. Shah, Memorandum on Minorities, March/April 1947, in *The Framing of India's Constitution: Select Documents,* ed. B. Shiva Rao et al., 5 vols. (New Delhi: Universal Law Publishing, 1966), 2:378.

182. Through this measure, Minto took the "principle of counterpoise"—which had been used for the representation of classes in measures such as the Councils Act of 1892—and applied it to communities. See K. B. Krishna, *The Problem of Minorities or Communal Representation in India* (London: George Allen and Unwin, 1939), 74–91.

183. The importance of partition to the Constituent Assembly's deliberations has recently been highlighted in Kanika Gauba, "Forgetting Partition: Constitutional Amnesia and Nationalism," *Economic and Political Weekly* 51 (2016): 41–47.

184. Pratap Bhanu Mehta, "On the Possibility of Religious Pluralism," in *Religious Pluralism, Globalization, and World Politics,* ed. Thomas Banchoff (New York: Oxford University Press, 2008), 82.

185. See Vallabhbhai Patel, Letter to Nihchaldas C. Vazirani, June 2, 1946, in *Sardar Patel's Correspondence,* 3:105.

186. See Speech by Govind Ballabh Pant, August 27, 1947, in *CAD,* 5:222–223. Bajpai has rightly underlined the importance of this speech in her valuable if somewhat different account of the retrenchment of communal measures. See Rochana Bajpai, *Debating Difference: Group Rights and Liberal Democracy in India* (New Delhi: Oxford University Press, 2011), 119–120.

187. Speech by Govind Ballabh Pant, August 27, 1947, in *CAD,* 5:224.

188. This is one key reason, for example, why descriptive representation was seen as antidemocratic in Victorian Britain. See Gregory Conti, *Parliament, the Mirror of the Nation: Representation, Deliberation, and Democracy in Victorian Britain* (New York: Cambridge University Press, 2019).

189. In thinking about how responses to us shape our sense of identity, we can take note of Appiah's recent observation: "My theoretical thinking about identity began, actually, with thoughts about race, because I was genuinely puzzled by the different ways in which people in different places responded to my appearance." Kwame Anthony Appiah, *The Lies That Bind: Rethinking Identity* (New York: Liveright, 2018), 6.

190. On descriptive representation and its limitations, see Hanna Fenichel Pitkin, *The Concept of Representation* (Berkeley: University of California Press, 1967), 60–91.

191. Ibid., 61, 80–81.

192. Ibid. 61.

193. See K. T. Shah, *Provincial Autonomy* (Bombay: Vora and Co., 1937), 33.

194. See, generally, Conti, *Parliament.*

195. Indian Franchise Committee, *Report of the Indian Franchise Committee* (Calcutta: Government of India Central Publication Branch, 1932), 1:20.

196. See Richard Tuck, *The Sleeping Sovereign: The Invention of Modern Democracy* (New York: Cambridge University Press, 2016), 260–262. On voting and individual agency, see also Richard Tuck, *Free Riding* (Cambridge, MA: Harvard University Press, 2008), 30–62; Richard Tuck, "Active and Passive Citizens" (unpublished draft on file with author).

197. On majority decision-making, see Kenneth O. May, "A Set of Independent Necessary and Sufficient Conditions for Simple Majority Decision," *Econometrica*

20 (1952): 680–684; Amartya K. Sen, *Collective Choice and Social Welfare* (San Francisco: Holden-Day, 1970), 71–74; Partha Dasgupta and Eric Maskin, "On the Robustness of Majority Rule," *Journal of the European Economic Association* 6 (2008): 949–973.

198. Mahmood Mamdani, *Define and Rule: Native as Political Identity* (Cambridge, MA: Harvard University Press, 2012), 44.

199. Kaviraj, "On Thick and Thin Religion," 351. See also Sudipta Kaviraj, *The Imaginary Institution of India: Politics and Ideas* (New York: Columbia University Press, 2010), 194; Cohn, *Anthropologist among the Historians,* 224–254.

200. See Speech by Begum Aziz Rasul, Constituent Assembly of India, November 22, 1949, in *CAD,* 11:775; Speech by Alladi Krishnaswami Ayyar, Constituent Assembly of India, November 23, 1949, in *CAD,* 11:835.

201. Sudipta Kaviraj, *The Enchantment of Democracy and India* (Ranikhet: Permanent Black, 2011), 170–171.

202. Ibid., 171.

203. Speech by Jawaharlal Nehru, Constituent Assembly of India, May 26, 1949, in *CAD,* 8:330.

204. On pluralism as a feature of the individual, see P. N. Furbank, *Behalf* (Lincoln: University of Nebraska Press, 1999).

205. One alternative put forth was proportional representation. Unlike separate electorates and reservations, it was understood as an inclusive measure that offered a genuine alternative. See Speech by Somnath Lahiri, Constituent Assembly of India, December 19, 1946, in *CAD,* 1:137; Speech by Hussain Imam, Constituent Assembly of India, November 8, 1948, in *CAD,* 7:303; Speech by Kazi Syed Karimuddin, Constituent Assembly of India, January 4, 1949, in *CAD,* 7:1233–1255; Speech by Z. H. Lari, May 25, 1949, in *CAD,* 8:283–285, 285–287. But proportional representation invited harsh criticism. In addition to its placing the same limitations on political life as communal representation did, it was viewed as a recipe for fragmented government and political instability. See Speech by K. M. Munshi, Constituent Assembly of India, July 17, 1947, in *CAD,* 4:643–644; Speech by B. R. Ambedkar, Constituent Assembly of India, January 4, 1949, in *CAD,* 7:1261–1263. It was also viewed as requiring a high level of literacy and was therefore taken to be inapplicable to India. See Speech by B. R. Ambedkar, Constituent Assembly of India, January 4, 1949, in *CAD,* 7:1261–1263. See also Speech by Begum Aizaz Rasul, Constituent Assembly of India, May 25, 1949, in *CAD,* 8:303; Speech by R. K. Sidhwa, Constituent Assembly of India, May 26, 1949, in *CAD,* 8:318; Speech by Shibban Lal Saksena, Constituent Assembly of India, May 26, 1949, in *CAD,* 8:319–320; Speech by Vallabhbhai Patel, May 26, 1949, in *CAD,* 8:352–353. On the relationship between proportional representation and the contemporary crisis of democracy, see Frances McCall Rosenbluth and Ian Shapiro, *Responsible Parties: Saving Democracy from Itself* (New Haven: Yale University Press, 2018).

206. See Sudipta Kaviraj, "The Curious Persistence of Colonial Ideology," *Constellations* 21 (2014): 186–198.

207. Kaviraj, *Enchantment of Democracy,* 172.

208. See Susan Bayly, *Caste, Society and Politics in India from the Eighteenth Century to the Modern Age* (New York: Cambridge University Press, 1999), 268–278.

209. See Anupama Rao, *The Caste Question: Dalits and the Politics of Modern India* (Berkeley: University of California Press, 2009), 23.

210. See Jayal, *Citizenship and Its Discontents,* 222–225.

211. I use the words "somewhat different" because the recognition of groups was permitted rather than required.

212. B. R. Ambedkar, "Annihilation of Caste," 1944, in *Dr. B. R. Ambedkar,* 1:47.

213. Ibid.

214. Ibid.

215. Ibid.

216. Ibid., 1:48.

217. Ibid., 1:49.

218. Ibid.

219. Jotirao Phule, *Slavery,* in *Selected Writings of Jotirao Phule,* ed. G. P. Deshpande (New Delhi: LeftWord, 2002), 40.

220. Ibid., 31–32.

221. Ibid., 38.

222. One might note that, at the time, an emerging strand of anthropological thought was interrogating the very idea of race itself. A leading statement of such interrogation was, of course, Franz Boas, *Anthropology and the Modern Life* (New York: W. W. Norton, 1928).

223. Ambedkar, "Annihilation of Caste," 51.

224. Ibid., 53.

225. Ibid., 57, 65, citing John Dewey, *Democracy and Education: An Introduction to the Philosophy of Education* (New York: Free Press, 1997 [1916]); Thomas Carlyle, *Sartor Resartus,* in *The Works of Thomas Carlyle,* ed. Henry Duff Traill, vol. 1 (New York: Cambridge University Press 2010 [1896]), 194–202.

226. B. R. Ambedkar, "Castes in India: Their Mechanism, Genesis and Development," 1916, in *Dr. B. R. Ambedkar,* 1:9.

227. B. R. Ambedkar, Evidence before the Southborough Committee on Franchise, 1919, in *Dr. B. R. Ambedkar,* 1:248–249.

228. B. R. Ambedkar, *What Congress and Gandhi Have Done to the Untouchables,* 1945, in *Dr. B. R. Ambedkar,* 9:193.

229. Ibid.

230. Ambedkar, Evidence before the Southborough Committee on Franchise, 255.

231. Ibid.

232. Ibid.

233. Ibid., 266–267.

234. Ambedkar, Report on the Constitution of the Government of Bombay Presidency, 1929, in *Dr. B. R. Ambedkar,* 2:465.

235. Ibid.

236. Ibid., 2:338.

237. Ibid.

238. Ambedkar, First Roundtable Conference, December 22, 1930, in *Dr. B. R. Ambedkar*, 2:533.

239. B. R. Ambedkar, *Mr. Gandhi and the Emancipation of the Untouchables*, 1943, in *Dr. B. R. Ambedkar*, 9:403–404, 407.

240. Ibid., 9:413.

241. Ibid., 9:416.

242. Ambedkar, *What Congress and Gandhi Have Done to the Untouchables*, 9:171.

243. Ibid., 9:203.

244. Ibid., 9:222–223.

245. Ibid.

246. I regard this framing to better capture the problem of negotiating caste than the more familiar description which sees the tension as one between equal citizenship for all and special treatment toward underprivileged groups. Though the latter does shed light on a number of important tensions, it does not quite shed light on the specificity of caste. See, for example, Partha Chatterjee, "The Nation in Heterogeneous Time," *Indian Economic and Social History Review* 38 (2001): 399–418.

247. See Nicholas B. Dirks, *Castes of Mind: Colonialism and the Making of Modern India* (Princeton: Princeton University Press, 2001). See also David Washbrook, *The Emergence of Provincial Politics: The Madras Presidency, 1870–1920* (Cambridge: Cambridge University Press, 1976).

248. In the United States, for example, such concerns have been expressed in the context of campaign finance and private corporations and public institutions. See, for example, Lawrence Lessig, *Republic, Lost: How Money Corrupts Congress—and a Plan to Stop It* (New York: Twelve, 2012).

249. See Speech by Vallabhbhai Patel, Constituent Assembly of India, October 14, 1949, in *CAD*, 10:249.

250. See Speech by K. M. Munshi, Constituent Assembly of India, November 30, 1948, in *CAD*, 7:697 (emphasis mine).

251. Speech by B. R. Ambedkar, Constituent Assembly of India, November 30, 1948, in *CAD*, 7:701.

252. Ibid.

253. Ibid., 7:701–702.

254. Ibid., 7:702.

255. See Report of a Sub-Committee appointed by the Advisory Committee on Minorities, Fundamental Rights, etc., available in *CAD*, 8:313–315.

256. Report of the Special Sub-Committee on Minority Problems affecting East Punjab and West Bengal, November 23, 1948, in *Framing of India's Constitution*, 4:592–593.

257. Speech by Sochet Singh, Constituent Assembly of India, November 23, 1949, in *CAD*, 11:853. See also Speech by Vallabhbhai Patel, Constituent Assembly of India, October 14, 1949, in *CAD*, 10:249; Letter from Vallabhbhai Patel to Baldev Singh, December 30, 1948, in *Sardar Patel's Correspondence*, 6:354.

258. Ambedkar, First Roundtable Conference, December 31, 1930, in *Dr. B. R. Ambedkar*, 2:530.

259. Ibid., 2:532.

260. See Articles 15–17, Constitution of India, 1950. There was a growing intellectual emphasis at the time on the role of constitutional rights in providing security to minorities like the lower castes. See, for example, C. Rajagopalachari,
Ambedkar Refuted (Bombay: Hind Kitabs, 1946), 6–7. On the link between antidiscrimination and representation, see also Report of the Committee of the All
Parties Conference, 1928, in *Selected Works of Motilal Nehru,* ed. Ravinder Kumar
and Hari Dev Sharma, vol. 6 (New Delhi: Vikas, 1995).

261. See Shefali Jha, "Rights versus Representation: Defending Minority Interests in the Constituent Assembly," in *Politics and Ethics of the Indian Constitution,*
ed. Rajeev Bhargava (New Delhi: Oxford University Press, 2008), 339–353; Daryl J.
Levinson, "Rights and Votes," *Yale Law Journal* 121 (2012): 1286–1363.

262. See, generally, D. R. Nagaraj, *The Flaming Feet: A Study of the Dalit Movement in India* (Bangalore: South Forum Press, 1993), 1–30; Eleanor Zelliot, *From
Untouchable to Dalit: Essays on the Ambedkar Movement* (New Delhi: Manohar,
1992), 150–183. On the Poona Pact—one of the most important episodes in the
Gandhi–Ambedkar contest—see Ramachandra Guha, *Gandhi: The Years That
Changed the World, 1914–1948* (Haryana: Penguin Random House, 2018),
421–447.

263. See Mohandas K. Gandhi, "Hindu–Muslim Question," February 19, 1925,
in *Collected Works,* 26:162.

264. Mohandas K. Gandhi, Speech at Indian Majlis, October 24, 1931, in *Collected Works,* 48:223.

265. Mohandas K. Gandhi, Speech at Public Meeting, December 28, 1931, in
Collected Works, 48:449. See also Gandhi, Letter to P. N. Rajbhoj, September 20,
1932, in *Collected Works,* 51:111.

266. See Rao, *The Caste Question,* 23.

Conclusion

1. See the Comparative Constitutions Project Chronology, available at www
.comparativeconstitutionsproject.org (last accessed on March 11, 2019).

2. See Martin Loughlin, "The Constitutional Imagination," *Modern Law Review* 78 (2015): 1–25.

3. On the present crisis of constitutional democracy, see Tom Ginsburg and
Aziz Z. Huq, *How to Save a Constitutional Democracy* (Chicago: University of Chi-
cago Press, 2018); Mark A. Graber, Sanford Levinson, and Mark Tushnet, eds.,
Constitutional Democracy in Crisis? (New York: Oxford University Press, 2018);
Steven Levitsky and Daniel Ziblatt, *How Democracies Die* (New York: Crown,
2018); Yascha Mounk, *The People vs. Democracy: Why Our Freedom Is in Danger
and How to Save It* (Cambridge, MA: Harvard University Press, 2018); Cass R.
Sunstein ed., *Can It Happen Here? Authoritarianism in America* (New York:
HarperCollins, 2018).

4. We have observed, such as in our study of Mohandas K. Gandhi, the presence of dissenting views on this matter. It should be noted that the questioning of

Western modernity on Indian soil found notable expressions even in India's post-colonial life. See, in particular, Jayaprakash Narayan, *A Plea for Reconstruction of Indian Polity* (Kashi: Akhil Bharat Sarva Seva Sangh Prakashan, 1959).

5. See Kwame Anthony Appiah, *In My Father's House: Africa in the Philosophy of Culture* (New York: Oxford University Press, 1992), 137–157.

6. Mohandas K. Gandhi, *Hind Swaraj and Other Writings,* ed. Anthony J. Parel (Cambridge: Cambridge University Press, 1997 [1909]), 56.

7. For a recent exploration, see Michael J. Klarman, *The Framers' Coup: The Making of the United States Constitution* (New York: Oxford University Press, 2016), 257–304.

8. Strictly speaking, such changes are not regarded as amendments.

9. See Granville Austin, *The Indian Constitution: Cornerstone of a Nation* (New Delhi: Oxford University Press, 1966), 255–264.

10. Speech by B. R. Ambedkar, November 4, 1948, Constituent Assembly of India, in *Constituent Assembly Debates,* 12 vols. (New Delhi: Lok Sabha Secretariat, 2009 [1950]) (hereafter cited as *CAD*), 7:36.

11. Ibid., 7:43.

12. Speech by B. R. Ambedkar, November 17, 1949, Constituent Assembly of India, in *CAD,* 9:1664.

13. The legitimation of any constitutional order is, of course, a complex matter, and India's order would be legitimized not merely through the formal structures of participation and representation but also by way of citizen involvement with institutions such as the courts. For a study of such engagement during the early years of the new constitutional order, see Rohit De, *A People's Constitution: The Everyday Life of Law in the Indian Republic* (Princeton: Princeton University Press, 2018).

14. See Klarman, *The Framers' Coup,* 405–417.

15. Akhil Reed Amar, *America's Constitution: A Biography* (New York: Random House, 2005), 7.

16. See Madhav Khosla, "Constitutional Amendment," in *The Oxford Handbook of the Indian Constitution,* ed. Sujit Choudhry, Madhav Khosla, and Pratap Bhanu Mehta (Oxford: Oxford University Press, 2016), 232–250.

17. See David Singh Grewal and Jedediah Purdy, "The Original Theory of Constitutionalism," *Yale Law Journal* 127 (2018): 644–705.

18. See Karuna Mantena, *Alibis of Empire: Henry Maine and the Ends of Liberal Imperialism* (Princeton: Princeton University Press, 2010), 184–185.

19. It is challenging to think of any major Indian figure who comprehended this as clearly as Jawaharlal Nehru. In his seventeen years as India's first prime minister, he approached the exercise of public power with noticeable care, mindful that freedom once acquired could be easily lost. Nehru sensed the repercussions of political action with a subtlety so detached from our practices that it can hardly be articulated. See Sunil Khilnani, "Nehru's Judgment," in *Political Judgment: Essays for John Dunn,* ed. Richard Bourke and Raymond Guess (New York: Cambridge University Press, 2009), 254–277.

ACKNOWLEDGMENTS

This work has been made possible by the support of a great many individuals and institutions. Foremost among those to whom I owe so much is the dissertation committee that supervised the thesis on which the work is based. Richard Tuck, who served as my advisor, revealed to me the intimacy that one could share with knowledge and taught me the meaning of intellectual imagination. Over the past decade, his gentle instruction has led me into an entirely new world and has left me with questions that feel inescapable. David Armitage made me expand my horizons, both temporally and geographically, while being an extraordinary source of advice and assurance. Karuna Mantena helped me problematize historical materials, making me see that arguments could be right even when historical interpretations were unconvincing. Nancy Rosenblum raised challenging questions at critical moments and allowed me to notice how political theory had a space for empathy. Mark Tushnet, with his quiet wisdom, ensured that I remained sensitive to the character of constitutional argument. I am grateful, above all, for the grace with which they have made me realize this project's limitations.

As a graduate student at Harvard, I benefited from the generous assistance offered by the Department of Government, the Graduate School of Arts and Sciences, the South Asia Institute, and the Weatherhead Center for International Affairs. Eric Beerbohm, Samuel Moyn, Eric Nelson, Parimal Patil, Michael Rosen, and Michael Sandel were kind enough to speak with me about my work. Even brief conversations often suggested an idea, or simply led me to pause. These years also presented the opportunity for the birth of profound friendships. It is hard to imagine that time without Greg Conti, Adi Dasgupta, Sungho Kimlee, Tsin Yen Koh, Abhilasha and Ashok Mehta, Zeynep Pamuk, Will Selinger, and George Yin. My final year of graduate school was spent at Columbia Law School as the inaugural B. R. Ambedkar Academic Fellow. I am thankful to Dean Gillian Lester for the chance to be part of such a terrific community. At Columbia, I learned considerably from my conversations with Akeel Bilgrami, Vincent A. Blasi, Jamal Greene, Olatunde

Johnson, Sudipta Kaviraj, Jeremy Kessler, Benjamin Liebman, Henry Paul Monaghan, Katharina Pistor, David Pozen, and Jedediah Purdy.

Daniela Cammack, David Singh Grewal, Ramachandra Guha, Devesh Kapur, and Srinath Raghavan watched over this project—and my own well-being—with great care and concern. In addition, Bruce Ackerman, Akhil Reed Amar, Shyamkrishna Balganesh, Aharon Barak, Sujit Choudhry, Rosalind Dixon, Tom Ginsburg, Samuel Issacharoff, Sunil Khilnani, Uday Singh Mehta, Martha C. Nussbaum, Rahul Sagar, Kim Lane Scheppele, and Arun K. Tiruvengadam provided much encouragement. The Centre for Policy Research, New Delhi, gave me an intellectual home during the long periods of time that I spent in India. Without Uday Raj Anand, Shweta Bansal, Justin McCarthy, Gopikaa Davar, Keshav Desiraju, Cyril Darlong Diengdoh, Gauri Gill, Keshava Guha, Rachael Israel, Prashant Jha, Amba Kak, Tahira Kathpalia, Karima Khalil, Parth Phiroze Mehrotra, Ananth Padmanabhan, Max Rodenbeck, Malvika and Tejbir Singh, Vinay Sitapati, Alex Travelli, and Raeesa Vakil, my time in India would have been rather different. Though they were neither in Cambridge nor in India, Kiel Brennan-Marquez, Abigail Fradkin, Hugo Leith, Neel Maitra, Jackie McArthur, Nicholas Mulder, Vishnu Vardhan Shankar, and Milan Vaishnav were present in vital ways.

Over the past couple of years, I have had the rare fortune of revising this work in the stimulating and congenial environment afforded by the Harvard Society of Fellows. My time at the Society, with its opportunities for unlikely intellectual exchanges and its incentives for reflection, was all the more special because of Gabriella Boulting, Sivan Goren-Arzony, Daniel Hochbaum, Kevin Holden, Alisha C. Holland, Kelly Richards Katz, Naomi Levine, Barry and Grace Dane Mazur, Ana Julia Novak, Andrew Ollett, Aspen T. Reese, Elaine Scarry, Amartya Sen, Emile Simpson, Paris Amanda Spies-Gans, Maria Tatar, William Todd, and Nur Yalman. I am especially grateful to Noah Feldman, who helped me understand that this work was as much about the constitution *of* democracy as it was about the constitution *as* democracy. Luckily, several elements of my graduate school community in Cambridge remained sources of comfort and joy, but additional persons who must be singled out include Ira Guha, Anna Lvovsky, and Arvind and Parul Subramanian.

In addition to the members of the dissertation committee, who were burdened with this project perhaps more times than they would care to remember, Kiel Brennan-Marquez, Greg Conti, Oran Doyle, Noah Feldman, Abigail Fradkin, David Singh Grewal, Ramachandra Guha, Sunil Khilnani, Sungho Kimlee, Pratap Bhanu Mehta, Ananth Padmanabhan, Jedediah Purdy, Srinath Raghavan, Will Selinger, Paris Amanda Spies-Gans, Milan Vaishnav, and Raeesa Vakil each read either significant portions or entire drafts, and offered invaluable comments and criticism. Various audiences at the universities of Ashoka, Columbia, Harvard, and Yale were subjected to presentations of the project, and their feedback was crucial. At Harvard University Press, Sharmila Sen and Heather Hughes were exceptionally supportive and helpful throughout the entire publication process. I am also thankful to John Kulka for his initial endorsement of the project.

To some individuals, my debt is greater still. This work would neither have commenced nor concluded without Pratap Bhanu Mehta. He has been the touchstone in matters of skill and matters of virtue. Bipin Pradip Aspatwar's friendship has been, in more ways than permit description, a most perfect gift. I am grateful to my family—Harish Khosla, Radhika Khosla, Akshay Mangla, Suchinta Sawhney—for their love and forbearance. What I owe to my parents, Amita and Rajiv Khosla, is of an altogether different nature. To say more about their contribution would be to debase the currency of gratitude.

INDEX

Ackerman, Bruce, 166n33

Adkins (1923), 65

Agarwal, Shriman Narayan, 89–90

agency, 138–139, 140–141

Aims and Objects Resolution, 1, 97

Alexandrowicz, C. H., 73

All India Congress Committee, 52

Ambedkar, B. R.: on universal suffrage, 10–12, 146, 167n53; and drafting of the Indian Constitution, 14; on copying Western constitutional arrangements, 19–20; on running of elections, 36; on prerogative writs, 37; on codification, 42, 43; on constitutional morality, 42–43; Memorandum and Draft Articles on the Rights of States and Minorities, 50–52; on civil-political and socioeconomic rights, 50–53; on value of the directive principles, 54–55; on Indian versus American approaches to rights, 58–59; on due process, 68, 69; on the grammar of anarchy, 70; on the Indian Constitution's centralized apparatus, 72; on democracy and modernization, 95–96; on regional autonomy, 96, 103, 104, 191n174; on radicalism, 97; and the decision to centralize, 98; on emergency powers, 102; knowledge of Indian history, 102; on supporting centralization, 103, 104–105, 191n174; on labor legislation, 105; on social reform, 108; statist commitment of, 108–109; on communalism, 130–133; *Pakistan or the Partition of India*, 130–133; on the caste system, 142–143, 144–145, 150–151; on communal electorates, 145–146; on backwardness, 148; on discrimination, 149; on the amendment process, 157; on the purpose of constitutions, 157

American Commonwealth, The (Bryce), 98

American Constitution, 158–159

Anderson, Perry, 168–169n76

anticolonial thought, 4–5, 47, 155

Appiah, Kwame Anthony, 171n102, 203n189

Athenian democracy, 42

Attlee, Clement, 7

Austin, Granville, 24

Ayyar, Alladi Krishnaswami: and the drafting of Indian Constitution, 14; on the adoption of suffrage, 19; on civil-political and socioeconomic rights, 48–49; on legal constitutionalism, 60; on U. S. due process, 67

Azad, Abul Kalam, 14, 118–120

213

Gandhi, Mohandas (*continued*)
electorates, 134; on the caste system,
150–151; on the English, 155; noninstitu-
tional orientation of, 200n104
Gokhale, Gopal Krishna, 77
Golwalkar, M. S., 127
Government of India Act (1919), 16
Government of India Act (1935), 16, 34, 46,
96–97, 100, 101, 104
Grote, George, 42–43
Grotius, Hugo, 107

habeas corpus, writ of, 37
Harel, Alon, 178–179n123
Hart, H. L. A., 30
Hartz, Louis, 18
Hastings, Warren, 31–32
Hegel, G. W. F., 4
Hind Swaraj (Indian Home Rule) (Gandhi),
75–81, 88, 124–125
Hinduism, 125, 126
Hindu Mahasabha, 126, 128
Hindu–Muslim conflict: Gandhi on, 78,
123–125; and Muslim representation,
114–120; Jinnah on, 115; Khan on,
115–118; Azad on, 118–120; Nehru on,
120–123; Savarkar on, 125–127;
Golwalkar on, 127; Rai on, 128–129;
Ambedkar on, 130–133; as engineered
by British, 139–140; breakdown of
Hindu–Muslim relations, 151
Hindu nationalism, 125–129
Hindustan, 133
Hindutva, 125, 126
history, anticolonial thought and the turn
to, 4–5
History of British India (Mill), 2
History of Greece, A (Grote), 42–43
Hobbes, Thomas, 2, 107
Hobhouse, L. T., 10–11

identity: representation and, 110–111,
137–140; colonial construction of,
137–140; forced, 147; responses to the
appearance and shaping of, 203n189
ideological decolonization, 171n102

illiteracy, and suffrage, 9, 10–11
India: turn to democracy, 4–15; democratic
origins of, 15–20; partition of British,
23, 112–115, 119–120, 122–123,
130–136, 139; inattention to the birth of
modern, 24, 25; choices underlying the
birth of modern, 25; Jinnah's conception
of, 115; conceptual foundations of
modern, 154
Indian Constitution: challenges facing
founders of, 5–6; Spratt on, 7; impact of,
13; drafting and adoption of, 13–15;
scholarship on, 15–16, 24, 25; length of,
27–28, 36, 172n1; as a statist document,
37; codification and the creation of,
41–42; "Directive Principles of State
Policy," 44–45; enforcement and
limitation of rights in, 55–63; due process
under, 63–69; as federal in character,
72–73; emergency provisions in, 100;
amendments to, 156–159; three paths to
change specified by, 157; individualism
and the legal structure of, 169–170n90;
Baker on preamble to, 172n3
Indian Councils Act (1861), 34
Indian Franchise Committee, 138
Indian National Congress, 120, 126
Indian nationalism, 128
Indian Penal Code 1860, 33
"Indian Problem, The," 91
Indian revolt (1857), 116
individualism, 147, 152, 169–170n90
industrialization, 91–92, 93–94, 96
inequality, Ambedkar on fraternity and
democracy and, 144–145
Instrument of Instructions, 54–55
International Bill of Rights of Man, An
(Lauterpacht), 53–54

Jayal, Niraja Gopal, 198n57
Jennings, Ivor, 8–9, 40
Jinnah, Mohammad Ali: concern of, with
the particularistic use of power, 23; on
representation, 112–113, 114–115, 141;
on Hindus and Muslims, 114–115;
Gandhi's exchange with, 115; similarities

Nehru, Jawaharlal (*continued*)
centralize, 98, 99; on regional units, 102;
on social reform, 108; statist commitment of, 108–109; on the rejection of
communal politics and identity-based
representation, 120–123; on the
partition of British India, 122–123;
on the Soviet Union Constitution,
193–194n230; relationship to religion,
199n93; approach to the exercise of
public power, 208n19
Nehru, Motilal, 56–57
New Deal, 165n26

Pakistan, 113, 114, 119–120, 122–123,
130–133
Pakistan or the Partition of India
(Ambedkar), 130–133
panchayats, 79, 80, 88, 90
Pant, Govind Ballabh, 136–137, 203n186
parliamentarianism, 88, 184–185n9
Patel, Sardar, 134
Patel, Vallabhbhai, 14, 106
Phule, Jotirao, 143–144
Plato, 144
pluralism, political, 74–90, 106–108,
194n235
political constitutionalism, 35–38, 70,
174n30
political freedom, relationship between
socioeconomic freedom and, 44–55
political pluralism, 74–90, 106–108,
194n235, 194n242
popular authorization, 20–21
poverty, 46, 93–94
power: dynamic between sovereignty and,
2–3; changing character of, in the modern
world, 3
practices, shared, 29
Prasad, Rajendra, 14, 15, 41–42
prerogative writs, 37
princely states, 95, 96–97, 98, 101. *See also*
regional governments; village
communities
procedural due process, 63, 64–65, 67–69
property, 52, 82–83

proportional representation, 204n205
Prosperity through Industry (Visvesvaraya),
93–94

race, caste and, 143–144. *See also* ethnicity,
Mukerjee on the problem of
Rai, Lala Lajpat, 128–130
railways, 79
Ranade, Mahadev Govind, 55, 189n123
Rau, B. N.: and the drafting of the Indian
Constitution, 14; on the directive
principles and the fundamental rights, 53,
55; on the judicial power to restrict
rights, 60; on the limitation of rights in
the U. S., 61; on blanket constitutional
guarantees, 62–63; on substantive due
process, 65–67
Raychaudhuri, Tapan, 17
Reconstructing India (Visvesvaraya),
90–91
regional autonomy, 191n174, 191n175
regional governments, 100, 194n235. *See
also* princely states; village communities
Regulating Act (1773), 33–34
Report of the Indian Franchise Committee, 9
*Report of the Indian Statutory Commis-
sion*, 9
Report on Indian Constitutional Reforms
(1918), 9
representation, 110–112, 151–152; prior
to Indian independence, 112–133; Nehru
on, 120–123; Gandhi on, 123–125;
Savarkar on, 126; Rai on, 128–130;
Ambedkar on, 130–133; Constituent
Assembly's approach to, 133–141;
colonial vision of, 137–140; descriptive,
138, 147, 203n188; caste and, 141–151,
152, 206n246; failure of, 151; territorializing of, 151–152; proportional,
204n205
Republic (Plato), 144
reservations, 148–149
Roundtable Conferences, 104, 120,
149–150
Rousseau, Jean-Jacques, 8
Roy, Manabendra Nath, 194–195n243

Russell, Bertrand, 46
Russia, 84, 105. *See also* Soviet Union

Sabine, George H., 86–87
Saha, Meghnad, 91
Sapru Committee's report (1945), 10, 39, 57
Sastri, V. S. Srinivasa, 16, 57
Savarkar, V. D., 125–127, 200n107
Schmitt, Carl, 27–28, 36
scientific advancement, 92–93
segregation, 144–145
self-determination, 22–24
Setalvad, M. C., 7
Shah, K. T., 14, 49–50, 58, 134
Shani, Ornit, 167–168n64, 170n97
sharia, the, 118
Sieyès, Abbé, the, 3
Sikh community, 149
socialism, 46–47, 91
social welfare, relationship between
  economic welfare and, 44–55
society, discovery of, 2
socioeconomic freedom, relationship
  between political freedom and, 44–55
socioeconomic rights, 29, 47–49, 51, 53,
  178n119
sovereignty: dynamic between power and,
  2–3; and suffrage, 8–9; Sabine on, 86–87
Soviet Union, 46, 91–92, 105, 193–194n230.
  See also Russia
Spratt, Philip, 7
Stephen, James Fitzjames, 16, 33
Stewart Dry Goods (1935), 61–62
Stokes, Eric, 33
Strachey, John, 17
Studies in History and Jurisprudence
  (Bryce), 39–40
subcastes, 143
Sub-Committee on Fundamental Rights, 52
substantive due process, 64–68
suffrage, for lower castes, 145. *See also*
  universal suffrage
Swaraj Bill (1895), 28

taxation, graduated, 61–62
technology, 79
territoriality, 114–115, 119, 127
Tigner (1940), 60, 61
Tocqueville, Alexis de, 1

uncertainty, 30, 38, 181n187
United States: limitation of rights in, 60–63;
  substantive due process in, 65–67;
  centralization in, 105; origins of the
  Constitution of, 158; amendments to the
  Constitution of, 158–159; British versus
  American constitutionalism, 174n30
universalism, 120, 125, 154–155
universal suffrage: institution of Indian, 6;
  sovereignty and, 8–9; literacy and, 9,
  10–11; support for, 9–12; Ambedkar on,
  10–12, 146, 167n53; and the drafting of
  the Indian Constitution, 14–15; Ayyar on,
  19; and popular authorization, 20–21;
  rejected by the Indian Franchise
  Committee, 138; democratic character of
  India partly enabled by, 156–157

Vaisya Dharma, 83
village communities: Gandhi on, 80, 87;
  Mukerjee on, 81–84, 85, 86, 87–89;
  resilience and the political remoteness of,
  85–86; Agarwal on, 89–90; Nehru on,
  92; Ambedkar on, 96, 103, 104; support
  for, 102. *See also* princely states; regional
  governments
Visvesvaraya, M., 90–91, 93–94

welfare, social and economic, 44–55,
  179n125
welfare state, emergence of, 27
West Coast Hotel (1937), 65
Western political institutions and civilization, 75–76. *See also* United States
Wheare, K. C., 73
Working Committee, 13, 94
worldliness, 76